Praise for *Landed*

"If you are purchasing overseas property, *Landed Global* is a must read. It's well written, easy to follow and bound to protect your interests and save you money."

Craig Shute
Senior Managing Director, Hong Kong, Macau & Taiwan
CBRE
Hong Kong, China

"I strongly recommend *Landed Global*. In addition to covering a wide spectrum of questions, this useful guidebook offers an excellent research framework for anyone buying property across international borders."

Mazen Salha
Chairman
Société des Grands Hotels du Liban (Hotel Phoenicia)
Société Hoteliers Vendôme (Hotel Vendome)
Beirut, Lebanon

"*Landed Global* is well written, thoroughly researched and essential reading for anyone thinking of buying international property."

Ashley Osborne
Head of Residential UK & Managing Director
of International Properties–Asia
Colliers International
Hong Kong, China

"*Landed Global* offers a wealth of clear, practical advice for finding, buying and financing recreational, residential and investment property. It's a great resource for minimizing the stress and headaches that can accompany an international property purchase."

Steven Aldridge
Director
Cityscope Developments
London, England

"*Landed Global* is the single most comprehensive guide for buying a home abroad. Millions of miles of travel would not give you the wealth of knowledge in this book."

Jun Homma
Deputy Editor
Nikkei Real Estate Market Report
Tokyo, Japan

"While the world is increasingly interconnected, the real estate market remains fragmented and thus difficult to understand. *Landed Global* provides prospective property owners with the knowledge to navigate through this challenging market."

Ernst Herb
Asia Correspondent
Finanz und Wirtschaft
Zurich, Switzerland

LANDED GLOBAL

Christopher Dillon

Landed Global © 2014 Dillon Communications Ltd. (www.dilloncommunications.com). All rights reserved.

No part of this book may be used or reproduced in any manner whatsoever without written permission, except in the case of brief quotations in articles and reviews.

ISBN: 978-988-17147-6-3

The author and publisher have made every effort to ensure the accuracy and completeness of the information in this book but assume no responsibility for errors, inaccuracies or omissions.

This book is published as a general reference and is not intended to be a substitute for professional legal, investment or tax advice. Readers should always obtain independent, professional advice before signing any legal document.

CONTENTS

Acknowledgements	7
Introduction	9
Where and Why?	**13**
Where to Buy?	15
Why Buy Abroad?	23
Buying Basics	**45**
Agents	47
Laws and Lawyers	57
Ownership and Property Rights	63
Negotiating	73
Demographics	79
Risk Factors	85
Pre-owned Homes	**133**
The Buying Process	135
Home Inspections	145
Land Surveys	151
Renovations	155
New Homes	**161**
New versus Old	163
Buying Off the Plan	167
Custom-built Homes	177
Money	**187**
Paying for Your Home	189
Mortgages	197
Insurance	213
Tax	219
Resources	**229**
Property Buyer's Checklist	231
Information Sources	239
Notes	267
Index	281
About the Author	293

ACKNOWLEDGEMENTS

I am grateful to the following people for generously sharing their time, expertise and contacts: Louise Alexander-O'Loughlin, Jennifer Kay Chan, Charlotte Cochrane, Jack Jackson, Charles Kelly, Rosemarie Kreisel, Grzegorz Laszczyk, Rickie Lo, Shoichi Muromura, Teymoor Nabili, Mike Nardella, Toshi Ota, Mark Panday, Karim Salha, Jonathan Sharp, Idalina Silva, Christopher Slaughter, Paul Stocker, Carrie Tan, Jim Thompson, Dr. Enzio von Pfeil and William Young.

Photo credits
Page 158, Jim Thompson; page 183, Teymoor Nabili; page 281, Idalina Silva. All other photos by the author.

INTRODUCTION

Landed Global is written for anyone buying or thinking of buying real estate across an international border. It guides you through the entire process—from choosing a location and selecting a property to negotiating and financing your purchase. With data and examples from more than 110 countries and territories, *Landed Global* will help you avoid common problems and make the most of your budget, whether you are buying a house, a weekend retreat or an income property.

The book draws on my experience as a Canadian who has lived abroad for 25 years and owned commercial, residential and industrial property in Hong Kong and Tokyo. *Landed Global* also features academic research, information from industry experts and case studies about successful cross-border purchases in France, Ireland, Japan, Sri Lanka, Thailand and the United States.

Inside *Landed Global*

Landed Global opens with a look at common reasons for buying abroad and highlights related opportunities and pitfalls. This section includes resources to help you choose a location and alternatives to purchasing bricks and mortar.

Next, Buying Basics introduces agents and lawyers and the services they provide. This section outlines common ownership structures and the fundamentals of property rights. It concludes with a description of the demographic trends and risks that can affect the value of your investment.

Section three examines the process of buying a pre-owned home, with examples from Italy, New Zealand, the United Kingdom and the United States and information about home inspections, land surveys and renovations.

Section four focuses on new dwellings, including off the plan purchases and custom-built homes.

The next section, Money, describes cross-border financing as well as mortgages, insurance and tax.

Landed Global closes with a series of checklists for property buyers and an international directory where you can find the people, products and services to make your purchase a success.

A final note

The inclusion of a company or organization in *Landed Global* is not a recommendation. Conversely, the omission of a company does not mean you should avoid it.

Throughout the book, I use "home" to refer to residential dwellings, including apartments and detached houses. To avoid using "he or she" and "s/he," I alternate between male and female pronouns.

Unless otherwise indicated, all dollar figures are in United States dollars. Other currencies are converted into U.S. dollars at exchange rates prevailing in May 2014.

I hope you find *Landed Global* helpful, and I look forward to including your comments and suggestions in the next edition of this book.

WHERE AND WHY?

Where to Buy?
15

Why Buy Abroad?
23

WHERE TO BUY?

Your reasons for buying will influence your choice of location. The following entries should help you consider the possibilities, spark a discussion and fuel a daydream (or two). Unless otherwise noted, cities and countries are listed from highest to lowest score. Many of these resources cover additional cities and countries, so you can evaluate a potential location on a number of criteria.

Antifragility

In his 2012 book *Antifragile*, Nassim Nicholas Taleb identifies a category of things, like human bones, that get stronger when exposed to stress and uncertainty. This effect is also seen in real estate markets. Research by Professor Tarun Ramadorai and Dr. Cristian Badarinza from the University of Oxford shows that London neighborhoods with high income levels experienced unusual price appreciation following higher levels of political uncertainty in China, the Middle East, East Asia and Russia, while areas with lower income levels saw gains after turbulence in Southern Europe and South Asia.[1]

Beaches

In 2008, *National Geographic* compiled a list of the world's best beaches: Seychelles, the Maldives, Bora Bora (Tahiti), the Hamptons (New York), Lanikai Beach (Hawaii), Nantucket Island (Massachusetts), Fraser Island (Australia), St. Bart's, Langkawi (Malaysia) and Kauna'oa Bay (Hawaii) (http://travel.nationalgeographic.com).

Commuting time

People who have long commutes have "systematically lower subjective well-being"[2] and a greater incidence of divorce and high blood pressure.[3] Among residents of 40 countries surveyed by the Organization for Economic Cooperation and Development (OECD) in 2011, South Africans and South Koreans had the longest daily commutes. Irish, Danish and Swedish respondents had the shortest.

Mapnificent, an interactive isochrone map, may be helpful if you are looking for a city or a neighborhood that offers manageable commuting time. The website shows how far you can travel on public transport from a user-selected point in a given period of time (www.mapnificent.net).

Connectivity

Loughborough University's Globalization and World Cities Research Network rates cities in terms of their global connectivity. In its 2010 survey, London and New York ranked alpha++. Hong Kong, Paris, Singapore, Tokyo, Shanghai, Chicago, Dubai and Sydney were alpha+. This program also rates cities by their importance to the global advertising, banking, accounting and legal industries—information that could be helpful for multi-career families (www.lboro.ac.uk/gawc).

Corruption

Transparency International publishes an annual corruption perceptions index. Where a score of 100 is corruption-free, the least corrupt nations in 2013 were Denmark (91), New Zealand (91), Finland (89), Sweden (89), Norway (86), Singapore (86), Switzerland (85), the Netherlands (83), Australia (81) and Canada (81) (www.transparency.org).

Cost of living

Human resources consultant Mercer conducts an annual cost of living survey for expatriates in over 200 cities. In 2013, the most expensive cities were Luanda (Angola), Moscow, Tokyo, N'Djamena (Chad), Singapore, Hong Kong, Geneva, Zurich, Bern and Sydney (www.mercer.com).

Economic freedom

The Heritage Foundation and *The Wall Street Journal* produce an annual ranking of the countries and territories with the freest economies. In 2014, the top 10 were Hong Kong, Singapore, Australia, Switzerland, New Zealand, Canada, Chile, Mauritius, Ireland and Denmark (www.heritage.org).

Education

If you are investing in student housing or sending your children to a university, consider these cities, which are from the *Times Higher Education* 2014 reputation ranking: Boston (Harvard and Massachusetts Institute of Technology), Palo Alto (Stanford University), Cambridge (University of Cambridge), Oxford (University of Oxford), Berkeley (University of California, Berkeley), Princeton (Princeton University), New Haven (Yale University), Pasadena (California Institute of Technology), Los Angeles (University of California, Los Angeles) (www.timeshighereducation.co.uk).

Experiments

If you have money, an ideological streak and a taste for adventure, there are social and economic experiments around the world seeking investors and residents. Examples include the charter cities movement in the Honduras, the Free State Project (http://freestateproject.org) to create a libertarian enclave in the American state of New Hampshire and Blueseed (http://blueseed.co), an entrepreneurs' community on a cruise ship 12 miles from the coast of San Francisco. These experiments range in risk from low to life-threatening, with financial commitments from thousands to millions of dollars.

Gastronomy

According the 2014 list compiled by The World's 50 Best Restaurants, the best dining can be found in Copenhagen (Noma); Girona, Spain (El Celler de Can Roca); Modena, Italy (Osteria Francescana); New York City (Eleven Madison Park); London (Dinner by Heston Blumenthal); San Sebastián, Spain (Mugaritz); São Paulo, (D.O.M.); San Sebastián, Spain (Arzak); Chicago (Alinea) and London (The Ledbury) (www.theworlds50best.com).

In its 2014 guide, Michelin awarded three stars to 14 Tokyo-area restaurants, versus 10 in Paris.[4]

Growth

In July 2013, consulting firm Stratfor compiled a list of 16 countries that were either benefiting from or poised to take advantage of rising labor costs in China. In alphabetical order, these countries were Bangladesh, Cambodia, the Dominican Republic, Ethiopia, Indonesia, Kenya, Laos, Mexico, Myanmar, Nicaragua, Peru, the Philippines, Sri Lanka, Tanzania, Uganda and Vietnam (www.stratfor.com).

Happiness

Published by the United Nations Sustainable Development Solutions Network, the *World Happiness Report* 2013 surveyed people in over 150 countries between 2010 and 2012. The happiest countries were Denmark, Norway, Switzerland, the Netherlands, Sweden, Canada, Finland, Austria, Iceland and Australia (http://unsdsn.org/happiness).

Immigration

In some countries, buying real estate entitles you to a passport, or to residency with the possibility of applying for a passport later. Minimum purchase amounts, holding periods and other conditions apply. See the "Why buy abroad?" chapter for more information.

Internet

In 2013, urban planing website UBM's Future Cities compiled a list of the top 10 Internet cities, based on connection speed, availability of citywide WiFi, openness to innovation, support of public data as well as security and data privacy. In alphabetical order, the top cities were Amsterdam, Geneva, Hong Kong, Montreal, Prague, Seattle, Seoul, Stockholm, Tokyo and Vienna (www.ubmfuturecities.com).

For up-to-date global information about Internet download and upload speeds, prices and service quality, see www.netindex.com.

Private islands can be purchased for as little as $50,000, but this figure increases rapidly when you include staff, equipment and upkeep.

Islands

Private islands are available on a leasehold and freehold basis in warm climates, like the Caribbean and the South Pacific, and in cooler countries, such as Canada, Scotland and Sweden. Islands cost as little as $50,000, although infrastructure like generators and desalination plants, taxes and groundskeepers can quickly add to this price. Islands are a particularly illiquid market, so experts recommend renting before you buy.

Market transparency

Every two years, Jones Lang LaSalle produces a global real estate transparency index, which is based on corporate governance, the regulatory environment, market data and other factors. In 2012, the top 10 countries were the United States, the United Kingdom, Australia, the Netherlands, New Zealand, Canada, France, Finland, Sweden and Switzerland (www.joneslanglasalle.com).

Potential turnarounds

Buyers with a long horizon and steady nerves can invest in destinations that are experiencing problems. For example, Greece offers culture, farms and beaches, although the country's finances are a mess and problems with land titles are common. Before civil war broke out in 1975, Beirut was known as "the Paris of the Middle East." Some beautiful architecture remains, although neighboring Syria is dangerously unstable. Japan's rural population continues to shrink as farmers retire and die, and young people move to Tokyo and other cities. In rural Japan, you can buy a house on an acre of land for $10,000. Some brave souls are moving into Rio de Janeiro's infamous *favelas* (slums), which became gentrified ahead of the World Cup in 2014 and the Olympics in 2016.

Press freedom

Reporters Without Borders publishes an annual press freedom index that offers useful insights into global censorship. In 2014, the freest countries were Finland, the Netherlands, Norway, Luxembourg, Andorra, Liechtenstein, Denmark, Iceland, New Zealand and Sweden (http://en.rsf.org).

Quality of life

The Economist Intelligence Unit produces an annual livability index, which is based on stability, access to health care, culture and the environment, education and infrastructure. In the 2013 edition, the top-ranked cities were Melbourne, Vienna, Vancouver, Toronto, Calgary, Adelaide, Sydney, Helsinki, Perth and Auckland (www.eiu.com).

The World Economic Forum publishes *The Human Capital Report*, which profiles 122 countries on the basis of education, health and wellness, workforce and employment and enabling environment. In 2013, Switzerland ranked first, followed by Finland, Singapore, the Netherlands, Sweden, Germany, Norway, the United Kingdom, Denmark and Canada (www.weforum.org).

The OECD maintains Your Better Life Index, an interactive tool that ranks 34 countries according to 11 user-selected topics: housing, income, jobs, community, education, environment, civic engagement, health, life satisfaction, safety and work-life balance (www.oecdbetterlifeindex.org). The OECD also produces *Society at a Glance*, a biennial overview of 25 social indicators for 42 nations (www.oecd-ilibrary.org).

The United Nations Office on Drugs and Crime maintains a homicide database that shows which countries and cities are most dangerous (www.unodc.org).

Resilience

In 2014, real estate group Grosvenor completed a three-year study into the resilience of global cities. The report assessed vulnerability to climate, environmental, social and resource-based threats and the adaptive capacity of the cities' institutions, governance, technology and funding. The top 10 cities were Toronto, Vancouver, Calgary, Chicago, Pittsburgh, Stockholm, Boston, Zurich, Washington, D.C., and Atlanta (www.grosvenor.com).

Retirement

International Living produces an annual list of the top global retirement destinations based on real estate, special retirement benefits, cost of living, ease of integration, entertainment and amenities, health care, retirement infrastructure and climate. The magazine's top picks for 2014 were Panama, Ecuador, Malaysia, Costa Rica, Spain, Colombia, Mexico, Malta, Uruguay and Thailand (http://internationalliving.com).

HelpAge produces the Global AgeWatch Index, which ranks countries by how well their elderly are treated, based on income, health, employment and education and enabling environment (www.helpage.org).

Walkability

Walkability is a measure of how friendly a community is to pedestrians. Walkable neighborhoods are more sustainable than car-dependent ones and offer environmental, health and social benefits. Research by Gary Pivo of the University of Arizona suggests that they have a lower risk of mortgage default.[5]

The Community Builders blog has a helpful checklist for walkability. You need wide, well-maintained sidewalks, with access ramps for wheelchairs and strollers. Second, you need destinations: schools, workplaces, shops, food and beverage outlets, parks and other public spaces, transit stops and cultural outlets. Finally, these destinations should be within a 10-minute walk, or about 800 meters, from your doorstep. To that list, I would add clean air, a low crime rate and a visually interesting environment.

According to Walk Score, which ranks cities in the United States, Canada and Australia for their friendliness to pedestrians, in 2014 the top three locations in those countries were New York, Vancouver and Sydney (www.walkscore.com).

WHY BUY ABROAD?

This chapter examines common reasons for buying abroad. To help you make an informed decision, it includes issues that accompany and influence those reasons and as well as alternative investments.

Status

An overseas property is a powerful way to signal your success, especially when you offer your home to friends or invite family to holiday with you. There are several ways to make a statement.

Apartments attached to luxury hotels are available in London, New York, Shanghai and many other destinations. These apartments include access to the hotel's facilities and services and have very large price tags.

Another strategy is to purchase something unique. For example, you can buy a home designed by Frank Lloyd Wright in the United States for the same price as a pre-owned, 100-square-meter apartment in Hong Kong. Or, for $2 million you can own a country house with outbuildings in Scotland or a similarly equipped manor house in France's Dordogne region. Classic Art Deco apartments are available in Miami, Paris and Shanghai. Renovations and repairs to historic homes may be subject to conservation regulations and you should include a generous budget for maintenance and upkeep.

Happiness

Whether you're motivated by something positive, like a cash windfall; a life-changing event, such as a divorce or the death of a spouse; or simply the desire for adventure, you may be considering a home abroad as a way to increase your happiness.

Several researchers have studied the relationship between home ownership and happiness. In a 2009 paper, Wharton's Grace Wong Bucchianeri analyzed survey data—gathered in 2005, before the subprime crisis—on 600 female homeowners in the U.S. state of Ohio.[1] The data showed that the homeowners spent less time with friends and, on average, were about five kilograms heavier than renters. Bucchianeri concluded, "Overall, I found little evidence that homeowners are happier."

In another study, from 1991 to 2007, Naoki Nakazato, Ulrich Schimmack and Shigehiro Oishi tracked 3,600 people in Germany who moved into a better house because their old home was too small, too expensive or in a poor location. The researchers noted that participants had a "strong and persistent" increase in housing satisfaction, but there was "no increase in average life-satisfaction."[2]

Despite these findings, a home abroad may increase your happiness if it lets you live in a greener, healthier environment, brings you into closer contact with family and friends or improves your access to museums and other cultural outlets. The lower cost of living in some destinations could also be beneficial. All of these benefits, however, are available to renters as well as owners.

For the price of a conventional property, you can often buy something distinctive. Edifício Triângulo is one of many buildings in São Paulo designed by the legendary Oscar Niemeyer.

Recreation

A holiday home abroad can let you swap cold, gray winters for warm, summer sun. It can also provide a welcome break from the stresses of day-to-day life and put golf, skiing and sailing at your doorstep.

A key consideration is the number of weeks per year that you will use the property. Beware the gym membership trap, where you buy an annual membership thinking that it will motivate you to exercise more frequently. A pay-as-you go plan is usually a less expensive way to work out.[3] Similarly for many people, renting a holiday home makes more economic sense than buying one.

Transportation costs and ease of access will influence how often you use your property. Trans-Pacific flights and jet lag can turn a week-long ski holiday into a three-day break. Also, beware of single-carrier destinations. The round-trip flying time from Hong Kong to Danang, for example, is 3 hours and 20 minutes on Dragonair, the only carrier currently offering nonstop service. Flying to the Vietnamese beach resort via Ho Chi Minh City or Hanoi, on the other hand, increases the total time to between 12 and 18 hours.

If you are buying a ski chalet, investigate the off-season activities. Many ski resorts organize bicycle and hot-air balloon races, white-water rafting, fishing and other diversions to draw people during the summer months. In addition, the ski runs should offer enough variety to keep you from becoming bored.

Before you buy, rent several times to confirm that you really like the destination. Visit during different seasons to ensure the area is attractive year-round. If possible, spend an extended period to understand the location's strengths and weaknesses. Living somewhere is different than vacationing, and a minor annoyance for two weeks—unreliable Internet service, for example—can become a major irritant over two months.

Ensure the residents are receptive to your presence. Between 1979 and 1994, for example, some 220 holiday homes in Wales were burned to the ground by arsonists protesting against wealthy English buyers, who they believed were making housing unaffordable for local people.[4]

Whether it's a detached home or a unit in a condominium complex, the quality of the management is vital. Incompetent or corrupt managers can add to your operating costs, reduce the value of your property and raise your stress level. Talking to existing owners and visiting other properties that are run by the management company can provide useful insights.

Consider long-term trends and how they will affect the property's value and your ability to sell it. For example, could new nearby developments add to the value of your home or erode it? What effect will changing tourism trends, such as the growing number of travelers from China, have? Is climate change a risk?

At the end of a vacation, when you are rested and relaxed, the idea of owning a holiday home can be tempting. Timeshare and resort salespeople use high-pressure techniques to capitalize on this vulnerability. If you find yourself tempted to buy, put the idea aside and revisit it a week after you return home.

Finally, treat claims that a holiday home is an investment with skepticism. Recreational property is a discretionary purchase and—even in mature markets—prices can be volatile. On Australia's Gold Coast, prices dropped 50% after the Lehman Brothers collapse in 2008.[5]

Alternatives to buying
If you are thinking of buying an overseas home for recreational use, you should consider the alternatives. For example, you could:

- ▲ Buy a timeshare. In exchange for the purchase price and recurring maintenance fees, a timeshare gives you the right to use a unit in a development at agreed times. The timeshare industry has a reputation for aggressive sales techniques, timeshares depreciate rapidly and are difficult to resell, and many owners complain about rapidly rising maintenance fees. Despite these drawbacks, you may find an attractively priced timeshare that fits your needs.

- Join a vacation club, where you buy points that you use to stay at resorts around the world. Vacation clubs are also known as vacation interval plans and are operated by major hotel chains or companies licensing a chain's name.

- Buy a room in a hotel. Under this arrangement, which is known as a "condotel," "apartotel" or fractional, you own the hotel room and use it when you want. When you are not using it, the property—which can range from a standard hotel room to a villa—is added to a rental pool and you receive part of the rental income. These properties are often managed by a well-known hotel chain. Capital gains are possible when you buy a unit off the plan, but it can be difficult to arrange a mortgage because lenders treat these properties as commercial, not residential. You are also dependent on the management company to ensure that the hotel is effectively marketed and properly maintained.

- Buy an income property or shares in a real estate investment trust (see below), and use the revenue to pay for a vacation in a hotel or resort. While lacking the emotional satisfaction of ownership, this approach gives you the greatest flexibility in terms of where and when to spend your holidays.

Renting your recreational property

Recreational properties are often sold as a source of income. While you can earn money from your property, it's wise to assume that the revenue numbers provided by the marketing people are optimistic and the expenses are understated. Your income and expenses can be affected by everything from weather and airline schedules to foreign exchange rates and political disputes. Treating the rental revenue as a bonus, not a reliable income stream, is sensible.

If you plan to rent your property, pick a location with year-round appeal and an internationally recognized brand, like the Indonesian island of Bali. Emerging markets have more potential for capital appreciation, but they also have more risk. Established markets generally withstand downturns better and have more of the commercial and tourism infrastructure—such as good restaurants, internationally accredited hospitals and foreign banks—that visitors and owners demand.

For maximum appeal, buy within a 90-minute drive of an international airport. Differentiating your home, for example, by child-proofing it and stocking it with toys, can boost revenues. For anything other than rustic, get-away-from-it-all retreats, guests expect broadband Internet and cable or satellite TV.

Public liability insurance is essential. Ensure that you have an appropriate level of coverage, particularly if your home is in the United States or you rent to Americans.

If you buy in a resort, the quality of the management will be critical to ensuring guests' happiness and minimizing your headaches. Some resorts offer a turnkey program that handles the marketing and guest logistics in exchange for a percentage of the income.

Check that there are no local laws prohibiting vacation rentals, as there are in parts of Florida and Spain and in cities like New York and San Francisco. Portals like Airbnb (www.airbnb.com), HomeAway (www.homeaway.com) and Housetrip (www.housetrip.com) make it easy to market your property. But these sites have also sparked a backlash from hotel and motel operators, who complain that homeowners compete unfairly because they do not comply with lodging regulations and pay taxes, and from neighbors, who object to strangers in their midst and increased demand for parking and other services.

Another approach is to simply make the property available to family and friends. This generates less cash, but eliminates the risk of dealing with strangers and the hassle of running a marketing campaign.

You will need to pay tax on your rental income. Some jurisdictions will view your rentals as a business that requires permits and inspections.

A vacation home in France

Mark Panday, a British communications executive who lives in Hong Kong with his wife, Alicia, and their three children, describes the process of buying a second home in Normandy as "trouble free." The couple paid cash for a 380-square-meter farmhouse in January 2013, after selling a home near Sees in Lower Normandy that they had owned for eight years.

The 17th century house is set in rolling countryside, equidistant from Saint Lo and Bayeux, and within easy reach of Normandy's beaches, Caen and Brittany. The property is on the outskirts of a village with a good *boulangerie* (bakery) and *boucherie* (butcher). Supermarkets are within a 15-minute drive.

The farmhouse comprises two reception rooms, a pair of kitchens, a study, five bedrooms and three bathrooms. Much of the home was original and did not require major repairs before the new owners took possession. The Pandays did decide to install a central heating system in time for the 2013 Christmas holidays and are considering improvements to the outbuildings that came with the 2.6-hectare plot.

After the hustle of Hong Kong, the Pandays were pleasantly surprised by the tranquility of the area, something they did not fully appreciate when they were viewing the home. Through the previous owner, the family was introduced to a local network of English and English-speaking friends, as well as a gardener and maintenance staff.

In August 2012, the French government introduced tax increases on second homes owned by foreigners and nonresidents. Capital gains tax increased to 34.5%, from 19%, while tax on rental income rose to 35.5%, from 20%. Appreciation in the value of the Pandays' first home in Normandy, which was also a 17th century farmhouse, largely offset the increase in capital gains tax.

The Pandays opened a local bank account, which is used to automatically pay utility bills and other expenses. Funds for the purchase were routed through this account and a local *notaire* (notary), who handled the conveyancing. Mark notes that in rural France, it is easier use a local bank than an international bank.

Owning a home in France made buying a second one much easier. The Pandays obtained legal advice from the same bilingual solicitor in Norwich, England, for both purchases. They were also familiar with Normandy and local prices and had a clear idea of their budget and the type of property they wanted to buy.

The family spent one week in France completing the sale of their first home. During that week, they viewed about 10 properties and shortlisted two before buying their new home. The farmhouse now serves as a venue for summer and Christmas holidays for the new owners, their friends and family and is not rented out.

A second home can put sun, surf and a range of recreational activities at your doorstep.

Retirement

If you plan to retire abroad, start by researching how your government treats expatriate retirees. This can affect your tax status as well as your ability to vote, collect a pension and obtain health care. If you have a retirement destination in mind, your government may have recommendations about that country. For example, Australia offers this information at www.smartraveller.gov.au.

Consider whether you will live in the new location full time (and sell or rent out your home in your country of residence) or split your time between the two countries. The latter arrangement is common among Canadians who spend their summers at home and winters in Florida, Arizona or Nevada. If you are dividing your time between two countries, ensure you don't violate the terms of your visa or stay too long and trigger an unexpected tax bill.

Much of the advice about buying a recreational property also applies to buying a retirement home. You'll want to ensure that you like the location, that it is pleasant year-round, that it has the infrastructure and services you need, that the management is competent and that transportation to and from your country of residence is accessible and affordable. Check the availability of products and services that are important to you, whether that is food or television coverage of your favorite football team.

But some things are different. For example, most people's health care needs increase as they age, so investigate the cost, availability and quality of local medical care. For people over 65, including registered foreigners, Ecuador offers health care for about $50 per month.

Look for a home with universal design, such as wheelchair-friendly counters, ramps and grab-bars that will let you age in place, or find a complex that is designed for retirees.

Investigate the availability of public transportation—buses, subways, taxis, paratransit services for the elderly and disabled, and ride-sharing services such as Uber (www.uber.com)— in your new home. Research conducted in 2011 by AARP showed that 88% of American adults continued to drive cars at age 65. But by age 75, that number dropped to 69%. As you age, living in a walkable neighborhood where everything you need is nearby and having access to public transport will improve your quality of life.[6]

If you plan to live out your days in your new country, look into the availability of long-term nursing care and ensure that your will is up to date and recognized in your new home and in all of the places where you live and have assets.

Bay views and fresh air

Eva Lee* was working in South Korea when she bought a vacation home in Alameda County on the east shore of San Francisco Bay. A U.K. native and resident of Hong Kong, Lee was drawn to the area by its fresh air, proximity to San Francisco and excellent public transport.

In May 2012, she purchased a 1,500-square-foot (139-square-meter), low-rise condominium for $553,000 in cash, $46,000 less than the asking price. The penthouse unit includes two bedrooms, two bathrooms, six closets, a balcony and a deck. Completed in 1972, the complex has heated outdoor swimming pools, jacuzzis and tennis courts. The building was designed by Wurster, Bernardi & Emmons, an award-winning firm noted for their modern designs.

As a U.K. passport-holder, Lee can participate in the ESTA visa-waiver program operated by the U.S. Department of Homeland Security (https://esta.cbp.dhs.gov). Under the ESTA program, visitors are limited to 90-day stays in the United States. She has since obtained a 10-year, multiple-entry visa that lets her stay for up to six months at a time.

Lee found California expensive. For example, property taxes are more than three times higher than for a more valuable home in London. Annual homeowners' association fees are almost as high as the property taxes, and home contents insurance is more expensive in California than in London or Hong Kong.

The buying process in California was more hands-on than in England and Scotland, where Lee had purchased property previously. "The paper burden was minimal in these countries compared to the U.S.," she observes, "and the conveyancing lawyer does all the work."

A lot of mandatory paperwork accompanied the California purchase. For example, there was:

---

* Eva Lee is a pseudonym.

- ▲ The residential purchase agreement and joint escrow instructions (Form RPA-CA), an eight-page standard sale and purchase agreement

- ▲ The statewide buyer and seller advisory (Form SBSA), a 10-page document that covers everything from the death of someone with HIV on the premises to nearby natural gas pipelines

- ▲ The state natural hazard disclosure, more than 30 pages of information about nearby flood, fire and earthquake risks

- ▲ The preliminary title company report, 10 pages detailing the home's ownership history

- ▲ A homeowners' association disclosure packet, over 70 pages of information, including newsletters, covenants, codes and restrictions, board meeting minutes, financial statements, insurance certificates and more.

Lee describes the local bureaucracy as "a wonderful puzzle." For example, without a Social Security Number, you can't get a credit card, buy an insurance policy or open an account with most of the utility companies. But you can open a bank account and get a California driver's license. State law requires carbon monoxide alarms for all dwellings intended for human occupancy that have a fuel-burning appliance, a fireplace or an attached garage. And if Lee were to rent her home out, she would need the approval of the homeowners' association, which monitors the number of rental units in the complex, as well as a city business license.

For non-Americans thinking of buying in the U.S., Lee recommends finding a good real estate agent who can manage the paperwork. She also suggests granting power of attorney to a trusted local person, if one is available, and buying the property through a trust to minimize taxes and expedite probate.

Despite the challenges, Lee is happy with her home, particularly the marvelous views of San Francisco Bay and the friendliness of her neighbors. Asked if she would do anything differently, she says, "I would have bought two condos because prices are rising big time."

Investment

There are many reasons for investing in overseas property, including income, portfolio diversification or sheltering your wealth. The following ideas may be helpful if you are thinking of investing abroad.

Boom towns
Buying property in boom towns can produce outsize returns for investors who enter the market early and exit before the inevitable crash. For example, in Maputo, Mozambique, discoveries of oil, gas and coal have caused prices and rents to spike. Homes in prime locations now rent for $7,000 per month and sell for $500,000.[7] Natural resources are also behind high prices in Fort McMurray, Canada, where the average single-family home sold for more than C$769,000 ($680,000) in September 2013.[8] The average bachelor apartment in the city, which is near northern Alberta's oil sands, rents for C$1,428 per month. The relaxation of sanctions by the United States and the European Union prompted a similar increase in Yangon, Myanmar, where four-bedroom homes rent for $6,500 per month.[9] In Afghanistan's capital, Kabul, prices of luxury property have dropped by half between 2011 and 2013, as speculators sold ahead of the departure of NATO forces in 2014.[10] If you have a taste for risk, it is possible to illegally buy a home in Pyongyang, where home prices are reported to be soaring as market forces spread.

Boom towns are rare in developed economies. In emerging markets like Mozambique, Myanmar and North Korea, it is often difficult to arrange financing or obtain clear title.

Cross-border arbitrage
As prices rise in hubs like Hong Kong and Singapore, people look to neighboring areas for cheaper accommodations and for recreational property. For example, an estimated 90% of the 130,000 foreigners

who own property in Malaysia's Johor are from nearby Singapore.[11] Senior citizens from Hong Kong, meanwhile, are able to retire and collect pensions in China's Guangdong Province.

Improvements at the border between Malaysia and Singapore and the boundary between Hong Kong and Mainland China make it possible to live on one side and work on the other.

Distressed property
Since the 2008 subprime crisis, value investors have sought opportunities in the United States. While it is possible to find bargains, many of these homes have issues that can cause problems for unsuspecting buyers. This includes "vampire REOs," which are bank-owned dwellings that are still occupied by the foreclosed homeowner, and "zombie foreclosures," which are homes that are still in the foreclosure process, but have been abandoned by the homeowner. You will have to evict the residents of the vampire REOs and hope they don't damage or destroy the home in the meantime. Zombie homes have often fallen into disrepair and represent a threat to the value of surrounding homes. Vampire REOs and zombie homes frequently have years of deferred maintenance that can be expensive to fix. According to RealtyTrac, in October 2013 Miami, Los Angeles and Houston had large numbers of vampire REOs. In March 2014, RealtyTrac estimated that zombie homes represented one in five foreclosures in the United States, with Miami, Chicago and New York City having the largest numbers of these properties.[12]

These problems are not limited to the United States: there are millions of vacant homes in Europe. Criminals in Madrid break into homes that are being foreclosed and "sell" or rent them at below-market prices until the foreclosure is complete.[13]

"Shadow inventory"—properties that are seriously delinquent, in foreclosure or held by mortgage servicing companies but not offered for sale on a listing service—is another pitfall. In October 2013, CoreLogic estimated that 1.9 million U.S. homes were in this category. If these homes were released onto the market all at once, prices would collapse.

Large investors have been converting foreclosed homes into rental properties. Companies including Blackstone Group, Oaktree Capital Group, American Homes 4 Rent, Colony Capital and Silver Bay Realty Trust Corp. bought 100,000 homes in southern California, Florida, Arizona and Nevada. Many of these companies are now trying to exit the business or monetize their investments. American Homes made an initial public offering in August 2013. In September 2013, Oaktree announced plans to sell a portfolio of 500 foreclosed homes. The following month, Blackstone said it would issue $479 million in bonds that would be backed by rental payments from these homes. If you are thinking of investing in distressed residential property, watch these companies. They are among the most sophisticated investors in the business and if they are cashing out, the market may well have peaked.

It is hard to overstate the importance of research in cross-border purchases of distressed property. A 2013 report by Harvard University's Joint Center for Housing Studies found that nearly one-third of the 38,931 REO sales in Cleveland, Ohio, between 2000 and 2012 had a negative outcome, such as abandonment, condemnation, demolition or tax delinquency. Out-of-state investors, many of whom bought the homes "sight unseen," fared particularly badly. They often underestimated the extent of the homes' deterioration and the rate at which prices were declining. Many buyers were also surprised at how aggressive local governments were in enforcing housing codes.[14]

Education
Buying a home near a desirable school is a proven investment strategy. In the United Kingdom, homes near top private schools in Oxford, Newbury, Winchester and Surrey command premium prices. Homes near schools offering the International Baccalaureate program are popular in countries ranging from Dubai and Malaysia to France and Spain. In March 2013, the *Global Times* reported that the average price of homes in Beijing's Wudaokou neighborhood, which is near some of China's top universities and primary schools, was more than 100,000 yuan ($16,000) per square meter.

Another strategy is to invest in student accommodations near universities, either for rental income or for your children's use. This approach can work near top-name universities, where off the plan and buy-to-let deals are available, or on a more modest scale with existing apartments in cities like Edmonton, Canada.

Some analysts have warned of a higher education bubble in the United States. If that bubble bursts, returns on student accommodations could suffer.

Gentrification usually starts with a building that is architecturally interesting, like this mansion near the center of São Paulo.

Gentrification

Gentrification happens when middle-class people and professionals move into a working-class, inner-city neighborhood. The newcomers are drawn to the neighborhood's proximity to the city center and its older homes, as well as the property price increases that accompany gentrification.

Gentrification is a global phenomenon, occurring in cities as diverse as Berlin, London and Rio de Janeiro. Gentrification is controversial because it displaces poorer residents and reduces a city's stock of low-income housing. It also pits long-term residents—who see their way of life disappearing—against newcomers who want to remake the area to accommodate their tastes.

Gentrification happens in waves, with pioneers taking the greatest risks and potentially reaping the greatest rewards. As the conversion takes root, prices begin to rise, crime rates fall, services improve and mainstream residents appear.

There are several signs that a neighborhood may undergo gentrification. Poor precincts that are surrounded by or adjacent to thriving, up-market districts are often annexed. A shift in the retail mix in local stores—from malt liquor to craft beer, for example—may indicate that gentrification has begun. Architecturally interesting neighborhoods, with older, well-built homes are desirable, as are areas where the government is investing in infrastructure, like public transit. In the United States, gay men gravitate toward neighborhoods with older, historic housing stock. Many of these "gayborhoods" reported rising income levels that are commonly associated with gentrification.[15] Finally, look for strong local employment and property prices that are below the city average—but rising quickly.

Rental accommodations
Owning rental property can add geographic and currency diversification to your investment portfolio. However, becoming an international landlord makes you dependent on local service providers, including agents, property managers, tradespeople, banks, lawyers and accountants. Finding and retaining the right suppliers can make the difference between a positive experience and enormous frustration for you and your tenant. Tales of woe—like the Singaporean investor who paid a New York property manager $260,000 to outfit 13 one-bedroom apartments and received $40,000-worth of junk furniture instead—are legion.[16]

Before you start looking at property, do some basic research about the rental market and its quirks. For example, a million apartments in New York City are subject to rent controls. Under a system known as *jeonse*, tenants in South Korea don't pay rent. Instead, they give their landlord a deposit, typically equal to 25%–50% of the property's value, to invest over the life of the lease. The owner keeps the returns and repays the deposit at the end of the tenancy. In Seoul, some *jeonse* deposits now exceed the value of the homes.[17]

Retirement housing
Around the world, there is growing, unmet demand for seniors' housing. In the United States, Canada, Australia, New Zealand and several European nations, the need comes from retiring baby boomers. In China, which will see the number of people aged over 65 grow from 119 million in 2010 to 330 million in 2050,[18] demand is being driven by longer life expectancies, the effects of the one-child policy and the reduction of state-supplied social welfare programs.

Seniors' housing is an interesting investment opportunity. However, high staffing costs and shortfalls in government pensions and retirees' savings make it difficult to turn a profit.

An income property in Tokyo

After publishing my second book, *Landed Japan*, in May 2010, it was time to use what I had learned to buy an apartment in Tokyo.

With Erik Oskamp, an agent I had met while researching the book, I spent the afternoon of September 30, 2010, looking at apartments in Nakano-ku, in Tokyo's western suburbs, and in Itabashi-ku, Adachi-ku and Katsushika-ku in the north. The apartments were 16–42 square meters in size and 22–36 years old. Some buildings had hundreds of units, while others had fewer than 40, and the group included buildings made of steel-reinforced concrete as well as steel frame construction. All were priced at less than ¥6 million ($58,600) and served by a train or subway line, although one apartment was a 20-minute walk from the nearest station.

In Japan, prospective buyers cannot view the inside of tenanted apartments. But we were able to walk around the neighborhoods, some of which were quasi-industrial. Overflowing mailboxes indicated buildings with high vacancy rates, while rust stains and peeling paint hinted at maintenance problems.

I shortlisted three apartments and, on October 1, made an offer for one in Itabashi-ku. The offer, which was 5% less than the asking price, was rejected and I subsequently met the original ¥4.2 million asking price. When that offer was accepted, I started doing the paperwork, which included a notarized declaration that I was not a resident of Japan. I also signed two powers of attorney, one authorizing Erik's company to purchase the apartment on my behalf and a second enabling a judicial scrivener, Kawanabe-san, to register the property in my name. Erik also began the due diligence process to ensure that there were no problems with the building, title or tenant.

This was followed by two video chat sessions on Skype. One was with Kawanabe-san, who needed to verify my identity and confirm that I was buying the property. The second was with Wakabayashi-san, a licensed real estate agent employed by Erik's company, who read me the "explanation of important matters." This is essentially the sale and purchase agreement, along with disclosures of any known issues with the property, and background on the tenant if there is one. Reading the explanation of important matters is mandatory when you buy real estate in Japan.

The recitation took 70 minutes and degenerated into comedy when the agent told me that the tenant, a retired civil servant, "had a problem with his waist." I asked for clarification, wondering if he was confined to a wheelchair or if there was a rubbish-related problem. After consulting a dictionary and much discussion among the office staff, Wakabayashi-san told me that the tenant had a severe case of hemorrhoids, which was the reason that he had retired.

The sale closed on November 15, 2010, and the tenant has remained in the apartment. Built in 1974 from steel-reinforced concrete, the unit is 21 square meters, plus a six-square-meter balcony. The apartment is adjacent to the Shuto Expressway, one of Tokyo's main highways, and is a 10-minute walk to the Mita subway line, from which it is 30 minutes to central Tokyo.

I paid cash for the apartment, which I still own. With all taxes and fees, the total purchase price was ¥4.9 million, or about US$58,000 at 2010 exchange rates. In calendar 2011, the apartment generated revenue of ¥491,000, after management fees, maintenance charges, possession tax and income tax. That's a net yield of over 10%.

As a nonresident Canadian living in Hong Kong, rental income from the apartment does not create a tax liability in Canada or in Hong Kong.

The apartment is in Itabashi-ku, a working class neighborhood in northern Tokyo. The Shuto Expressway can be seen on the right.

Alternative investments
In addition to owning physical property, there are several ways to gain exposure to real estate. You can:

- ▲ Buy shares in a company listed on a stock exchange like those in New York (http://nyse.com), London (www.londonstockexchange.com), Tokyo (www.tse.or.jp), Hong Kong (www.hkex.com.hk) or Singapore (www.sgx.com). Developers, builders, real estate agents, lenders, hoteliers, consultants and other companies are listed on these bourses.

▲ Buy shares in a real estate investment trust (REIT), which is a mutual fund that invests in real estate. REITs legally avoid corporate taxes by distributing the bulk of their income to shareholders. Specialty REITs invest in individual countries, market segments like offices or according to other criteria. For example, the Sabana REIT (www.sabana-reit.com), which is listed in Singapore, is Shariah-compliant. For more information, see the National Association of Real Estate Investment Trusts (www.reit.com) and the European Public Real Estate Association (www.epra.com), the British Property Federation (www.bpf.org.uk) and Japan's Association for Real Estate Securitization (www.ares.or.jp).

▲ Purchase shares in an exchange-traded fund or a mutual fund. Like REITs, ETFs and mutual funds invest in a variety of sectors and markets, are liquid and are accessible to small investors.

▲ Invest through a private equity real estate fund. Because these funds are usually illiquid and require an investment of $1 million or more, they are suitable for institutions and wealthy individuals.

A second passport

Having a second passport provides many benefits. It can facilitate travel when your primary passport is being renewed or held for a visa, enhance your privacy, allow you to work abroad and simplify tax planning.

Antigua and Barbuda, Australia, Austria, Cyprus, Greece, Ireland, Portugal, Malta, Latvia, Spain and St. Kitts and Nevis allow individuals to acquire citizenship or residency by purchasing real estate.

These programs come and go in response to political and economic pressures. In February 2014, for example, Canada's federal government scrapped an immigrant investor program, under which individuals with a minimum net worth of C$1.6 million could lend the Canadian government C$800,000 for five years in exchange for residency. Some 59,000 applications, many of them from people in China, Hong Kong and Taiwan, were canceled.

If you are thinking of obtaining a second passport through a property purchase, you need to know:

- ▲ When you will be eligible for citizenship
- ▲ The minimum investment amount and availability of financing
- ▲ The type of real estate that qualifies and how long you must hold the property
- ▲ If there is a residency requirement to obtain citizenship
- ▲ Whether your current and new countries allow dual citizenship
- ▲ The nations to which your new country's passport offers for visa-free entry
- ▲ If your new country has national-service requirements, especially if you have children
- ▲ How the new passport will affect your tax liabilities
- ▲ If you can renounce your new citizenship

BUYING BASICS

Agents
47

Laws and Lawyers
57

Ownership and Property Rights
63

Negotiating
73

Demographics
79

Risk Factors
85

AGENTS

A real estate agent is an intermediary between the buyer and the seller of a piece of property. Also known as estate agents and brokers, real estate agents can act on behalf of the buyer, the seller or for both parties in what is known as dual agency. In some places, agents act as facilitators or transactional agents and do not represent either party.

Representation

In general, if an agent acts on behalf of a seller or a buyer, they have a fiduciary duty to that party. The agent is expected to maintain client confidentiality, act with care and diligence and disclose any conflicts of interest. In practical terms, that means getting the best possible price and terms for the client; not telling a potential buyer that their client is in the middle of a divorce and is anxious to sell; and advising their client if the home they are buying is owned by the agent's brother.

In the United States, the agent is hired by and paid by the vendor. A subagent handles the buyer's side of the transaction. The subagent's commission is paid from the 6% that the vendor pays his agent. The subagent has a fiduciary duty to the vendor, not the buyer. If you are the buyer, for example, and make the vendor an offer of $200,000 but tell the subagent that you were prepared to pay $250,000, the subagent is required to convey that information to the vendor.[1]

Dual agency is illegal in Singapore and other places. Where dual agency is permitted, agents are usually required to provide a written disclosure that they are working for both parties. Agents may be limited in the services that they can offer and may have to disclose their commission to both parties. Agents prefer dual agency, because it allows them to earn higher commissions. Dual agency arrangements can result in situations where the client's interests do not align with those of the agent. But because the agent is receiving a larger commission, she may be more willing to offer a discount.

In many markets, anyone can call themselves a real estate agent. For instance, in Cuba real estate agents were only recognized as an authorized occupation in 2013.[2] In the United States, agents must complete training programs, pass exams and participate in continuing professional education. In Japan, where agents are licensed, it is not unusual for the owner of a real estate agency to be unlicensed, but for property sales to be processed by a licensed agent. Likewise, an unlicensed salesperson may show you a property and then hand the transaction off to a licensed agent to compete the formalities.

In the United States, real estate salespeople and brokers are both real estate agents. But a salesperson works for a broker, who may work for herself or for another broker. Brokers have more training and assume more legal responsibility than salespeople.

Dual agency is forbidden in Singapore but is common in many other markets.

The agent's role

At an absolute minimum, agents introduce buyers and sellers. But national regulations can greatly expand that role. In Sweden, for example, agents have a duty to gather and disclose information—such as listing all encumbrances and confirming that the vendor has the right to sell the property—and draw up the sale and purchase agreement. In Sweden, agents must be an impartial counselor to the buyer and seller and are forbidden from representing either party.[3]

An agent's greatest contribution is her local knowledge. Google Maps and 360-degree photographs are useful, but they cannot replace the expertise and access to information (including data that is not in the public domain) that an agent gains from operating in a neighborhood day in and day out. In small markets—for example, Monaco's 202 hectares or luxury villas in Tahiti—one agent or agency may be able to cover the entire sector. But in most locations, knowledge is gained one neighborhood at a time.

Some people hire a buyer's agent (BA) to help them locate a property. Research in the United States, where the BA is paid from the 6% commission that the seller pays to his agent, suggests that BAs do not negotiate lower prices for their principals. They do, however, save clients money by reducing the amount of time it takes to find a home.[4]

A buyer's agent can help you in several other ways, such as preparing the offer, ensuring your strategy is right and including conditions to protect your interests. A BA can also help you negotiate more effectively because they are not emotionally invested in the transaction.

If you use a BA, carefully review the contract. Three areas deserve particular attention: your liability for paying the BA's commission if the seller's agent does not pay; your liability for paying the BA a commission if you buy or rent a home from another agent, even if this happens after the expiry of your agreement with the BA; and your liability for paying the BA's commission if you do not complete the sale.[5]

Agents in certain markets offer overseas inspection trips, where you enjoy subsidized airfare and accommodations while visiting prospective homes. This can be an efficient way to view property, but the agent will expect to recoup the travel subsidies with commission from a sale. Ensure that you know the extent of your liability if you don't buy.

An agent's market knowledge can be especially helpful if you are buying distressed property. At a minimum, you will want to know why the home is distressed, the agent's motivation for showing you a specific property, how long the agent expects it will take for the property to turn around (and why she believes it will recover) and your exit strategy. The building's physical and financial conditions are critical. You don't want to buy a unit in a building that has large, unfunded or deferred repairs. You'll also want to avoid buildings where other owners are not paying their maintenance fees—a common situation with Japanese resorts built during the 1980s. Properties are distressed for a reason, and if something seems too good to be true, it probably is.

In addition, a good agent can add value by:

▲ Helping you find and evaluate sources of financing

▲ Providing data and context, such as market trends, opportunities and threats in a particular neighborhood

▲ Recommending other service providers, such as contractors

▲ Anticipating and resolving problems that might derail a transaction

▲ Giving you access to properties before they reach the broader market

▲ Providing cultural insights that help you make a better purchase

Finding an agent

Recommendations from friends and colleagues are a good place to start when searching for an agent. Follow this up with checks of online forums and with the local regulator and trade association. In some markets, there are online registries where you can confirm that the agent is licensed. Websites operated by regulators, trade organizations and consumer protection groups can be a good place to learn about local standards and practices.

Real estate agencies use a variety of ownership and operating structures. This includes one-person companies, local and regional corporations and global franchises. Small, local agencies can provide more flexible, personal service. Large businesses offer the reassurance of a familiar brand, plus marketing, staff training and quality control programs. Big companies and franchises have higher overheads, which are reflected in their fees. They are also less likely to offer discounts.

Ideally, the agency should have been in business for a long time and have deep roots in the community. Companies that meet these criteria have spent time and effort building a reputation and are unlikely to jeopardize their brand by acting unethically.

First, to get the best out of your agent, be an informed, educated consumer. Start by understanding the local market, which will allow you to ask questions and determine how much—or how little—the agent knows. If you get vague, evasive or incorrect answers, it may be time to find another agent.

Second, by knowing your budget and schedule, as well as your preferred location, features, size and other requirements, and communicating this clearly to the agent, you demonstrate that you are a serious buyer. Tell the agent what is essential and where you can compromise. This approach saves everybody time and reduces the likelihood that the agent will show you homes that don't meet your needs.

Third, identify people who have purchased homes in your target city and neighborhood. These homeowners can be an excellent source of referrals and insights about local problems and opportunities.

Incentives and sales techniques

In their book *Freakonomics*, Steven Levitt and Stephen Dubner suggest that agents have an incentive to encourage vendors to accept lowball offers. They note that in the United States, the selling agent and buying agent (or subagent) typically split the 6% commission on the sale of a home, and the agents then split the commission again with their respective agencies. As a result, the selling agent receives $4,500, before taxes and expenses, of the $18,000 commission from the sale of a $300,000 home. But if the agent makes an extra effort and sells the home for $310,000, it only puts an extra $150 in her pocket. A faster sale is clearly preferable.

This conclusion was supported by research conducted by Steven Levitt and Chad Syverson, in which they analyzed data from the sale of 100,000 Chicago-area homes between 1992 and 2002. Levitt and Syverson found that when agents sold their own homes, they kept them on the market for an average of 9.5 days longer and sold them for 3.7% more than comparable homes sold for clients.[6]

Agents have numerous techniques for making homes appear attractive. For instance, beware what Professor Robert Cialdini calls "set-up properties" in his book *Influence: The Psychology of Persuasion*. An agent will show you ugly, overpriced homes to set your expectations before showing you nicer, better priced ones. The second group will seem far more appealing after you've seen the first batch, even if the second group isn't particularly desirable.

Duke University Professor Dan Ariely describes another technique for focusing a buyer's attention. The agent shows a customer three desirable, similarly priced homes: two colonial and a contemporary. One of the colonial homes, which Ariely calls the decoy, needs repairs and is offered at a discount. The decoy serves as a point of comparison and makes the customer more likely to ignore the contemporary and buy the undiscounted colonial home.[7]

In *Freakonomics*, Levitt and Dubner also note there is a "strong positive correlation" between the use of certain words—granite, maple, gourmet and state-of-the-art—and higher sale prices. The authors observe that these words are specific and useful, unlike other common terms—fantastic, spacious, "!", charming and great neighborhood—that are ambiguous and subject to interpretation. Levitt and Dubner point out that an ad full of vague words may indicate that the home has nothing special that is worth describing.

In Australia, Canada, the U.K., the U.S. and other countries, agents will use fresh flowers or the smell of cinnamon, coffee, bread or cookies to make a home seem more attractive. Some agents employ "home stagers"—a cross between a film set designer and an interior designer—to decorate a property with antiques and artwork, highlight its strengths and minimize any weaknesses. This is most common in expensive, empty homes.

Both the buyer and seller pay 3% commission to the real estate agent when a home is sold in Argentina.

Fees

Agents' commission rates and practices vary widely, and may be subject to sales tax or value-added tax. For example, in:

▲ Argentina, the buyer and seller each pay 3% of the sale price

▲ Colombia, the seller pays 3% of the sale price. Some agents offer a buyer's agent service, in which the buyer pays the 3% commission and the vendor reduces the sale price accordingly.

▲ Hong Kong, the buyer and seller each pay 1% of the sale price. Rates are negotiable.

- ▲ Japan, the buyer pays 3% of the purchase price, plus ¥63,000 ($616)

- ▲ Malaysia, a maximum of 3% of the sale price is payable by either the buyer or seller

- ▲ Mexico, the seller pays 5%–10% of the sale price

- ▲ New Zealand, the seller pays an administrative fee of about NZ$500 ($429), plus 4% of the sale price. Discounts may be negotiated.

- ▲ Russia, the buyer pays 2%–6% of the purchase price, with higher rates applying to less expensive homes

- ▲ South Africa, vendors pay 4%–8% of the sale price. Rates are negotiable and flat-rate agreements are possible.

- ▲ The United Kingdom, the vendor pays 1%–3% of the sale price. Commissions are lower in competitive markets and higher for non-exclusive contracts. Flat-rate agreements are possible.

- ▲ The United States, the vendor pays 6% of the sale price. Rates are negotiable and flat-rate agreements are possible.

For sale by owner

In Canada and the United States, about 10% of homes are sold without an agent, in what is known as an FSBO transaction.[8] Approximately 13% of owners in the United Kingdom sell their home without an agent.[9] For buyers, this can be an opportunity to save money because vendors will usually discount the home's price by an amount equal to all or part of the agent's commission.

However, this approach is not risk-free. Buyers are vulnerable to problems that could have been avoided by an experienced agent, or paid for by her professional insurance or industry indemnity fund.

That said, many people have successfully sold property without an agent. If you are buying an FSBO home, I suggest the following:

▲ Research the vendor, builder or developer, neighborhood, value of comparable properties on the market and the local disclosure regulations. In the United States, with the owner's permission, you can buy a Comprehensive Loss Underwriting Exchange (CLUE) report, which lists the home's insurance claim history and provides information on possible defects, like mold. You can also obtain a professional appraisal. With a little effort and ingenuity, you can close the gap between an agent's knowledge and your own.

▲ Hire a professional inspector to check the home. Use an inspector with a reputation for being thorough. Every issue that he discovers is a bargaining chip that you can use to reduce the price of the home, or a reason to buy another property. Either way, you win.

▲ Retain an experienced real estate lawyer to review the documents and advise on the transaction.

▲ Use an escrow account instead of giving the deposit (also known as earnest money) directly to the vendor.

▲ Consider hiring a buyer's agent to represent you either on a commission or a flat-fee basis.

There is a growing body of research into the effectiveness and value of agents in the sales process. Papers released in 2007 by Stanford University[10] and Northwestern University[11] in the United States concluded that vendors using agents did not achieve a higher sale price. However, both papers found that agents sold homes more quickly. The Northwestern University paper, which compared sales using an electronic listing service operated by real estate agents and an FSBO Website in Madison, Wisconsin, found that 22% of the FSBO vendors ultimately moved to to the electronic listing service.

LAWS AND LAWYERS

In general, the jurisdiction where your property is located determines the law that governs the buying process and your ability to enjoy, rent out, mortgage and sell it.* As a result, the stability, transparency and efficiency of the local legal system are important.

From the perspective of an overseas property buyer, some jurisdictions are more desirable than others. For instance, England has a long history of welcoming foreigners, and litigants from around the world choose English courts as a venue for settling international disputes. On the other hand, in just over a decade, Sri Lanka went from allowing foreigners to buy freehold property, subject to a 100% tax, to permitting foreigners to buy tax-free, to only allowing 99-year leases with a 100% tax.

In addition, some jurisdictions are investor-friendly. Until recent market cooling measures were introduced, Hong Kong, which has no capital gains tax, fell into this category. Other places, like California, tend to be more tenant-friendly.

Legal systems

International legal systems can be divided into four broad categories:

- ▲ Civil law can be traced to the Justinian Code from sixth-century Rome. Countries using this system have a written code of laws that judges use to decide cases. Scotland, Mexico and many nations in Europe, Central and South America and Africa use civil law.

- ▲ Common law derives from English case law. Under this system, judges' decisions are based on precedents set by other judges in earlier, similar cases. Common law is used in the United States and former members of the British Empire, such as Australia, Canada, Hong Kong, India and New Zealand.

---

*   Exceptions include properties owned by offshore companies and trusts.

▲ Muslim law is based on the Koran. It is used in Afghanistan, the Maldives and Saudi Arabia.

▲ Mixed systems combine features of civil, common and Muslim law, and sometimes elements of customary law. China and Japan, for example, combine civil and customary law. There are also anomalies, like Louisiana and Quebec, which use civil law in common law countries.

In Canada, Quebec uses civil law while the other provinces use common law. Quebec's French heritage is also reflected in Montreal's architecture.

Practitioners

There are different kinds of professionals who can assist you in a real estate transaction. In the United States, for example, lawyers and attorneys provide legal advice and represent clients in court. England has a split system, where solicitors offer legal advice and instruct barristers, who represent clients in court. In England, Australia and New Zealand, buyers may use licensed conveyancers, who specialize in transferring property. Japan has similar specialists, called judicial scriveners (*shiho-shoshi*).

In common law countries, a notary (also known as a notary public) administers oaths, witnesses statutory declarations and authenticates certain types of documents. In civil law countries, however, notaries have a different function. They are professional lawyers who draw up and record civil contracts and handle conveyancing, among other services.

Services

Lawyers and solicitors can provide advice on many aspects of home ownership, including:

▲ Reviewing the transaction to ensure that your interests are protected

▲ Structuring the purchase, including the use of companies, trusts and other vehicles

▲ Preparing a will that will be recognized in the country where you live, where you own property and where you are domiciled

▲ Ensuring that you comply with foreign ownership regulations

▲ Checking the title to make sure it is defect-free

▲ Ensuring that all taxes and fees are paid

▲ Preparing a tenancy agreement, if you plan to rent your home out

▲ Introducing you to other professionals, such as accountants

▲ Reviewing your financing

▲ Explaining local laws and customs, such as the use of seals (*hanko*) in Japan

Retaining a lawyer

Purchasing property is complicated enough in your home country. When you add a second language, a different legal system and unfamiliar customs, the potential for problems grows. Legal advice can help you avoid and minimize those problems.

That said, you need to balance the cost of legal advice against the property's value. Spending $10,000 for a $50,000 home doesn't make sense. You'll also want to find a commercially savvy lawyer, who understands where she adds value to the buying process.

The lawyer should be licensed to practice in the jurisdiction where your new home is located. In general, a lawyer who practices in a given country will be more knowledgeable about local laws and commercial realities than a nonresident. Furthermore, if you receive bad advice, your ability to obtain compensation is greater if the lawyer, property and transaction are all in the same jurisdiction.

Unlike litigation, most property transactions are predictable. Ask for a cost estimate, with an explanation of the services that are included, the hourly billing rate and expected disbursements. You may be able to negotiate a flat rate.

Find your own lawyer and check her credentials. It is essential that the lawyer has experience in international real estate and expertise in international tax and estate planning can also be helpful. The lawyer you use in your home country may be able to provide a referral.

Global law firms offer the comfort of a well-known brand, attractive offices and English-speaking staff. However, their rates tend to be higher than those of local firms. In some countries, such as China, foreign law firms may not practice local law.

If you use a lawyer who has been recommended by a developer or agent, you run the risk of a conflict of interest. Local-language contracts normally take precedence over translations, so do not rely on a translation prepared by the developer or agent. If your counterparty tells you, "There's no need to bring lawyers into this," getting independent legal advice is often the smartest thing that you can do.

Ensure you know who the lawyer is representing. For example, civil law notaries are required to act impartially, for both the buyer and seller. In Hong Kong, lenders will often appoint the purchaser's solicitors to draw up the mortgage. Purchasers are required to sign a warning letter acknowledging that, if there is a conflict with the lender, they will have to hire a second solicitor to represent their interests.

Criminal matters

Understanding the local laws is smart, particularly if you are moving to a country with a different legal system or conservative values.

In Singapore, for example, if you are found in possession of more than 500 grams of cannabis, you face the death penalty. In the United Arab Emirates, if you write a check that is dishonored, you are guilty of a criminal act and can go to jail, even if the check bounces by accident.

Many nations have a version of the U.S. Foreign Corrupt Practices Act, which makes it a criminal offense to pay a bribe while abroad. This can cause problems if you are living in country where kickbacks are a way of life.

Documents and identification

To buy a home, open a bank account or take out a mortgage, you will need to provide a range of documents. A photocopy, a notarized copy or the original document may be required, and you may be asked to provide a certified translation or a translation by an officially approved translator.

Institutions and bureaucrats have different ways of handling document authentication, and they may request something—like a seal on each page of a multipage document—that the issuing government refuses to provide. There is not much you can do about this, except remain pleasant, negotiate and try not to lose your temper. Common forms of certification include:

- ▲ A notary public can witness (or notarize) a signature on a document. In some jurisdictions, notaries can make "certified true copies" of documents. Note that notaries do not certify the contents of a document.

- ▲ A consularized document is certified by an embassy or consulate, sometimes with a ribbon and a wax seal. For example, to be recognized in China an American birth certificate would be consularized by the Chinese embassy in Washington, D.C.

- ▲ An apostille authenticates a public document like a birth or marriage certificate. Apostilles are issued by the government that issued the original document and are either placed on or attached to the original document. See the Hague Conference Website (www.hcch.net) for more information.

In addition, you should note that:

- ▲ Documents have expiry dates. A three-month-old phone bill may be acceptable as proof of residency, but an older one may not.

- ▲ Documents need to be whole and unaltered or they may be rejected. If a document has five pages, bring all five, including the ones that say, "This page intentionally left blank."

- ▲ Your documents should be consistent. Most native English-speakers understand that "Chris" and "Christopher" are the same person. A non-native speaker may not.

OWNERSHIP AND PROPERTY RIGHTS

The twin cornerstones of a functioning real estate market are a transparent legal system and a property registry that identifies the owner of a piece of property and the owner's holdings and rights and ensures that those rights can be enjoyed and transferred with certainty and predictability.

Ownership structures

Condominiums
In a condominium, you have exclusive title to the space within your unit. You share ownership of the building's common elements, such as hallways, elevators and swimming pool, with other owners. You are free to mortgage or sell your unit, and all owners pay their share of the cost of operating, maintaining and repairing the building. Owners also contribute to a reserve fund, which is used to pay for major repairs.

Condominiums are run by an owners' committee, which is responsible for enforcing the rules that owners accept when they buy a unit, and for maintaining the common elements of the building. Owners' committees have the power make expensive decisions, like replacing a roof, and obliging all owners to contribute to the cost.

Condominiums can be built on leasehold or freehold land. If the condominium is built on freehold land, each of the unit owners has a share of the land under the building.

Cooperatives
A cooperative is a form of corporate ownership, whereby the corporation's shareholders are tenants who are permitted to use a specific dwelling. As a shareholder/tenant, you don't own any real estate—the corporation owns the entire building. You pay monthly rent or a maintenance fee, which is a prorated share of the corporation's mortgage, operational, maintenance and repair costs, taxes and reserves.[1] In the United States, co-ops are most common in New York City and

Chicago, but they can also be found in Canada and Europe. Co-op buildings can be on leasehold or freehold land.

Co-ops are managed by a board of directors. Unlike condominiums or single-family homes, which can be bought and sold freely, buying into a co-op requires the board's approval. Some people describe this process as being similar to joining an exclusive club. The existing members want to ensure that you will be a good neighbor, fit in and have the financial resources to meet your obligations. The vetting process can be invasive, and a board can reject a prospective buyer without giving a reason.

Freehold and fee simple
In common law, fee simple is a subset of freehold property and is the highest form of ownership. If you buy a home on land that is held on a fee simple basis, you own the house and the land that it sits on. For condominiums, you own a share of both the building and the land. If you buy property on a fee simple basis, you own it in perpetuity and can sell it or leave it to your heirs. Fee simple property is still subject to taxation, eminent domain (also known as expropriation or resumption), police power and encumbrances. Fee simple and freehold properties are more desirable and more expensive than comparable leasehold properties.

Leasehold
When you buy a home that is built on leased land, you own the house or a share of the condominium, but the land underneath is leased from a private or public landlord. In some jurisdictions, like China, all land is owned by the state or by collectives. In other places, like Canada and the United Kingdom, leasehold and freehold are both available.

The term of the lease varies: 50-, 75- and 99-year leases are common and 999-year leases are sometimes available in the United Kingdom and its former colonies. In China, residential land is leased from the state for 70 years, industrial land for 50 years and commercial land for 40 years. Some leases, like that for residential land in China, are automatically renewable. Others have a fixed term.

The term begins when the developer leases the land from the owner, not when you buy the home. For example, if you buy a 25-year-old home on land with a 75-year lease, your lease expires in 50 years. Depending on the contract terms, you may be able to negotiate an extension to the lease. The landowner may take the house or condominium back at the end of the lease. Or you may have to demolish the building and return a vacant lot to the landlord. Demolition can be expensive if asbestos or other hazardous materials are involved.

Leasehold dwellings are cheaper than comparable freehold homes, but they have several disadvantages.

▲ It can be difficult to get a 30-year mortgage if there is only 25 years left on the land lease.

▲ Monthly costs are usually higher than for freehold property because they include land rent.

▲ Leasehold homes can be hard to sell, especially near the end of the lease.

Property Rights

Air rights
When you buy land, you also obtain air rights above the property. In general, your air rights extend to the height limit in the local zoning regulations. Planes and satellites may pass overhead without trespassing on your property. Some places, notably Japan, recognize the right to unobstructed sunlight. Like mineral rights, air rights can be detached from surface rights and sold.[2]

Encumbrances
An encumbrance is any right to, or interest or legal liability in a property that affects its value.

Encumbrances can be financial, like a lien or unpaid taxes. Encumbrances can also be non-financial, like an easement that allows a utility to bury a pipeline on your property or a right-of-way that lets bathers cross your land to reach a beach. A covenant—for example stipulating that a parcel of land will only be used for single-family homes or requiring that certain materials be used in the homes' construction—is another form of encumbrance.

In the deeds registration system used in the United States, the title company provides a list of encumbrances affecting a parcel of property. In Hong Kong, which uses a variation of the deeds registration system, the buyer's solicitor conducts a search for encumbrances. In Australia and other countries using the Torrens system, encumbrances are listed on the certificate of title.

Mineral rights

In most countries, when you buy land, you only own the surface rights. Any oil, gas, coal, gold, silver or other natural resources in or under the land belong to the state. The rights to these resources can be detached from the surface rights and sold or licensed separately. However, there are exceptions to this pattern.

In the United Kingdom, buried oil, gas, coal, gold and silver are owned by the state. In general, other minerals are privately owned. Information about the ownership of mineral rights is held by the land registry together with details of surface ownership.[3] In Australia, Canada and the United States, ownership of surface rights may include mineral rights.

Two recent developments brought mineral rights to the attention of homeowners. In the United Kingdom, the Land Registration Act 2002 required anyone with interests owned through manorial rights—privileges originally enjoyed by lords of the manor—to register those rights with the land registry by October 13, 2013. Otherwise, the rights, which include hunting, grazing and mining, would lapse the next time the property was sold.[4] When the owners of these rights (including the Church of England, which owns mineral rights beneath an estimated 500,000 acres of land) registered their interests, affected homeowners received notices from the land registry. Many people were shocked to learn that they did not own the resources under their homes and were worried that "fracking," or hydraulic fracturing, would take place nearby.

In the United States, tens of thousands of people bought new houses that do not include mineral rights. The home builders separated the surface rights from the mineral rights and kept the mineral rights in hope of cashing in on the fracking boom. Splitting the surface and mineral rights is legal, but many of the affected homeowners failed to read the fine print when they bought the homes.[5]

It is unlikely that these homeowners will wake up one morning to discover an oil well on their lawn. But their anxiety could have been avoided if they had scrutinized the paperwork accompanying their purchases or hired a lawyer to review the documents for them.

Surface rights

Surface rights are the ability to use or modify the surface of the property, for example by building a home. When people talk about buying property, they are usually referring to surface rights.

In the Philippines, Filipinos and Filipino-controlled groups may lease foreshore lands for nonagricultural activities, including tourism.

Waterfront rights

The littoral zone lies between a lake or ocean and the land; the riparian zone is between a river or stream and the land. The terms littoral and riparian are often used interchangeably.

Littoral rights apply to the foreshore, which is the area between the high- and low-tide marks, and vary with jurisdiction. For example, in the United Kingdom, with some exceptions, the Crown is presumed to own the foreshore.[6] In most of the United States, the foreshore is public property. But in parts of California and Oregon, some titles extend past the low-tide mark to include land that is normally submerged.[7] Filipinos and Filipino-controlled groups may lease foreshore lands in the Philippines for nonagricultural, productive purposes.[8]

In places where the foreshore is public property, people normally have the right to use it for fishing, navigation or recreation. Obstacles like rocks or vegetation may make it difficult for people to reach the foreshore in front of your property, effectively giving you a private beach. But someone could still legally land a boat on "your" beach.

In general, owners of property adjacent to a river or stream have the right to use the waterway as long as their use does not harm their upstream or downstream neighbors. That includes swimming, boating and fishing, and the use of water for domestic purposes. In British Columbia, Canada, the province owns "nearly all" the freshwater and saltwater foreshore. Individuals may obtain leases, licenses of occupation, statutory rights of way and temporary permits from the province.[9] In some circumstances, Canadian citizenship may be required.

If your property includes a river or a stream, in many jurisdictions you are responsible for keeping the banks clear of debris and preventing them from eroding. You may have additional responsibilities. In the United Kingdom, for example, landowners must notify the Environment Agency and relevant risk management authority if they plan to build or alter a structure that obstructs a watercourse.[10] In September 2013, the United States Environmental Protection Agency released a draft report that would put ponds, streams and wetlands on private land under the agency's control for the first time.[11]

Registration systems

There are two basic approaches to record keeping: deeds registration and the Torrens system.

Torrens system

The Torrens title system is named for Sir Robert Torrens, who created and implemented it in Australia in 1858. Now used in parts of Canada as well as England, Iran, Ireland, Madagascar, Malaysia, New Zealand, Singapore, Wales and other jurisdictions, the Torrens system is based on three principles:

- ▲ The certificate of title in the register accurately and fully reflects the ownership of a parcel of property. This includes the chain of ownership, starting with the original property grant and ending with the current owner, as well as encumbrances and claims on the property, such as mortgages and judgments.

- ▲ Because the certificate of title in the register is accepted as accurate and complete, the owner does not have to produce a long, complex series of deeds and other documents to prove she owns the property.

- ▲ If a person suffers a loss as a result of incorrect information in the register, she is compensated by the government.[12]

The Torrens system eliminates grounds for most disputes and the problem of lost certificates. Under the Torrens system, land sales and transfers are faster, simpler and less expensive.

Deeds registration

Deeds registration is found mainly in common law jurisdictions, including most of the United States, parts of Canada, and India and Hong Kong. The deeds registry is a record of all of the instruments registered against a parcel of property. Unlike the Torrens system, there is no guarantee that the person or entity listed as the "owner" in the deeds registry is the actual owner of the property.

In the deeds registration system, ownership is proven by:

- ▲ Showing that all of the title documents have been properly executed

- ▲ Establishing an unbroken "chain of title" from the original government land grant (which may have taken place a century earlier) to the current owner

▲ Demonstrating that there are no encumbrances, such as mortgages or easements that will harm the title of the land

In the United States, deeds registration is complicated by the fact that instruments are entered in the register chronologically and are not organized by property as they are under the Torrens system,[13] and instruments may be in several locations, including county and municipal offices. According to the American Land Title Association, about one-quarter all residential real estate transactions have title issues.[14]

Title insurance

When you buy a home in an American state that uses the deeds registration system, a title company will conduct a search of the registry and produce a preliminary title report, which is also called an abstract. This document includes the name of the owner or owners, a precise legal description of the property, an account of any outstanding property taxes that must be paid before the property can be conveyed to you and a list of encumbrances. Title companies maintain proprietary "title plants," which are databases containing information about maps, deeds, mortgages, taxes and liens, divorces and probate records.

The title search may be conducted separately or bundled with title insurance, which protects against errors in the public records, forged documents, unknown claims against the property and other surprises. Unlike other forms of insurance, which protect against future occurrences, title insurance covers past events. Only one premium payment is made when a property is purchased or refinanced. Title insurance covers any decrease in a property's value from a successful challenge to its title, as well as lawyer's fees associated with litigating these claims.

There are two types of title insurance: owners and lenders. Most lenders demand that home buyers purchase title insurance to protect the lender's interests. Lenders title insurance does not protect the owner's interests, which are covered by a separate owners title insurance policy.

Title insurance can add several thousand dollars to the cost of a home, and buyers are often unaware that they can shop around for cheaper coverage. In the United States, title insurers have been accused of making excessive profits and have paid millions of dollars in refunds and penalties for providing illegal kickbacks to agents, banks and builders.[15]

Conveyancing involves 14 separate steps in Brazil. In other countries, the process can be completed online with the push of a button.

Conveyancing

Conveyancing is the process of changing the registration of the property from the vendor to the buyer.

The speed and complexity of the conveyancing process varies widely. In New Zealand and Portugal, for example, title can be transferred in less than a day using a secure Website. In Georgia and Norway, title transfer involves a single process versus 14 steps in Brazil and Uzbekistan.

Developed economies are generally fast. On average, it takes 16.5 days in Canada, 21.5 days in the United Kingdom and 12 days in the United States.

At the other end of the spectrum are countries like Haiti, where title is transferred by writing an entry in a book by hand, a process that averages 312 days. That's fast compared to Kiribati, where it takes 513 days and requires a review by a magistrate.

There can also be significant variations within a country. In Egypt, for instance, it takes 18 days in the city of Sohag, 50 days in Cairo and 130 days in Damietta.[16]

Sole, spousal and joint ownership

There are several ways for you to own property, starting with sole ownership.

You can also buy a home with your spouse or bring an existing property to a marriage. In the event of death or divorce, countries and states have different ways of distributing marital property. Property rights for unmarried, cohabiting couples and gay and lesbian couples also vary by jurisdiction.

Joint ownership with a friend or a family member other than your spouse is another option. If you buy jointly, have your lawyer draw up a co-ownership agreement that specifies the rights and obligations of each owner and a mechanism for both parties to sell their stake in the property. If you don't have an agreement and there is a dispute among the owners, you could be stuck with large legal bills or forced to sell the home.

See the "Tax" chapter for information about using a company to buy property.

NEGOTIATING

In any market, buying a home involves negotiating—with agents and vendors and sometimes with lenders, tenants, inspectors, lawyers, architects and contractors. There are many opportunities to negotiate, so polishing your bargaining skills can save you a lot of money.

Research

A key component in a successful negotiation is research, so that you understand your counterparty's goals and motivations. It also helps to understand market conditions and sentiment. Your approach will be different if you have found a just-listed, one-of-a-kind home in a buoyant market like Mayfair than if you are sifting through a backlog of distressed properties in Detroit.

Research also includes self-knowledge: how much can you spend, where are you willing to compromise and what is nonnegotiable? At what point will you walk away?

Find out what can be negotiated. Typically, this encompasses the purchase price, the completion date, the down payment amount and the fixtures and fittings that are included in the sale. But I have also negotiated discounts on agents' commissions, lawyers' fees, renovations and many other things. It never hurts to ask for a discount or an upgrade, particularly if you are buying in the off-season or in a depressed market.

That said, some items can be difficult to negotiate. For example, fee schedules may be set by national cartels. Developers generally prefer to provide extras, like appliance upgrades or additional landscaping, rather than precedent-setting discounts. Developers are more likely to negotiate on completed or nearly completed homes, which cost them money to carry on their books.[1]

Language

Buying across borders adds several elements to the negotiating process. Being able to speak the local language—even if you don't let on that you do—gives you an advantage in the form of insights and information.

Language skills can also help you build rapport with the vendor and avoid paying the "foreigner premium" that is common in many markets.

Developers prefer to provide upgrades, like higher-quality finishes and better appliances, rather than discounts.

Law and contracts

Buying a home is usually a one-shot deal—it is unusual to buy a second dwelling from the same vendor. You are even less likely to buy another home from the same owner, agent or developer in a second country. That encourages some people to behave unethically or criminally, knowing that it is often impractical or impossible to resolve problems like fraud and misrepresentation across borders. Choosing legitimate, competent suppliers is essential.

A cross-border purchase can highlight important cultural differences, such as attitudes towards corruption and attention to details like zoning and construction permits. Behavior that is commonplace in one country, like bribing a building inspector, will land you in jail in another.

Culture also influences the choice of a detailed contract that addresses every eventuality or a brief, general agreement, where the relationship provides the framework for resolving future differences. Americans prefer the former, while sale and purchase agreements in Japan are short. This also extends to how commitments are perceived. Some people take commitments as ironclad. Others see them as subject to modification if circumstances change.

Negotiating styles

Negotiating styles vary, and conventional behavior in your home country may be ineffective or offensive elsewhere. Sarcasm, humor, threats and ultimatums can easily backfire in the wrong setting. Even sports metaphors can knock an unsuspecting counterparty or supplier for six.

Here are some examples of national and regional differences:

- ▲ Americans are noted for being informal and using first names. Germans prefer formal titles.[2]

- ▲ Swiss are punctual. Meetings in Brazil often start and end late.

- ▲ Anglo-Saxons see items that have been verbally agreed as final. Southern Europeans will revisit and renegotiate items.

- ▲ Americans are action-oriented and make fast decisions. Japanese make decisions more slowly.

- ▲ Germans and English people don't show emotion while negotiating, while individuals from Spain and Latin America are more likely to do so.

- ▲ Israelis and Americans expect clear, unequivocal responses to the proposals. Egyptians and Japanese favor a vague, less precise style. This can make it difficult to understand and resolve objections.

- ▲ Americans and Scandinavians use compromise to break a deadlock. The French are less inclined to do so.

- ▲ Chinese logic is influenced by Confucianism and Taoism and their concepts of virtue. Anglo-Saxons' logic often uses the Hegelian concepts of thesis and antithesis to form a synthesis, or compromise.[3]

Sensitivities

National sensitivities can become an issue, particularly if there is history between the buyer and seller's countries. In 2009, for example, the Japanese media carried scare stories about Chinese people buying land in Hokkaido, much the way that the Australian media panicked about Japanese purchases in the 1980s.

Buying a vendor's primary residence requires tact. If you loudly enumerate the home's shortcomings or make an aggressive lowball offer, you could insult the vendor. Some people will be so offended that they will refuse to sell to you—no matter how much you offer later.

Negotiating guidelines

Here are some guidelines that can be helpful in any market.

- ▲ Never accept the vendor's first price, even if it is a bargain. If you accept the asking price, the vendor will wonder if he sold too low, which can cause a problem before settlement. Offer 3%–5% below the asking price.

- ▲ The more contingencies there are attached to your offer, the weaker your negotiating position. Some contingencies—like your ability to obtain a mortgage and the home passing an inspection—are standard. But multiple contingencies can make your offer less attractive than a lower-priced one.

- Vendors like cash offers because they close more quickly and are less likely to be derailed by lenders.

- A vendor is more inclined to make concessions and sell a home to someone he likes. My father got a discount on our family's first home because the vendor thought he was "a nice young man starting a family."

- Know when to stop. Pushing for the last dollar or concession can ruin a good deal.

- "Yes, but" is often better than "no." As in, "Yes, I can meet your counteroffer, but you will need to replace the dishwasher."

- If you buy a home in the United States, unless you use a buyer's agent, the agent showing you homes is paid by the listing agent. "Your" agent is legally bound to share anything that you tell him—including the maximum price you are willing to pay—with the listing agent. For more information, see the "Agents" chapter.

DEMOGRAPHICS

The population trends in the city, state and country where you buy a home can have a dramatic impact on your investment. Birth, migration, aging and death rates influence your ability to enjoy your home today and sell it tomorrow.

Questions to ask

Here are some demographic questions to consider when buying a home:

▲ Is the city's population growing, stable or shrinking? By 2020, for example, Euromonitor International predicts the population of Istanbul will surpass that of London and Ankara will have more people than Berlin.[1]

▲ Are local housing needs changing? Analysts predict a glut of single-family homes in parts of the United States as aging baby boomers downsize into condominiums. Many people in this cohort hope to finance their retirement by selling their homes, and a flood of sellers is likely to depress prices for single-family homes and boost rents and prices for condominiums.

▲ Are there enough taxpayers to finance roads, police departments and other public goods and services? In rural Japan, for instance, between 31% and 39% of the population will be over age 65 by 2030.[2]

▲ If you are retiring abroad, will there be younger people—particularly doctors and nurses—to care for you? In 2012, 4% of the people in the Philippines and 5% of those in Indonesia were aged over 65. In Spain and Portugal, seniors represented 18% and 19% of the population, respectively.[3]

▲ If you are buying a recreational property, does the resort benefit from demographic trends? For example, there are far more 80-year-old golfers than skiers.

▲ Is the population balanced on gender and economic lines? In 2012, 117.7 boys were born in China for every 100 girls.[4] As those boys mature and confront a shortage of brides, their frustration could boil over into social unrest. Likewise, growing income inequality and a sense of hopelessness contributed to the Arab Spring, which crushed Egypt's tourism industry.

▲ Does the city have a diversified economy? Single-industry cities—common in Canada, where they are built around natural resources, and in centrally planned economies like Russia and China—are vulnerable to political and economic shifts that can turn them into ghost towns overnight. Kitsault, British Columbia, a town built to support a molybdenum mine that was abandoned when the price of the mineral collapsed, is one example of this phenomenon, which can even affect national capitals. In 2005, for example, the ruling junta moved Myanmar's government from Yangon to a greenfield site in Naypyidaw.

▲ Are events in nearby countries shaping your destination's demographics? For example, by the end of 2013, more than a million Syrians had taken refuge in Lebanon. One estimate claimed that the number of Syrian children in Lebanon exceeded the entire population of school-age Lebanese children.

▲ Does your new home have an appropriate mix of kindergartens, primary schools, high schools and universities? What about creches and daycare centers for senior citizens? Pediatricians and geriatricians?

Long-term trends

Demographic trends change slowly, but small shifts can have a large cumulative effect. Demographic patterns are influenced by many factors, including politics, religion, education, medicine, technology, economics and immigration. Here are some trends to watch:

▲ The United Nations expects the global population to grow from 7.2 billion in 2013 to 10.9 billion in 2100. Thirty-five of the U.N.'s least-developed countries will see their populations triple by 2100. The populations of Burundi, Malawi, Mali, Niger, Nigeria, Somalia,

Tanzania, Uganda and Zambia are expected to increase five-fold. In order of contribution, more than half the world's population growth will come from Nigeria, India, Tanzania, Congo, Niger, Uganda, Ethiopia and the United States.

▲ By 2050, Belarus, Bulgaria, Croatia, Cuba, Georgia, Latvia, Lithuania, Moldova, Romania, Russia, Serbia and Ukraine will see their populations fall by 15% or more.

▲ Between 2010 and 2050, the United States is expected to receive 1 million immigrants each year; Canada, 205,000; the United Kingdom, 172,500; Australia, 150,000; and Italy, 131,250. Net sources of immigrants include Bangladesh at 331,000 annually; China, 300,000; India, 284,000; Mexico, 210,000; and Pakistan, 170,000.[5]

▲ The global population is getting older. In 2013, there were more people over age 60 than children under 5. By 2050, there will be more people over 60 than under 15.[6] In 2012, for every 100 women over 60 there were 84 men. For every 100 women over 80, there were 61 men.[7] China, Japan and Western Europe all face growing senior populations.

▲ More people are living alone. According to Eric Klinenberg, author of *Going Solo: The Extraordinary Rise and Surprising Appeal of Living Alone,* single-person households represent 60% of the total in Stockholm. Sweden, Norway, Finland and Denmark have the highest proportion of people living alone, while China, India and Brazil have the fastest-growing number of single-person households.

▲ More than half the world's population now lives in cities and the U.N. expects the urbanization trend to continue. Between 2010 and 2050, the top gainers will be India, which will add 497 million to its urban population; China, 341 million; Nigeria, 200 million; the U.S., 103 million; and Indonesia, 92 million.[8] While this growth is straining the infrastructure and creating urban sprawl in fast-growing centers, it also means that property prices in desirable cities should do well over the long term.

Fewer weddings and smaller families are contributing to the rapid aging of Japan's population.

It can be helpful to look backward to see how countries and cities have handled demographic challenges. For example, the University of Utah's Professor Arthur C. Nelson believes that in the run-up to 2040 the United States will see many of the trends—such as growth in the number of people aged over 65, childless households and single-person households—that are now shaping Japan.[9]

Comparisons between the American automobile and high-technology industries may seem unusual, but nearly half the people working in Cupertino, California, and in Redmond, Washington, are employed by Apple and Microsoft, respectively.[10] That proportion is comparable to the automotive industry's influence on Detroit: in 1950, there were 296,000 manufacturing jobs in Detroit, the bulk of which were in the automotive industry.

Detroit

Detroit is undergoing a demographic change that *The New York Times* called "the country's most startling example of modern urban collapse."[11] In 1950, Detroit was the fifth-largest metropolis in the United States with 1.8 million inhabitants. By 2010, it had dropped to 18th place, with just over 700,000 people. Three years later, the city declared bankruptcy with debts of more than $18 billion.[12]

Detroit's problems have many sources. The city was reliant on the automotive industry, which faced stiff competition from cheaper and more efficient producers. Detroit lost jobs to Japan, South Korea and right-to-work states, such as Tennessee, Missouri and Kentucky, which are less union-friendly than Michigan.

The city's income and property taxes, which are the highest in the state, made Detroit a less attractive place to live. As people and businesses left, the city's tax base crumbled. In 2013 dollars, total revenues fell from $2.0 billion in 1960 to $1.1 billion in 2013. Meanwhile, aggregate property values fell from $45.2 billion in 1958 to $9.6 billion in 2012.

Detroit's financial woes were compounded by generous salaries and benefits—in 2012, the city had more pensioners than employees. Corruption was widespread: in 2013, Kwame Kilpatrick, Detroit's mayor from 2002 to 2008, was sentenced to 28 years in prison for accepting bribes, rigging city contracts and other crimes.

Mismanagement is another factor. In March 2014, the Detroit Water and Sewerage Department had more than $260 million in delinquent accounts. More than half of the department's customers, including Detroit's public schools, were behind on their payments.[13]

Detroit's public schools are among the worst in the United States and the city's homicide and violent crime rates are high.[14] In 2013, Detroit had the same number of murders as New York City, which has a population 12 times larger.[15]

Local business groups are working to revitalize the city. For example, Why Don't We Own This? (www.whydontweownthis.com) offers an online database of Detroit's real estate, complete with ownership, property tax and foreclosure information. Several other initiatives are recruiting businesses and investors to Detroit and while there have been some successes, many problems remain. For example, in 2013 the city had some 78,000 abandoned buildings[16] and 1,500 vacant lots were converted into a 57-hectare urban forest,[17] 40% of Detroit's 88,000 streetlights were burned out,[18] 50,000 abandoned dogs roamed the streets[19] and at one point the bankrupt city was unable to issue birth and death certificates because it did not have enough cash to buy special embossed paper.[20]

In January 2014, the *Detroit Free Press* reported that there were shortages of rental accommodations in central neighborhoods, such as Midtown and Corktown, where tenants faced rent increases of $200–$400 per month. But in less desirable districts, houses could still be purchased for $500 or less. Most of the homes were uninhabitable and had been stripped of anything salvageable, up to and including the kitchen sink.

RISK FACTORS

Not all of the risks described below apply to every property, but these examples will help you evaluate potential homes and jurisdictions and avoid common pitfalls. For a summary of common risk factors, please see the "Property Buyer's Checklist" at the end of the book.

Air pollution

In October 2013, the World Health Organization (WHO) classified outdoor air pollution as carcinogenic. Five months later, the WHO estimated that in 2012, seven million people died—equal to one in eight total global deaths—as a result of air-pollution exposure. Children are vulnerable, due to the immaturity of their respiratory systems, as are the elderly.

The main measures of air pollution are PM10 and PM2.5, which refer to particulate matter with diameters of less than 10.0 and 2.5 microns, respectively. The coarse PM10 particles typically come from road dust and grinding operations. PM2.5 particles are smaller and can lodge deeply into human lungs, making them more dangerous than PM10.

Air quality is an issue at both the neighborhood and city levels. Research published in December 2013 by the University of California at Los Angeles and the California Air Resources Board showed that air pollution is hyper-local, with neighborhoods surrounded by highways and arterial roads having much higher concentrations of ultrafine particle pollutants. But on January 12, 2013, when PM2.5 levels in Beijing reached 993 micrograms per cubic meter—nearly 40 times the WHO's guidelines—your health was at risk wherever you lived.

The WHO maintains a database of PM10 and PM2.5 levels in more than 500 places around the world (see www.who.int/phe for details).

Aluminum wiring

In the 1960s and 1970s, aluminum wiring was used in residential buildings in Canada, Hong Kong, the United States and other places.

Aluminum was used because it was less expensive and weighed less than copper, which is commonly used for electrical wiring.

Aluminum wiring is safe, but it poses two problems. First, when aluminum is heated and cooled, it expands and contracts at a different rate than other metals, including copper, which is often used in the terminals of circuit breakers, light switches and wall outlets. Over time, heating and cooling can make a copper–aluminum connection loose, creating a fire hazard. Second, aluminum oxidizes. Aluminum oxide is an insulator that adds electrical resistance to aluminum–aluminum connections, causing heat buildup and a fire hazard.

These problems can be overcome by adding special terminations, called pigtails, to the ends of the aluminum wire. You can also replace the breakers, switches, outlets etc., with products designed to accommodate aluminum wire and apply antioxidant paste to the connections. Finally, the home's entire electrical system can be replaced. Each of these solutions is expensive, and repair work should be carried out by a licensed electrician who has experience working with aluminum wiring.

In duplexes, condominiums and other multifamily dwellings, the entire building's wiring must be fixed to eliminate the fire hazard. In some places, it can be difficult to obtain insurance for homes with aluminum wiring.

American citizenship

Americans are finding it increasingly difficult to obtain financial services, including bank accounts and mortgages, outside the United States. The situation is likely to get worse, as the Foreign Account Tax Compliance Act (FATCA) takes full effect on July 1, 2014.

Unlike most countries, the United States taxes its citizens on worldwide income. FATCA requires that foreign financial institutions report information about accounts held by American taxpayers to the Internal Revenue Service. Complying with these regulations is estimated to cost thousands of dollars per client and, in some cases, violates the privacy laws of the institution's home country. As a result, some foreign banks are deciding that American clients are simply not worth the trouble.

British Columbia has more than 38,000 archaeological sites, most of which are associated with Canada's First Nations.

Artifacts

The discovery of human remains, artifacts and other archaeologically significant items is a common problem, particularly in cities with a long history, like London and Rome, and in places like China that have large numbers of construction sites.

Laws governing archaeological sites vary among jurisdictions, as does the attention paid to those laws. The discovery of artifacts on a building site can cause long delays and considerable expense, as relics are excavated, cataloged and evaluated. The involvement of multiple levels of government and aboriginal groups can complicate things further.

In some places, builders treat the fines that are levied for failing to preserve an archaeological site as a cost of doing business. Others simply bury the evidence and hope no one notices, or sell the artifacts to thieves. Homeowners who find artifacts on their property and report the discovery to the authorities are often quoted as saying that they wished they had just kept digging.

As these examples from Canada illustrate, problems can occur under a variety of circumstances:

▲ In 2013, a Vancouver Island woman who began building a home in 2006 estimated that a government-mandated archaeological inspection resulted in C$750,000 ($680,000) in losses from construction delays and reduced property values. That figure includes C$6,000 in inspection fees and C$51,000 for archaeological work.[1]

▲ In 2012, the construction of a five-story condominium in Vancouver was halted when the developer and an aboriginal band could not reach an agreement. More than 70 units in the complex, which was situated on a sacred burial ground called the Marpole Midden, had been pre-sold. The developer said he expected to refund the buyers' deposits.[2]

▲ In 2013, a couple in Sarnia discovered a 400-year-old skeleton while installing a fence in their backyard. Under local law, they were required to undertake an archaeological survey of their property at a cost of $5,000.[3]

The simplest way to minimize this risk is to avoid areas that are known to be archaeologically important. If you are intent on buying in such an area, conduct extensive research beforehand. Newspapers, libraries, historical societies and neighbors are useful sources of information. You can also hire a consulting archaeologist to conduct research for you.

City and regional governments can also be helpful. For example, Chichester in the United Kingdom (www.chichester.gov.uk) and Australia's New South Wales (www.environment.nsw.gov.au) maintain searchable listings of archaeological sites. To protect its more than 38,000 archaeological sites, British Columbia does not list this information on land titles. But the Canadian province's archaeological branch will advise a prospective buyer of a property's archaeological status if the buyer requests this information.

Asbestos

Asbestos is a naturally occurring family of minerals prized for its tensile strength and resistance to heat, electricity and chemicals.

Inhaling asbestos fibers, however, causes lung cancer, mesothelioma, asbestosis and other diseases. The WHO notes, "There is no evidence for a threshold for the carcinogenic effect of asbestos and that increased cancer risks have been observed in populations exposed to very low levels." Cigarette smokers exposed to asbestos are more likely to develop lung cancer than nonsmokers.

In 1983, Iceland was the first country to ban the use of asbestos. Today, more than 50 countries have banned it. One notable exception is the United States, where asbestos continues to be used in construction materials.

Despite these bans, there is a substantial amount of "legacy" asbestos in buildings around the world. Typically, it is found in flooring, joint compounds, ceiling tiles, roofing, wallboard and insulation.

Asbestos was also discovered in vermiculite, a mineral used in thermal insulation and fireproofing. W.R. Grace & Co. produced vermiculite at a mine and milling facility in Libby, Montana, from 1963 to 1990. Vermiculite from the Libby mine—which represented 80% of the global supply—was used in W.R. Grace's Zonolite® attic insulation that was installed extensively in Canada and the United States and has been found in buildings in Japan.[4]

Asbestos in building materials is generally regarded as posing a low risk, unless the materials are cut or broken and asbestos fibers are released into the air. This can occur during renovations, demolitions and earthquakes.

Trained technicians and specialized equipment are required to safely remove building materials that contain asbestos. The costs involved can be prohibitive and some homeowners decide to seal, rather than remove, the asbestos. Other homeowners leave items like asbestos-based floor tiles in place.

In many jurisdictions, vendors are required to advise buyers if they know that asbestos is present in a home that they are selling. Asbestos tests and related services are available in most cities.

Censorship and surveillance

In May 2013, former CIA contractor Edward Snowden leaked information about secret surveillance programs operated by the United States and British governments. In light of Snowden's disclosures, it is safe to assume that electronic communications are insecure and subject to government interception.

This can cause problems if you buy a home in a country where your sexual orientation, religious beliefs or political views are discouraged or outlawed. In 2013, for example, the government of Argentina began criminally prosecuting economists who published inflation data that contradicted official numbers. If you are retiring or buying a vacation property abroad, you may also find that your legal protection is weaker than it is at home.

Censorship can also have public health implications. Official stonewalling has been associated with the spread of SARS (severe acute respiratory syndrome) in China in 2002 and 2003. In 2013, researchers expressed concerns that censorship in Saudi Arabia may have helped another viral respiratory illness—MERS (Middle East respiratory syndrome)—take root around the Arabian Peninsula.[5] Between its discovery in September 2012 and April 2014, at least 93 people died from MERS.

Countries also impose restrictions on local and international information sources. In China, for example, Internet access is filtered through "the great fire wall of China" that blocks searches for forbidden subjects, and the Websites of *The New York Times* and Bloomberg have been blocked after they ran stories about sensitive topics.

Facebook, Twitter and YouTube are blocked in China. At various times, Germany, Indonesia, Malaysia, Thailand, Turkey and other nations have instituted full or partial bans on YouTube. This is important because social media can be a useful source of information in times of crisis or when the mainstream media is being less than forthcoming. Media restrictions and censorship can make it difficult to research developers, lenders, vendors and other business partners. Internet restrictions can usually be circumvented by using a virtual private network (VPN), although this may be illegal.

For more information about international censorship, see the Electronic Frontier Foundation (www.eff.org), Freedom House (www.freedomhouse.org) and Reporters Without Borders (http://en.rsf.org).

Climate change

Climate change is associated with rising ocean levels; increases in extreme weather events, such as floods, landslides and tropical cyclones; and changes to weather patterns in general.

Unfortunately, the science surrounding climate change is complex, and therefore accurately predicting its effects and chronology is difficult and public discussion of this topic has become politicized. These factors make it difficult for buyers to formulate a climate change strategy, other than avoiding coastal property that could be damaged by a storm surge or end up submerged.

That strategy can eliminate many neighborhoods. In Florida, for example, 300,000 homes, 4,100 kilometers of roads and nearly 1,000 sites registered with the Environmental Protection Agency are on land that is less than one meter above the high-tide mark. Miami is already vulnerable to flooding from rain and storm surges, and the South Florida Regional Planning Council currently projects a 60-centimeter sea level increase by 2060.[6]

Reinsurance companies like Munich Re (www.munichre.com) and Swiss Re (www.swissre.com) produce climate change research that is accessible and commercially, not ideologically, oriented.

Crime and corruption

A foreigner buying a home abroad is an attractive target for con artists. "Special" arrangements to help foreign buyers evade taxes or local laws and ownership restrictions are a common way of scamming them. In some countries, there are legal ways of overcoming these barriers, such as the use of trusts, offshore companies and nominees but such techniques are usually costly and have risks of their own. If you take this route, employ a reputable law firm and ensure that you understand the risks and costs. As the Americans who used Swiss bank accounts to evade U.S. taxes discovered, what worked in the past may not work in the future.

You can reduce the risk of being scammed by using common sense. Avoid deals that seem too good to be true and take time to learn about the country's legal system as well as the city and neighborhood where you are buying. It's also a good idea to know (or research) the people with whom you are doing business.

In some countries, corruption is common during construction and renovations. An inspector may request a bribe to overlook a defect or expedite an approval, or a builder will offer a discount for a cash payment that is not reported to the tax authorities. Bribes and cash payments make foreign homeowners vulnerable to prosecution in an unfamiliar and potentially corrupt legal system and make it difficult to have defective work rectified. Furthermore, foreign homeowners are a tempting target for local bureaucrats who want to appear tough on crime.

Holiday homes and dwellings that are used infrequently are often burgled, especially in buildings with many unoccupied units. To manage this risk, make friends with your neighbors and look out for each other's homes. An alarm system, appropriate insurance, a good property manager and advice from the local police can also be helpful.

Death

A death in a dwelling can have a negative impact on the home's price. In some jurisdictions, vendors are required to reveal this information. In Japan, for example, deaths and violent crimes must be divulged in the explanation of important matters, but after two title transfers, no disclosure is required. In Hong Kong, agents are also required to reveal this information.

In and outside China, Chinese buyers avoid homes near funeral parlors, cemeteries and crematoria.

But this requirement is not universal. In 2006, a judge in the province of Quebec, Canada, ruled that a vendor did not have to disclose that a suicide had taken place on a property a decade earlier.[7]

In the United States, a trade association for real estate agents advises, "Generally speaking, if someone died of natural causes, this involves no disclosure."[8] But they also advise that if a buyer asks if a home has any "negative history," the vendor should share this information.

While the vendor may not be obliged to disclose a death, it can be a wise strategy. Full disclosure reduces the chance that the sale will be canceled or that the buyer will sue you if they discover a death or violent crime had taken place.

This issue is complicated by the range of emotions that death can trigger. For example, a crib death that occurred two decades ago or a pensioner expiring from old age are clearly different from a grisly murder that is front-page news. Residential deaths are more common in Europe, where homes may be centuries old, than in Asia, where much of the housing stock is new.

Death near a home can also have a negative impact. Chinese buyers avoid homes near funeral parlors, cemeteries, crematoria and those associated with the number four, which is a homophone for death. The value of the apartments adjacent to a murder or suicide scene can also be affected.

However, this trend did not carry over to the United States. According to a 2013 survey by Redfin, homes less than 50 feet (15 meters) from a cemetery sold for an average of $162 per square foot versus $145 for homes more than 500 yards away. However, homes less than 50 feet from a graveyard took a week longer, at 48 days, to sell compared to more distant dwellings.

A home with a history can usually be purchased at a significant discount, but you may encounter resistance from children and family members with concerns about the supernatural. Asking a priest to say prayers for the victim or conducting a purification ritual in the home may help to overcome their anxiety.

In addition to asking the vendor if someone has died in the property, you can check online databases, such as www.diedinhouse.com in the United States and www.hk-compass.com in Hong Kong.

If you are new to the area, investigate your neighborhood's history. Nearly a million people are buried in a potter's field on Hart Island in New York. While rumors that London's Blackheath was a mass burial site for Black Death victims are unfounded,[9] the Crossrail project has unearthed a plague pit and several graveyards. Up to 50,000 plague victims are believed to have been buried in an emergency cemetery in London's Farringdon district.[10]

Deceptive data

Pay close attention to the quality and source of the data that you are using when buying a home. Governments, trade associations and other organizations frequently "massage" data to present their case in the best possible light, and statistics are often adjusted retroactively. This can affect everything from general economic statistics—in China, for example, national numbers rarely tally with provincial totals—to sales volumes and market trends that are used to convince prospects to become buyers. A few minutes searching the Internet can highlight suspicious data and help you find more accurate information.

Defective design and construction

Design and construction problems—ranging from minor aesthetic issues to structural failure—are a global issue. In developing economies, shortages of skilled tradespeople, weak inspection and quality control procedures and pressure to cut corners contribute to these problems. In 2009, for example, a 13-story apartment building in Shanghai fell over, killing one person. The incident, which occurred while the building was under construction, was due in part to the use of hollow pilings.[11]

Defective construction is not unique to the developing world. In 1968, a corner of the Ronan Point apartment block in London collapsed, killing three people. In Vancouver, 50,000 condominiums built between 1982 and 1999 have serious water leaks, which can cost tens of thousands of dollars to repair.[12]

Economic booms provide fertile ground for building problems. Priory Hall in Dublin is one of more than 2,800 "ghost estates" that were erected in Ireland during the 2000s. In October 2011, the 187-unit complex was declared a fire hazard and over 250 residents were given 48 hours to leave.[13] Many owners continue to pay mortgages on homes they cannot occupy; the developer is bankrupt; and the Dublin City Council has spent €3 million ($4.1 million) securing the estate and re-housing residents, with the final bill expected to exceed €7 million.[14] Worse, there is no resolution in sight.

Defective and dangerous materials like asbestos (see above) can make life miserable for homeowners. Between 1975 and 1994, polybutylene (PB) water pipe was installed in up to 10 million new and remodeled homes in the United States and Canada. Marketed as an inexpensive replacement for traditional copper pipe, PB pipes began failing prematurely, causing leaks, water damage and other problems. PB pipes were the subject of class-action lawsuits in both countries, and affected homeowners face large bills to replace the pipes.

Building codes are not retroactive. If a product like PB pipe is approved for use and later found to be unsuitable, it will be removed from the list of acceptable products, but it can remain in existing installations unless it is found to pose a health or safety hazard.

Defective drywall is another source of problems. Between 2001 and 2008, Chinese-made drywall was installed in about 100,000 U.S. homes, where it was found to emit higher-than-normal levels of hydrogen sulfide, a chemical with a "rotten egg" smell. In addition to irritating homeowners' eyes and respiratory systems, hydrogen sulfide corroded electrical wiring and damaged their home appliances. Most of the drywall was installed in Florida, although there were reports of cases in other states and in Australia and Canada. The drywall, which was the subject of a class-action lawsuit, must be removed to rectify the problem.

How can you avoid these problems? If you are buying a new home, deal with a financially stable developer who has a proven track record. An established developer with a reputation to protect is more likely to resolve problems.

If you are buying a pre-owned home, know your legal rights, research common issues—like asbestos, lead paint, PB pipe and Chinese drywall—and ask the vendor if the home is affected. Hiring a professional home inspector is also wise. See the "Home Inspections" chapter for more information.

Divorce

The disposition of property in a divorce will be influenced by many factors, including the existence (and enforceability) of a prenuptial agreement, the jurisdiction where the divorce is filed and its requirements for disclosing assets, the location of the property, and whether the property was acquired during the marriage.

If the divorce involves a husband from country A, a wife from country B and they live in country C and own a home in country D, the complexity increases, as does the price. *The Economist* estimates that the cost of a bi-national divorce, "usually starts in six figures, in dollars, euros or pounds," and can easily reach seven figures.[15]

From a practical standpoint, ensuring that your name is on the title of any property that is jointly owned will make it easier to prove your interest in the property. It will also make it harder for the property to be sold without your knowledge and consent. Getting advice from a law firm with experience in cross-border family law is also sensible.

Drugs

Unless you are investing in distressed property, you are unlikely to buy a home in an area populated by drug dealers and addicts. But illegal drugs can complicate a home purchase, even in wealthy neighborhoods.

Homes that have been used as indoor marijuana farms, called "grow ops," can suffer from a range of problems. This includes mold and mildew, illegal alterations to the home's wiring to bypass the power meter and supply electricity to hydroponic lights, structural modifications like additional ventilation that may not have been repaired properly and contamination from fertilizer and other chemicals.

Marijuana growers often rent property, including new homes in expensive neighborhoods, for use as grow ops. According to the Royal Canadian Mounted Police, telltale signs that a home is a grow op include windows that are covered with paper or plastic, a distinctive, skunky smell, excessive condensation on windows and walls, residents who are rarely at home and trash that doesn't contain typical domestic waste.

If the police discover that a rental property you own is a grow op, you face the prospect of large bills from lawyers, cleaners to remove the accumulated mold and mildew, electricians to fix the wiring, construction companies to repair illegal modifications and engineers to certify the home is safe for occupancy. This can easily cost tens of thousands of dollars and underscores the importance of obtaining and checking tenants' references.

Some home inspectors can recognize dwellings that were used as grow ops. In some jurisdictions, police maintain a list of properties that are known to have been used for this purpose. But a home that isn't on the list may still have been used for cultivation. To help people recognize pot farms, Dutch authorities produced scratch-and-sniff cards infused with the scent of growing marijuana. After successful trials in The Hague and Rotterdam, the cards were rolled out nationwide in October 2013.

Homes can also be used as methamphetamine factories, or meth labs. Like grow ops, meth labs often have covered windows, elaborate ventilation systems and nondomestic trash. But where grow ops are essentially indoor gardens, meth labs are crude chemical factories that use toxic substances including acetone, ether, red phosphorus, toluene, lye, sulfuric acid and ammonia. Active meth labs are a fire hazard and produce large amounts of hazardous waste.

Meth labs are a major problem in the United States. The U.S. Drug Enforcement Administration (www.justice.gov/dea) maintains a list of houses in 50 states where meth has been manufactured. In 2012, the DEA reported over 11,000 meth-related incidents, including the discovery of labs and dump sites as well as seizures of chemicals and glassware.

Some of the chemicals used to make methamphetamines are carcinogenic. Many of these chemicals are toxic in small quantities and can leach into building materials like carpets throughout the house.[16] Children are particularly susceptible because they put things into their mouths and because their bodies are small and still developing. In the United States, regulations governing the disclosure that a house was a meth lab vary from state to state, as do clean-up standards. A home that was officially remediated can still be hazardous, and the clean-up costs can exceed a home's value.

Quick test kits are available for $50. If this test produces a positive result, a more detailed test can be ordered for about $500.

Residential meth labs have been discovered in Australia, Canada and New Zealand. The drug is also produced in India, Iran, North Korea, Pakistan and Sri Lanka.[17]

Earthquakes create a range of additional threats, including fires, explosions, landslides and tsunamis.

Earthquakes

Earthquakes present several threats to people and property. This includes tsunamis, explosions and fires, collapsing embankments, liquefaction of reclaimed land and the release of hazards such as asbestos and radiation into the environment. After a major earthquake, buildings may be uninhabitable, transportation, utilities and other key infrastructure may fail and essential services may be interrupted.

Earthquakes can occur anywhere. But more than 80% of the world's largest earthquakes occur along the circum-Pacific seismic belt, which extends from Chile up the west coast of North America, across southern Alaska and down through Japan, China, the Philippines and New Zealand.

Cities located in seismically active areas are at risk. However, the risk increases in poor countries and nations where there is a culture of corruption. A 2011 study by professors Nicholas Ambraseys of the Imperial College of London and Roger Bilham of the University of Colorado Boulder showed that "83% of all deaths caused by the collapse of buildings during earthquakes occurred in countries considered to be unusually corrupt." The authors compared New Zealand and Haiti, which were both struck by 7.0 earthquakes in 2010. There were no fatalities in New Zealand. At least 100,000 people died in Haiti.[18]

Corrupt practices include using substandard materials and construction techniques, erecting structures in dangerous locations and ignoring building codes. Many of the concrete buildings in Turkey, for example, use scrap metal instead of steel reinforcing bars (rebar) and sea sand, which corrodes and weakens the rebar. In 2000, the U.S. Geological Survey estimated the probability of a strong earthquake hitting Istanbul within 30 years at 62%. Mustafa Erdik, chairman of the Department of Earthquake Engineering at Boğazici University, estimates that such a quake would kill 200,000–300,000 people.[19] By comparison, the Japanese government estimates that a severe earthquake in the northern part of Tokyo Bay would result in 11,000 deaths. Istanbul and Tokyo have populations of about 13 million.

In Chile, building owners are liable during the first 10 years of a building's life for losses resulting from the inadequate application of the building code during construction.[20] In February 2010, Chile was hit by a massive 8.8 earthquake that killed 521 people. Chile's tough, rigorously enforced building codes saved thousands of lives.

You can minimize your earthquake risk by choosing your home carefully. High-risk cities include Bogotá, Cairo, Caracas, Dhaka, Islamabad, Jakarta, Karachi, Katmandu, Lima, Manila, Mexico City, New Delhi, Quito and Tehran. Large portions of Japan and California are also at risk, but they are expected to benefit from effective building codes and enforcement.

If you live in an earthquake zone, ensure that your home is well constructed and properly maintained. Older dwellings, built to less strict standards, are generally more vulnerable to earthquake damage than new ones.

Homes built on bedrock survive earthquakes better than those on loose sand, silty clay and gravel. Water-saturated soils, which are often found in reclaimed areas, change from a solid to a liquid in an earthquake. Known as liquefaction, this can result in buildings collapsing or settling unevenly.[21]

Skyscrapers pose a unique set of challenges. Modern high-rise buildings in earthquake zones are often equipped with stabilizers and shock absorbers. But after the Great East Japan Earthquake in 2011, the elevators in many Tokyo towers were disabled until technicians could confirm that they were safe.

If you live in an earthquake zone, buy a first-aid kit, fire extinguishers, water and survival supplies.

Expropriation

Expropriation occurs when the state takes an object or rights belonging to an individual for a public purpose. Known as eminent domain in the United States, compulsory purchase in England and resumption in Australia, expropriation takes many forms. For example:

- ▲ In 2000, Robert Mugabe began a series of land reforms in Zimbabwe that saw the transfer of eight million hectares from 4,500 farms to 160,000 households. Most of the land was taken from white farmers, often by force, and given to Mugabe's allies and supporters.

- ▲ In 2005, the U.S. Supreme Court ruled in favor of the City of New London in the Kelo case, which allowed the city to seize a neighborhood so that it could be used as the site for a pharmaceutical factory. Ironically, the factory was never built.

- ▲ Since 1979, an organization established by Ayatollah Khomeini has confiscated property in Iran worth tens of billion dollars. Religious minorities, expatriates and other victims allege that Setad has used violence, extortion and fraud to take their land and buildings.[22]

As Jane Jacobs notes in her book *The Death and Life of Great American Cities*, when a government expropriates property, it pays only for what it acquires and not for what it takes from the owner. That means an owner is compensated for the land that a drug store, for example, is standing on, but not for the value of the drug store as a going concern. The difference between the two amounts can be large.

Laws governing expropriation vary among jurisdictions, but most are based on the idea that the expropriation is in the public interest. Unfortunately, some politicians abuse this power, leaving an individual owner to battle against the state.

Expropriation occurs everywhere, but it is a particular problem in developing countries, where many roads, airports and other infrastructure projects are being built. Opaque urban planning processes, poor governance and corruption increase the risk from expropriation.

Fire

Wherever there are houses, there are house fires. Ensure your home meets local building codes and that your fire extinguishers and smoke detectors are checked and maintained regularly. If you are buying in an apartment block or residential compound, ensure that the building management keeps the fire exits clear and maintains the sprinkler and alarm systems.

There are also location-specific concerns. In the United States, the city of Flint, Michigan, has adopted a "let it burn" policy for abandoned homes. Flint had the nation's highest per capita arson rate in 2010 and 2011 and recorded more than 1,600 fires in vacant buildings between 2008 and 2012.[23] Michigan's anemic economy has contributed to a shrinking tax base and reduced services.

High winds, hot temperatures and low humidity make bush fires common in Australia, particularly in Victoria. The Black Saturday blaze on February 7, 2009, was the most lethal bushfire in Australian history, killing 173 people, many of them in the towns and villages northeast of Melbourne. The American states of Arizona, California and New Mexico are vulnerable to wildfires, as are parts of Greece, Italy, Portugal and Spain. The impact of these fires is usually focused on rural areas, but the suburbs of major cities, including Athens, Los Angeles and Sydney, have also been affected by wildfires.

Rural fires can also damage urban infrastructure. In August 2013, for example, a blaze on the edge of Yosemite National Park threatened water and electricity supplies to San Francisco, some 200 miles away, causing a state of emergency to be declared by the state government.

Fires also affect air quality. In June 2013, air pollution reached crisis levels in Singapore and Malaysia, as the region was blanketed with smog from fires in Indonesia. The fires were set in illegal slash-and-burn land clearance activities and spread to peatlands, where they can smolder for long periods of time.

Floods

Floods are caused by heavy rainfall; by rising river levels, which, in turn, are caused by heavy rainfall, snow melts and typhoons; by ocean storm surges and tsunamis; and by the failure of dams and other infrastructure.

Improvements in forecasting and flood management have helped reduce the number of people killed in floods, but they still have a large social and economic cost. The World Bank estimates that floods in 2010 caused $40 billion in damage and affected 178 million people in Pakistan, Australia, Sri Lanka, South Africa and the Philippines. The threat from floods continues to increase, driven by the growing number of people moving to cities, especially poorly planned cities in the developing world.

Climate change is believed to increase flood risk for coastal cities. The World Bank estimates that, based on projected socioeconomic change alone, average annual flood losses will grow from $6 billion in 2005 to $52 billion by 2050. With the addition of climate change and subsidence, global flood losses could exceed $1 trillion per year unless corrective action is taken. In terms of financial losses, the most vulnerable cities are Guangzhou, Miami, New York, New Orleans, Mumbai, Nagoya, Tampa, Boston, Shenzhen and Osaka.[24]

To manage flood risk, start by researching the city and neighborhood where you are planning to buy. While an area's risk profile can change with alterations to the built environment, population and climate, the past can be a useful guide to the future. The local archives can help you understand an area's history and many cities and countries prepare flood maps. For example, a flood risk map for the United Kingdom is available at http://watermaps.environment-agency.gov.uk. Neighborhood names can also provide useful clues. In Japan, for example, the words *numa* (marsh), *tani* (valley) and *bonchi* (basin) suggest that an area is prone to flooding. In the United States, the National Aeronautics and Space Administration uses satellites to monitor global flood risks in real time (http://pmm.nasa.gov/node/187).

It also helps to understand how flood risk is measured. As the World Bank notes, a "100-year flood" is not certain to occur once a century or guaranteed to only happen once in 100 years.

If you buy in a flood zone, ensure your home's foundation is sound and the sump pump, if installed, is maintained. Finally, if it is available, flood insurance can be a wise investment.

Foreign exchange risk

Changes to foreign exchange rates can complicate your life in several ways. For example, say you live and earn income in the United States, but buy a vacation home in Canada. Your C$1,000 monthly mortgage payment cost you $620 in January 2002. But by November 2007, the same C$1,000 payment would have jumped 75% in U.S. dollar terms, to $1,085.

If you buy a home in Japan with an Australian dollar–denominated mortgage and the yen increases in value against the Australian dollar, the unpaid balance of your mortgage (measured in Australian dollars) may exceed the lender's maximum loan-to-value ratio. If this happens, the lender may demand additional collateral or require you to make additional payments.

Foreign exchange rates can also affect rental property. For example, when Cristina Fernández de Kirchner's government in Argentina began introducing currency controls in 2011, landlords in Uruguay's Punta del Este beach resort saw double-digit drops in rental prices, as holidaymakers from neighboring Argentina were forced to buy U.S. dollars—the currency in which Uruguayan resort property is rented—on the black market.[25]

It is possible to hedge your foreign exchange exposure using forward contracts and other instruments, although the cost of the hedge may outweigh the benefits for smaller transactions.

Fraud

When you buy a home, you will give money to the vendor; to a person or company acting on the vendor's behalf, such as a lawyer or real estate agent; or to a developer. Each of these transactions represents an opportunity for problems.

Before handing over your money, ensure that the person or organization receiving the funds is who they claim to be and that they have the right to sell the property or to represent the vendor. In Nigeria, for example, it's not uncommon for con artists to break into a house, change the locks, print fake deeds and sell a home to several unsuspecting buyers.[26]

If you are paying a lawyer or an agent, ensure your funds are protected while they are in the intermediary's custody. This protection can take the form of an arrangement like the Legal Practitioners Fidelity Fund, which protects clients in the Australian state of New South Wales from a "solicitor's or firm's dishonest failure to pay or deliver trust money or property."

In China and Japan, where it is not unusual to buy a property with bricks of cash, ensure that you receive a properly completed receipt. If you pay by bank transfer, confirm the account name and number are those of the vendor. If you pay by check, ensure the payee's name is correct.

Consumer protection regimes vary widely. If you live in a country with strong consumer protection laws and buy a home in a developing country, ensure that your expectations are appropriate. Lawsuits are costly, unpleasant and time consuming. This is particularly true of cross-border disputes.

Galvanized steel plumbing

Galvanization is the process of coating iron or steel in zinc to prevent rusting. Galvanized steel pipe, which was used in homes in Australia, Canada, the United States and other countries until the 1960s, poses a risk because it corrodes internally. In the short term, the corrosion can discolor the home's water and cause an unpleasant taste. Over the longer term, the corrosion accumulates and reduces the water pressure. Ultimately the pipe will fail, which can cause a flood.

Galvanized plumbing has a lifespan of 40–50 years, depending on the thickness of the zinc coating, whether the pipe was coated on the inside and outside and the chemical composition of the local water. Galvanized pipes are gray in color and are typically about 25 millimeters in diameter.

Replacing the plumbing in a home can cost tens of thousands of dollars. In addition, some insurance companies may refuse to issue a homeowners' policy if galvanized plumbing is present. Without insurance, you may not be able to obtain a mortgage. See the Defective design and construction entry in this chapter for information about polybutylene pipe, another common cause of plumbing problems.

Government debt

City, state and national governments around the world are in financial trouble. For example:

▲ When Stockton, California, declared bankruptcy in 2012, it had $400 million in unfunded liabilities for retirees' healthcare.[27] After completing a one-month probation period, a janitor working for the city and her spouse were guaranteed health care for life.[28]

▲ At the end of 2010, provincial and local governments in China had borrowed a total of 10.7 trillion yuan ($1.7 trillion). Of that amount, 8 billion yuan in repayments were overdue and 35 billion yuan had been used for unauthorized purposes, such as stock market investments.[29]

▲ Greece's debt topped €300 billion, or 175% of gross domestic product, at the end of 2013.[30] In April 2014, the overall unemployment was 27%.[31] It was far worse for young people.

American cities like Stockton have seen businesses and residents flee, creating a negative feedback loop, where essential services are cut, crime rates soar and the tax base shrinks as more people leave. Stockton was the largest municipal failure in U.S. history until Detroit filed for bankruptcy.

Pension shortfalls are another issue. Research by State Budget Solutions in 2013 indicated that Ohio had a shortfall as a percentage of its gross state product of 56%, followed by New Mexico (53%), Mississippi (48%), Alaska (46%) and Illinois (41%). Even in financially sound states like Texas, local governments have taken on dangerous levels of debt and it can be hard to accurately gauge a community's total debt load.

Times of crisis can present opportunities for prepared buyers. If you had bought property in New York State in 1975—the year that New York City nearly declared bankruptcy—you would have seen prices rise on an index basis, from 100 on January 1, 1975, to a peak of 823.7 on January 1, 2007. Returns like this are by no means guaranteed.[32]

Anyone planning to buy property in a troubled country should be ready to pay cash, as it may be impossible to obtain financing, and view the purchase as speculative. Prepare to hold the property for the long term and anticipate periods when there is little or no market liquidity. You can also expect an increase in xenophobia, as has been reported in Greece, and foreign exchange controls, like those introduced in Argentina.

Health issues

An international move can create health and medical challenges. Some countries share medical standards, allowing products that have been approved in one country to be sold in another, but this is not universal. Oral contraceptives, for example, were not available in Japan until 1999, decades later than in the West. If there is a drug, product or service that you depend on, check to see if it is offered locally, if a substitute is available or if you can import a supply.

You may also want to consider how your new home would respond to a pandemic. In 2009, the United States Northern Command prepared CONPLAN 3551-09, a concept plan to synchronize pandemic influenza planning for the Department of Defense. The plan assumed that a flu pandemic would last 12–24 months and could kill 2 million Americans. It would take 4–6 months to prepare an effective vaccine and when one was available, production capacity would be limited to 1% per week of U.S. demand. The plan assumed that state and local governments and civilian hospitals and mortuaries would be overwhelmed, and that local and international transportation would be restricted.[33]

Moving from a developed to a less developed country can diminish the quality of your medical care, but it can also produce benefits. Hungary, India, the Philippines, South Africa and many other nations are developing their medical and dental tourism industries, and you can can obtain anything from a facelift to open heart surgery, often with a shorter wait and for less money than you would pay at home. Hospitals in many countries are certified by organizations such as Joint Commission International (www.jointcommissioninternational.org), which promote global health care standards.

International moves can also expose you to diseases, many of which are controlled or eradicated elsewhere. For example, in 2013 and 2014, there were outbreaks of measles in the United States,[34] multi-drug-resistant tuberculosis in Myanmar and polio in Pakistan. In some cases, outbreaks are due to misinformation, like rumors that vaccines cause autism or contain pork products. Counterfeit pharmaceuticals and patients abandoning a course of treatment before they have taken all of their medicine also contribute to the spread of diseases such as tuberculosis and malaria.

Illiquidity

As an asset class, real estate is illiquid. Transaction costs, travel expenses, foreign exchange and communication delays make overseas property even less liquid than domestic real estate.

If you will need to cash out quickly, buying overseas may be a poor choice. That's doubly true if you buy in a developing market where prices are volatile and regulations change frequently.

China has embarked on history's largest infrastructure spree, building hundreds of new subways, airports, rail lines and other facilities.

Infrastructure

Infrastructure can cause a variety of issues for homeowners. Age is one problem. Much of the infrastructure in the United States is reaching the end of its useful life. For instance, 15% of the water mains and 11% of the bridges in New York City are more than a century old.[35] The American Society of Civil Engineers' 2013 Report Card for America's Infrastructure gives the country an overall rating of D+ and notes that $3.6 trillion needs to be invested by 2020.

Some aging infrastructure is particularly dangerous, like the 54-year-old natural gas main that exploded in 2010 in San Bruno, California, killing eight people. A 2014 paper noted that 5,900 leaks from the natural gas pipelines under Washington, D.C., were large enough to be detected above ground,[36] while Boston had more than 3,300 leaks, some of which were large enough to pose a risk of explosion.[37] The cities with the largest number of major leaks since 1984 are Houston, Austin and Phoenix.[38] Natural gas leaks are also the largest anthropogenic source of the greenhouse gas methane in the United States.[39]

Infrastructure issues can reduce your quality of life and add to the cost of ownership. For example, plans are now underway to upgrade London's overloaded Victorian-era sewers. The project will cost an estimated $6.6 billion; result in large increases to residents' water bills; and create noise, dirt and traffic problems.

Infrastructure can also be affected in unexpected ways. In parts of Germany, for example, the population is too small to keep the sewage system functioning properly.[40]

New infrastructure can pose a different set of problems, especially in places with expanding economies. China is in the middle of the largest construction boom in history, and the 12th Five Year Plan (2011–2015) calls for the creation of 82 new airports and the expansion of 101 existing ones.[41] Homes in China are often expropriated to make way for infrastructure projects and the construction of new subway lines has caused cave-ins, damaged the foundations of nearby buildings and released poison gas.[42]

Unfortunately, there isn't much that an individual homeowner can do to avoid infrastructure shortages or construction projects. Modern buildings usually have better support systems, like backup generators, to minimize the effects of service interruptions. Paying attention to the local media and talking to your neighbors will minimize the chance that you will be blindsided by a new project. Finally, get involved in your community. Research by Daniel Aldrich at Purdue University suggests that once technical factors have been eliminated, communities with a strong civil society, like farmers' and fishermen's cooperatives, are less likely to have controversial facilities built in their backyards.

Knob-and-tube wiring

Knob-and-tube (KT) wiring was used in Canada and the United States from the 1880s to the 1940s. It comprises insulated copper wires that are pulled through porcelain tubes that pass through holes in joists and studs. The wires are anchored to cleats and porcelain knobs that are nailed to the joists and studs. KT wiring is not inherently unsafe, but because it is old and many installations have been improperly modified, it can be dangerous. KT wiring is a two-wire (i.e., hot and neutral) system that does not include a ground wire, which makes it unsuitable for use in wet environments, such as bathrooms, laundry rooms and kitchens. KT wiring can also cause fires if the wires are covered with combustible material, like some kinds of thermal insulation.

In general, if KT wiring was installed properly, has not been damaged or improperly modified and has been inspected by a qualified electrician, it does not pose a safety hazard. However, insurance companies may refuse to provide coverage unless the KT wiring has been replaced. In some jurisdictions, insurers may provide coverage, subject to an electrician's inspection and payment of an increased premium. Without insurance, you may not be able to obtain a mortgage.

Landslides

According to David Petley at the U.K.'s Durham University, between 2004 and 2010, landslides killed more than 32,000 people worldwide. Petley's figures are believed to be conservative because they exclude landslides caused by earthquakes, many landslides occur in remote areas where reporting is poor and fatalities often occur long after the landslide and are under-reported.

Landslides affect both wealthy and developing countries. Locations with steep slopes and high levels of rainfall from monsoons, hurricanes and typhoons are vulnerable. Earthquakes, erosion and deforestation are contributing factors, and some scientists believe that increased rainfall associated with climate change will increase the number of landslides.

Landslides are difficult to predict and are another reason why it is helpful to understand the history and geology of an area before buying. In the United States, the National Aeronautics and Space Administration uses satellites to monitor global landslide risks in real time (http://pmm.nasa.gov/node/187).

Lead paint

Lead is added to paint as a pigment and to increase durability and moisture resistance. Even a small amount can damage the brain and nervous system, and lead is especially harmful to children. Scientists have long been aware of lead's toxicity—it was first banned in house paints in Europe in 1935.[43]

Lead was used extensively in house paint in the United States, Canada, Australia and many other countries until the 1970s, when the allowable limits were gradually reduced. A 2001 report prepared for the U.S. Department of Housing and Urban Development estimated that 38 million homes, or about 40% of the total, had lead-based paint somewhere on the building, with 26 million having "significant lead-based paint hazards somewhere in the building or on the premises."[44] Today, the maximum allowable lead content in house paint in the United States is 90 parts per million.

Lead paint is still used in many countries. According to Occupational Knowledge International, studies conducted between 2005 and 2011 showed that a "substantial portion of new residential paints contain lead at levels at or above 90 ppm" in Belarus, Brazil, China, Cameroon, Ecuador, Egypt, India, Indonesia, Lebanon, Malaysia, Mexico, Nigeria, Paraguay, Peru, the Philippines, Russia, Senegal, the Seychelles, Singapore, South Africa, Sri Lanka, Taiwan, Tanzania, Thailand and Uganda. The average of 10 samples taken in Ecuador was over 31,690 ppm, more than 350 times the U.S. maximum.

Lead paint is similar to asbestos in that it is most common in older homes and it becomes a problem when it is damaged or disturbed. Lead-based paint that is in good condition, that is not flaking or that is covered by lead-free paint is not hazardous. Lead paint can be dangerous when it is on surfaces that are subject to friction or impact, such as windows and doors, or on surfaces where children can chew it. Lead-based paint is often found on window frames, doors, skirting, kitchen and bathroom cabinets, interior walls and ceilings and exterior walls and gutters.

You can check for the presence of lead paint using a simple test kit that is available from hardware and paint stores for less than $20. Lab tests of paint samples and tests using X-ray fluorescence machines can provide more accurate analysis.

The United Nations Environment Program operates the Global Alliance to Eliminate Lead Paint. The alliance's Website offers a range of links and information (www.uncp.org).

Local quirks

Every market has local quirks. If you are purchasing a home in an area that you don't know well, it pays to ask open-ended questions, like "What else should I know about buying here?"

For example, in South Africa's Western Cape and Kwazulu-Natal, it is customary for the vendor to provide the purchaser with a certificate that the home is free from borer beetles.[45] In South and Central America, triatomine insects (known locally as *barbeiro* and *chupão*) live in crevices in the walls and roofs of substandard housing and spread a parasitic infection called Chagas disease.[46] And in the U.K., you can be liable for upkeep of your local church under an ancient right known as chancel repair. One case took 17 years to resolve and cost the homeowner £200,000 ($336,000).[47]

Money laundering

In markets ranging from Hong Kong and London to Miami and New York, real estate is a popular way for criminals to launder ill-gotten gains. Under global anti-money laundering programs, financial institutions must report suspicious transactions. But in many countries, real estate agents and developers are exempt from this requirement.

Criminals use several ways to launder money through real estate.

- ▲ In violation of national foreign exchange laws, people from Mainland China smuggle shopping bags of cash out of the country and buy apartments in Hong Kong. Mainland cash laundered through Macau casinos is also used to buy Hong Kong property.

- ▲ Elsewhere, criminals will buy a house valued at $700,000 for $500,000 in legitimate funds plus $200,000 in cash, which is paid to the vendor "under the table." The sale and purchase agreement lists the price as $500,000. When the criminal later sells the home for $700,000, he appears to have made a legitimate $200,000 profit.

- ▲ Offshore companies, bank accounts and trusts are used to conceal the ownership of a property or disguise the source of funds that were used to buy a home. In some American states, criminals use limited liability companies, the beneficial owners of which can remain anonymous.

- ▲ Criminals will create a fake loan agreement with an offshore company that they control, creating the appearance that the funds have a legitimate source.[48]

Money laundering has a damaging effect on real estate markets. It drives prices up, pushing local end-users out of the market. Price increases can fuel an unsustainable levels of construction that leave legitimate buyers in negative equity when the boom inevitably turns into a bust. Furthermore, criminals are usually more concerned about laundering their funds than negotiating the best purchase price or renting vacant homes out, further distorting the market.

Noise

Living in a noisy neighborhood can be stressful and lead to poor cognitive performance. Long-term exposure to environmental noise has also been associated with health problems ranging from hearing loss to obesity and increased incidence of Type 2 diabetes.[49] The connection between high blood pressure and aviation noise is so well established that it has its own acronym, HYENA, for hypertension and exposure to noise near airports.[50]

Living in a noisy environment is stressful and has been associated with an increased risk of obesity and diabetes.

Children, elderly people, the chronically ill and shift workers are worst affected by high noise levels.

Nuclear issues

Until the 2011 Great East Japan Earthquake, nuclear power had been enjoying a renaissance as governments and voters saw it as a way to reduce the greenhouse gases produced by fossil fuels. After the Fukushima disaster, many Western governments reconsidered this position. Germany, for example, closed eight of its nuclear power plants and announced plans shut the remaining nine plants by 2022.

Today, about 11% of the world's electricity is generated by 434 nuclear power stations. As of April 2014, the United States had the largest number of operable plants, with 100, followed by France, with 58. Globally, 72 nuclear power stations were under construction, 173 were on order or planned and 309 had been proposed. More than half the plants under development were in China and Russia.[51]

Nuclear installations pose several threats. In addition to a criticality (an uncontrolled nuclear chain reaction), there is the risk of fires, explosions and radioactive leaks. Nuclear materials being transported to and from these facilities are vulnerable to accidents and theft, and radioactive waste requires secure, long-term storage. Some power plants in the United States may be mothballed, now that cheap natural gas has made them uneconomical. However, as the WWII-era Hanford facility demonstrates, decommissioning nuclear facilities is an expensive, time-consuming process.

Nuclear power advocates maintain that it is safer than fossil fuels, when all of fossil fuels' impacts—air and water pollution, mercury emissions from coal-fired plants, oil spills, climate change, etc.—are considered. In addition, studies by the National Cancer Institute in the United States, as well as other neutral agencies, concluded that there is no increased cancer risk from living near a nuclear power plant.

Concerns about nuclear safety have been exacerbated by Tokyo Electric Power's handling of Fukushima. Nuclear operators in Japan, South Korea[52] and the United States[53] have been caught faking test data and component certification and the industry is surrounded by a culture of secrecy that does not inspire confidence. While air pollution causes over 1.3 million urban deaths each year, it does so slowly and quietly. Nuclear accidents, on the other hand, are dramatic events that generate large amounts of media coverage.

Power plants are the most visible part of the nuclear industry. But radioactive materials are also used in hospitals, universities and research institutes, the oil and gas industry and the military. *The Wall Street Journal* has an interactive database of more than 500 Cold War-era nuclear research and development sites in the United States, many of which are still hazardous (http://projects.wsj.com/waste-lands/).

Canada, meanwhile, has started its largest-ever nuclear remediation project. Cleaning up the former radium and uranium refinery in Port Hope, Ontario, 110 kilometers east of Toronto, will cost an estimated C$1.28 billion and be completed by 2022.

Policy risk

From approving building plans to enforcing zoning bylaws, governments play a central role in every property market. The large sums involved and immovable nature of real estate amplify that impact. For cross-border buyers, governments' role is even larger because there are at least two national governments involved—the one where your home is located and the one that issued your passport—and immigration laws, currency controls and other legislation can affect your ability to buy, enjoy and sell property.

If you buy across borders, look for a country with a stable government and a history of openness to foreigners and foreign investment. In addition, financially sound countries are less likely to confiscate property and impose capital controls than ones that are in distress. There are no guarantees, but a nation's past is often a good guide to its future.

Here is a sample of property-related policies affecting cross-border buyers. These policies can be tightened, relaxed or scrapped often on short notice.

- ▲ In Mexico, foreigners are forbidden from owning land within 50 kilometers of the coast or 100 kilometers of an international border.[54]

- ▲ In Thailand and the Philippines, foreigners can own an apartment but cannot own land.

- ▲ Foreigners must live in China for one year before they can buy a home. In China, individuals and companies may not own land, which belongs to the state or to collectives.

- ▲ In Australia, foreigners may buy new homes but cannot purchase existing homes without government approval. New Zealanders and permanent residents are exempt from this rule.[55]

- ▲ In Switzerland, there is an annual quota governing the number of homes that can be purchased by nonresident foreigners, as well as restrictions on the number of homes each foreigner can own.[56]

- ▲ In Malta, foreigners pay 35%–60% more for electricity, water and other services than natives.[57]

- ▲ A 2010 diplomatic spat resulted in Canadians needing a visa to enter the United Arab Emirates. A six-month, multiple-entry visa cost C$1,000, before it was cut to C$660 and then eliminated in 2013.[58]

- ▲ Changes to the U.S. federal flood insurance program began taking effect in 2013. As a result, over a million homeowners will see their premiums rise by as much as 600%. Home prices in some flood zones have dropped 30%.[59]

Property bubbles

Bubbles occur when valuations rise to unsustainable levels and then decline, often rapidly and dramatically. Bubbles are driven by a belief that prices will continue to rise and that buyers will be able to sell later at a profit. This is also known as the greater fool theory.

Bubbles have a long history, stretching back to tulip mania in the Netherlands in the 1600s. In the United States, land bubbles occurred in New York State in the 1790s, in Kansas in the 1850s, in California in the 1880s and in Florida in the 1920s. More recently, Australia, Brazil, Dubai, Hong Kong, Japan, Singapore, Spain, the United States, Vietnam and other markets have experienced bubbles. Many observers believe that China has now joined this group.

For people who buy early, bubbles can be lucrative. Those who buy late, as valuations peak, suffer the worst losses and often find themselves trying to sell into a falling market, where there are few, if any, buyers. When bubbles collapse, they frequently overshoot and desirable assets can be purchased at discounted prices. Patient, discerning investors who buy at this point in the cycle can do well.

How can you tell if a market is in a bubble? Checking current prices against historical ones is a good starting point, as prices eventually revert to the mean. You can also compare purchase prices with rents and with disposable incomes. Another way is to compare prices for homes in similar markets, for example between London and New York or between Hong Kong and Singapore.

The best clue that you are in a bubble, however, is when transactions don't make economic sense. For example, in 1636 five hectares of land was offered for a single tulip bulb.[60] Pay close attention when you hear people say "this time it's different."

Determining when a bubble will burst can be difficult and it can be frustrating to watch a market rise beyond any rational valuation. As economist John Maynard Keynes famously observed, "The market can stay irrational longer than you can stay solvent."

Radon

Radon is a colorless, odorless and tasteless gas. It is radioactive and occurs around the world from the decay of uranium in the soil. In the United States, 1 in 15 homes is estimated to be affected by radon. It is second only to smoking as a cause of lung cancer. Like asbestos, radon poses a greater hazard to smokers than nonsmokers.

Radon enters homes through the lowest level in the building that is exposed to open ground, such as cracks in the foundation, gaps around pipes and the water supply. Some jurisdictions have building codes that minimize the effects of radon, and measures can be taken to reduce radon accumulation in existing homes. Inexpensive radon testing kits are available and some jurisdictions, like Ireland, where radon is common produce online maps (www.rpii.ie).

Separatist movements

There are hundreds of active separatist movements in Africa, Asia, Europe and North and South America. Structured around economic, ethnic, racial and religious lines, these groups range from handfuls of "true believers," who do little more than talk, to well-established political parties like Canada's Parti Québécois.

Separatist movements pose a risk because they often use violence—ranging from the murders and kidnappings perpetrated by ETA in Spain to the civil war waged by the Tamil Tigers in Sri Lanka—to achieve their goals.

Separatist movements also create uncertainty. This can discourage tourists and foreign investors, boost unemployment and dampen economic growth, none of which is good for home prices.

Sick building syndrome

Sick building syndrome (SBS) is a group of nonspecific symptoms that includes headaches; coughing; irritation of the eyes, nose, throat or skin; dizziness; nausea; difficulty concentrating; and fatigue. There is no standard clinical definition for SBS, but people suffering from this condition usually feel better shortly after they leave the building.

A definitive cause for SBS has not been identified, but it is associated with indoor air pollution, particularly from the volatile organic compounds (VOCs) in adhesives, furniture, wall coverings, paint, flooring, wood products, solvents and cleaning solutions, pesticides and other products. Polluted outdoor air that is drawn into a building can also contribute to SBS.

Because VOCs are used in construction materials, SBS is common in new and newly renovated homes, especially dwellings that have been sealed to increase their energy efficiency. SBS has also been linked to biological contaminants such as mold, bacteria, viruses and pollen and is exacerbated by inadequate ventilation and poor building maintenance.

Children are more susceptible to SBS and other forms of environmental chemical exposure than adults. Homemakers and other people who spend a great deal of time at home are also at risk. Psychosocial factors such as stress and anxiety can play a role in SBS, and some researchers have questioned whether SBS (and related conditions such as multiple chemical sensitivity and idiopathic environmental intolerance) is a panic attack triggered by exposure to "chemical" smells.

Airborne chemicals can be removed via physisorption with activated charcoal, porous ceramics and natural fibers; by chemisorption using organic and inorganic compounds; and through decomposition using photocatalysts, negative ions and other techniques. Commercial products, such as electronic air cleaners and passive air cleaning boards that use manganese dioxide to convert formaldehyde into water and carbon dioxide, are also available, as are colorimetric detectors that indicate the presence of formaldehyde. Increasing the flow of outside air can also help.

Social housing

Vibrant cities welcome people of different backgrounds and income levels. This is often accomplished by providing social housing, which is also known as public or affordable housing.

Some social housing programs, like Fuggerei in Germany, which has been operating since 1519, are successful. Others, such as the infamous Pruitt-Igoe Project, an architectural experiment in the United States that was completed in 1956 and demolished in 1973, are not.

Social housing plays different roles in different places. City government owns or influences about half of Vienna's housing stock and social housing there is comparatively luxurious. In Hong Kong, nearly half the population lives in subsidized dwellings that they rent or own. Mainland China plans to complete 36 million units of social housing between 2011 and 2015.

Governments use different methods to encourage the construction of social housing. In Buenos Aires, developers of luxury properties are required to give 10% of their land, or an equivalent amount of money, to the government for social housing.[61] In the United Kingdom, local authorities sign "section 106 agreements" with developers that require the developer to provide social housing, or meet other conditions, in exchange for planning approval. Some London boroughs have set targets specifying that 50% of the dwellings in new developments be affordable housing. New York City and many other U.S. jurisdictions operate inclusionary housing programs that give developers additional floor area or similar concessions in exchange for creating or preserving affordable housing.

Social housing programs are controversial. A 2004 research paper by the libertarian Reason Foundation that examined cities in the San Francisco Bay Area found that inclusive housing programs did not add to the housing stock, were overly expensive, restricted the supply of new homes and did not address the underlying causes of affordable housing shortages.

Social housing can also lead to conflicts. In New York, a complex on Manhattan's Upper West Side sparked a controversy when people learned that it would include two entrances: one for owners paying market prices and a second for public housing tenants.[62] In one U.K. development, social housing tenants complained about being treated like second-class citizens while homeowners blamed the tenants for vandalism and bad behavior.[63]

For buyers, the key is knowing that a development includes social housing—something that developers do not always make clear—before you sign a contract. This is particularly true when buying off the plan, buying in an inner-city redevelopment or buying a home in London, for example, at a developer's road show in Singapore. Social housing does not have to be a problem, if the development is properly planned and managed and you know what you are buying.

Soil pollution

Contaminated soil is often found on brownfield sites, which are old industrial facilities like factories, mines, refineries and steel mills. Former dry cleaners, gas stations and warehouses may also be polluted. Around the world, these sites are common.

- ▲ In the United States, more than 400,000 brownfield sites await remediation. The Environmental Protection Agency estimates that one in four Americans lives within five kilometers of a hazardous waste site.[64]

- ▲ Between 2001 and 2009, 98,000 industrial enterprises in China moved from urban locations, including the site of Shanghai Expo 2010.[65] Until 2011, the Shougang Group operated a steel mill just 17 kilometers from Tiananmen Square in Beijing.[66]

▲ In 1998, the U.K. government announced a target of having 60% of the nation's housing built on brownfield sites. By 2008, an estimated 80% of all new homes met this goal.⁶⁷

Former factories—like the Taipei tobacco plant that became the Songshan Cultural and Creative Park—often need extensive remediation.

Brownfields are frequently polluted with heavy metals, including arsenic, cadmium, chromium, lead and mercury; electronic waste, such as flame retardants; organic chemicals like hydrocarbons and solvents; and persistent organic pollutants, including polychlorinated biphenyls (PCBs) and pesticides like DDT. These substances can accumulate in the soil, where they can form a toxic soup that poisons the groundwater. In 2008, soil under the proposed new site for the Tsukiji fish market in Tokyo was found to contain 43,000 times the allowable amount of the carcinogen benzene. In nearby groundwater, benzene was 10,000 times higher than the legal limit.⁶⁸

Soil pollution can also affect areas that were converted from industrial to residential use in the 1960s and 1970s, before there was much awareness or testing for hazardous waste. Illegal or undocumented dumping can also cause problems.

Brownfields can be successfully cleaned up. But remediation is expensive and time consuming, and environmental standards are stricter and more vigorously enforced in some places than in others. In New Zealand, for instance, a site that was once used for a hazardous activity or industry is subject to additional environmental regulations, regardless of whether the site is contaminated or not.[69]

There are also questions about the effectiveness of the cleanup programs. Thirty-five years after a state emergency was declared at Love Canal, which is probably the most infamous example of industrial pollution in the United States, there are new concerns about the site. Residents of the area, which was renamed Black Creek Village, have filed lawsuits alleging that chemicals continue to leach into the soil. More than 19,000 tonnes of chemicals remain in the Love Canal site.[70]

If you buy a new home on a former brownfield, deal with a reputable developer. With a brand to protect, they are more likely properly remediate the site and they have an incentive to treat you properly if there is a problem.

Homes on former brownfields may be difficult to resell. In a 2003 survey by the Japan Real Estate Institute and Meikai University Graduate School of Real Estate Sciences, just 9% of respondents said they would be willing to buy land or an apartment on a site that had been remediated. Nearly two-thirds would not purchase a property if there was a history of soil contamination.[71]

Subsidence

Subsidence is a drop or depression in the earth's surface. In cities, subsidence is most commonly associated with groundwater depletion, but it can also be caused by mining, oil and gas extraction, the dissolution of limestone and earthquakes.

Subsidence can occur imperceptibly or very quickly. In August 2013, a sinkhole with a diameter of 30 meters swallowed a 24-unit condominium in Clermont, Florida, in a matter of minutes.[72] Sinkholes are common in Florida, where limestone is weakened by acidic rainwater.

Subsidence is a global problem. It affects 50 cities in China alone, including Shanghai, which has sunk 2.6 meters since 1921. Bangkok, Jakarta, Mexico City, Osaka, Tokyo, Venice and many other cities are also affected. In London, several incidents have occurred when wealthy homeowners have excavated their basements and caused structural damage to neighbors' houses.

Subsidence can create large bills for homeowners, who must repair and reinforce foundations. It is also a major expense for cities, which spend billions of dollars each year fixing damaged roads, bridges and railways. These costs are ultimately borne by taxpayers.

Sustainability

Cities are dynamic, and the most livable ones include a diverse range of people, businesses, institutions and attractions. With that in mind, it's worth asking if the cultural, economic and environmental elements that attracted you to a place will be there in future. For example:

▲ Home prices in San Francisco have been bid up by Silicon Valley technology workers. Middle-class people, like kindergarten teachers and firefighters, can no longer afford to live in the communities they serve. Hong Kong, London and New York have similar problems.

▲ Macau was under Portuguese rule until 1999, when it became a special administrative region (SAR) of China. Macau's SAR status is guaranteed until 2049, after which its future is unclear.

▲ In Belgravia, Chelsea and other ultra-wealthy parts of London, many homes are second residences that are only occupied for a few weeks each year. There are too few year-round residents to sustain shops and other services.

▲ In 2013, the total fertility rate in nearly 100 countries was below the replacement level. Whether they increase immigration or watch their populations shrink, these countries will experience long-term social and economic change.[73]

▲ Record levels of air pollution, daily traffic jams and ongoing water shortages make life in Beijing difficult for rich and poor alike.

Termites

Termites are an important part of the global ecosystem, helping to break down plant matter and aerate soil. There are more than 2,600 species of termites, about 10% of which are considered pests. Termites can be grouped into four categories: dampwood, drywood, subterranean and arboreal/mound-builders.

All four categories can be found in Africa, Asia, Australia and South America, while all but the arboreal/mound-builders are seen in North America. The subterranean *Reticulitermes* termite is most common in Europe and North America.

Termites do billions of dollars in damage to buildings and infrastructure each year. Wood is their main target, but termites also consume plasterboard, carpets, electrical insulation and other material. A mature colony of Formosan subterranean termites, *Coptotermes formosanus* (Shiraki), can comprise millions of insects, consume over 400 grams of wood per day and wreck a building in months.[74]

New homes can be protected with stone, concrete or metal barriers that termites cannot penetrate. Chemicals are also used as barriers and to treat timber.

Termite damage can be difficult to detect until it has reached an advanced stage, so a professional inspection is wise if you are buying a pre-owned home in an area where infestations are common. The presence of shelter tubes, which termites use as protection from the elements and predators, frass (termite excrement) and shed wings are indications of a problem. Infested homes are usually treated by killing the colony with insecticides or chemicals and then introducing barriers to prevent the termites from returning.

Traffic

In 2011, road injuries were the ninth most common cause of death worldwide, resulting in 1.3 million deaths.[75] National fatality rates vary widely: Iceland had 2.8 traffic deaths per 100,000 people, versus 41.7 in the Dominican Republic.[76] Rates vary within countries: In 2010, the American state of Wyoming had more than 27 deaths per 100,000 while the District of Columbia had fewer than 4.[77]

Roads in developing countries are particularly dangerous. Brazil has 22.5 deaths per 100,000—a rate that jumps during *Carnivale*—and under-reporting is common. On the other hand, in 2013 North Korea and Uzbekistan awarded themselves perfect marks in the World Health Organization's road safety compliance survey.

Traffic jams also degrade your quality of life. In 2011, IBM conducted a "commuter pain survey" that covered 20 cities. The survey, which addressed travel time and nine other factors, rated Mexico City worst with a score of 108, followed by Beijing and Shenzhen, which were tied at 95. The best cities were Montreal (21), London (23) and Chicago (25).

Finally, traffic has environmental impacts that include noise as well as light and air pollution. Living next to a busy road can be bad for your health, especially in countries that have not switched to ultra-low-sulfur diesel. In addition, as of January 2013 leaded gasoline was still sold in Afghanistan, Algeria, Iraq, North Korea, Myanmar and Yemen. Leaded gasoline includes tetraethyl lead, which has been associated with brain damage.[78]

Tropical cyclones and tornadoes

Many kinds of extreme weather follow long-term patterns and should be part of your pre-purchase research. For example, each year Taiwan and the Philippines are hit by typhoons as those storms move toward the coast of China. Hurricanes are common in the Caribbean and the Gulf of Mexico, while tornadoes occur more frequently in Texas, Kansas, Oklahoma and Nebraska than in other American states.

Ensure that you are ready for extreme weather with insurance and emergency supplies, such as food, water, flashlights and a first-aid kit.

Urea formaldehyde foam insulation

Urea formaldehyde foam insulation (UFFI) is a form of thermal insulation that was used in hundreds of thousands of homes in the United States and Canada in the 1970s and early 1980s. UFFI was popular because it could be injected into confined spaces where it would be impractical to install other types of insulation.

UFFI releases formaldehyde—a known carcinogen—while it is curing, although the level of formaldehyde emissions becomes negligible within a couple of days. UFFI also shrinks, reducing its insulation value, and retains moisture, which can support the growth of mold.

As a result of health concerns, Canada banned UFFI in 1980. Its use was prohibited in the United States in 1982, but the ban was overturned in 1983. UFFI continues to be used in Europe. In some jurisdictions, vendors may be required to declare the existence of UFFI when they sell a home. However, many experts now believe that the health concerns surrounding UFFI were groundless.

Water

At the end of 2011, 89% of the world's population used an improved drinking-water source, while 55% had a piped water supply on the premises. In general, developed nations enjoy more reliable supplies of cleaner water than developing countries, while city dwellers have better access to clean water than rural residents.[79]

But this is only part of the story. Droughts, rapid growth and poor stewardship have created persistent water shortages in countries as diverse as Australia and Yemen. In China, more than a quarter of 4,000 urban water treatment facilities tested by the government in 2009 failed to meet national quality standards.[80] Meanwhile, the American Society of Civil Engineers notes that the United States experiences 240,000 water main breaks each year, as much of the nation's water infrastructure reaches the end of its useful life. Water pollution—from chemical spills, industrial effluent, sewage, and from livestock waste and fertilizer and pesticide runoff from farms—remains a global concern.

Water shortages are caused by a range of factors including droughts, pollution and depleted aquifers.

Each of these issues has the potential to reduce the amount of potable water that is available and lead to higher taxes to pay for repairs to existing infrastructure, build new water treatment and delivery systems and clean up polluted waters.

Xenophobia

If you live in a country where you stand out from the rest of the population, you may face discrimination. This can be relatively mild—like the case of Debito Arudou, a naturalized Japanese citizen who launched an anti-discrimination lawsuit after he was refused admittance to a Hokkaido public bath in 2000—or much more serious. During WWII, more than 20,000 people of Japanese ancestry, most of whom were Canadian citizens, were held in detention camps and had their homes, farms and other property confiscated by the Canadian government.[81]

Xenophobia is a particular risk during times of upheaval: the popularity of Greece's ultra-nationalist Golden Dawn political party has spiked as the country's economic fortunes have waned. High levels of immigration can provoke a backlash when the newcomers are not integrating. Geopolitical tensions, like the dispute between Japan and China over the Diaoyu Islands (known in Japan as the Senkakus), sparked China-wide, anti-Japanese protests in 2012.

Zoning and urban planning

If you are used to orderly, transparent urban planning, you may be in for a shock when you buy a home overseas. Differing legal processes, economic priorities and aesthetic values mean that assumptions you make in your home country may be invalid in a new location. This can influence everything from your ability to paint or renovate your home to the development of your neighborhood. For example, as this book was being written, the author was part of a community initiative to stop the construction of a 10-story, 37,000-niche columbarium in a Hong Kong residential neighborhood.

PRE-OWNED HOMES

The Buying Process
135

Home Inspections
145

Land Surveys
151

Renovations
155

THE BUYING PROCESS

While each country—and many states and provinces—have local variations, the process of buying a pre-owned home follows a basic pattern.

1. The buyer sets a preliminary budget and determines his requirements, including the home's size, style, location and facilities.

2. If a mortgage is required, the buyer researches lending rates, currencies and terms and creates a shortlist of lenders. This can be done directly with a bank or through a mortgage broker or financial adviser.

3. The buyer applies for and receives approval in principle from a lender.

4. The buyer reads online listings, views prospective homes and finds a suitable home.

5. The buyer makes the vendor an offer. When the offer is accepted, the buyer and the vendor sign a preliminary sale and purchase (S&P) agreement, which specifies the main transaction details, including the price, property description, items included in the sale, dates and amounts of subsequent payments, signing date for the S&P agreement and penalties for breach of contract.

6. The agent confirms the vendor's identity and verifies that the vendor owns the property.

7. The buyer pays a deposit, ranging from a few hundred dollars to as much as 20% of the purchase price. Depending on the market, the deposit is paid directly to the vendor or to an intermediary, such as an escrow company, a lawyer or an agent.

8. Several weeks later, the buyer makes a second payment to the vendor or his intermediary. By this point, the buyer has typically paid 10% or more of the purchase price.

9. A lawyer or title company reviews the property's title to ensure there are no defects or encumbrances.

10. The buyer arranges title insurance and fire insurance.

11. If needed, the buyer applies for a mortgage.

12. The buyer and vendor sign the S&P agreement and associated title transfer documents.

13. Title is formally transferred from the vendor to the buyer. The change in ownership is registered with the government.

14. Money is transferred from the buyer or his mortgage lender to the vendor or his intermediary.

15. The buyer pays stamp duty or other transfer taxes.

16. The buyer, vendor and agent make a final visit to the property, where the buyer checks that the property is in order and that there has been no damage. The vendor hands over the keys.

17. The utility accounts are transferred from the vendor to the buyer's name. Miscellaneous outstanding expenses, such as prepaid or unpaid utility bills, are settled.

18. The buyer and vendor pay their agents and lawyers, as necessary.

19. The transaction is complete.

Four examples

Here are sample purchases from Italy, New Zealand, the United Kingdom and the United States.

Italy

In Italy, the process usually starts with a *proposta* (written offer), which is accompanied by a check. When the offer has been accepted, the check is deposited into an escrow account and the offer becomes binding. A deadline is included in the written offer, after which the offer lapses. If the buyer defaults on the purchase, the vendor keeps the buyer's deposit. If the vendor defaults, he pays the buyer a sum equal to twice the deposit. Payments over €12,500 ($17,300) must be made by check or bank transfer.

When the offer is accepted, the buyer's lawyer makes preliminary searches to ensure that the property complies with building regulations. The buyer's lawyer and the vendor's lawyer work with the *notario* (notary) to produce a *compromesso* (preliminary contact). When the contract has been signed by the buyer and the vendor, it is lodged with the notary.

In Italy, *mediatore* (real estate agents) are registered with the Chamber of Commerce. Both the buyer and seller pay the agent 3% of the purchase price, plus value-added tax (IVA). The commission amount is written into the preliminary contract and is payable when this contract is signed. When the preliminary contract is signed, the buyer pays the vendor a deposit of 20%–30% of the purchase price. If the buyer or seller is a married couple, both the husband and wife sign the preliminary contact.

The preliminary contact also includes the names of the buyer, seller, agents and notary; the location and description of the property; the price; the payment terms; the completion date; details of any encumbrances; whether the buyer is assuming any existing mortgages or if they will be paid by the vendor; and information about easements, certifications and compliance with zoning regulations.

At this point, if the vendor is found not to have declared important information, the buyer can cancel the sale. However, if the buyer cancels the sale without just cause, he loses his deposit and may be liable for additional damages.

After the preliminary contact has been signed, the notary completes any outstanding searches and prepares the *rogito notarile* (final contract). When the final contract is signed, the buyer pays the vendor the balance of the purchase price. He also pays the notary's fee, which is approximately 1% of the purchase price, the lawyer's fee, if applicable, as well as IVA and registration, mortgage tax and cadastral taxes. Different taxes and tax rates apply, depending on whether the home is purchased from a private individual or from a construction company. First homes and luxury dwellings are also taxed differently, with acquisition costs representing 10%–12% the purchase price.

Before completion, the buyer must obtain a *codice fiscale* (Italian tax card). When the final contract has been signed, the notary transfers legal title of the property to the buyer.[1] If there is a long interval between the initial acceptance and completion, a large down payment has been made or if the vendor is a company that might enter bankruptcy, the buyer can protect her interests by registering the written offer with the Land Agency.[2]

New Zealand
The buyer starts by identifying a lawyer to advise on the purchase. Lawyer's fees are typically about NZ$1,500 ($1,286).

When the buyer has found a property that he wants to acquire, the seller's agent draws up the S&P agreement. The agent is required to give the buyer a copy of the New Zealand Residential Property Sale and Purchase Agreements Guide and the buyer provides written confirmation that he has received the guide. The buyer's lawyer reviews the S&P agreement and if it is acceptable, the buyer signs the S&P agreement and the agent presents it to the seller.

Conditional offers are common in New Zealand, and conditions are included in the S&P agreement. Buyers can make an offer that is contingent on a satisfactory title search, which costs about NZ$250; a builder or engineer's inspection (NZ$500); a lender's valuation of the property (NZ$100); a Land Information Memorandum report from the local council, which identifies issues such as soil pollution, drainage and landslip risks as well as any remedial work that needs to be conducted (NZ$300); on the buyer obtaining financing; or on the buyer selling their existing home. The offer also includes an expiry date.

The S&P agreement will specify the purchase price; any chattels (fixtures, fittings or appliances) that are included in the sale; whether the property is leasehold or freehold; any other conditions, such as repairs that the seller must make before the contract is settled (completed); the deposit that the buyer must pay; and the settlement date, when the buyer pays the balance of the purchase price and takes possession of the home. The buyer usually pays the balance through his lawyer.

The S&P agreement will also list the buyer and seller's obligations—such as the buyer's access to the home and which party is responsible for insuring the home before settlement—and penalties for delaying or defaulting on the sale.

The buyer and seller can negotiate and adjust the price and terms of the sale. When the buyer and seller have reached an understanding, and both parties have initialed any changes to the S&P agreement, the seller signs the S&P agreement. When all of the buyer's sale conditions have been met, the sale is "unconditional." At this point, the buyer is legally obliged to purchase the home from the seller. When the sale is unconditional, the buyer pays a 5%–10% deposit, which is held in the agent's trust account until settlement. Land transfer fees add another NZ$200–NZ$300 to the final bill.

While most homes in New Zealand are sold by the offer and negotiation process described above, tenders and auctions are also used.

In a sale by tender, the vendor works with a real estate agent, who prepares the tender documents and advertises the sale. Buyers then submit bids, usually to the agent's office. Unlike an auction, bidders in a tender do not know how much other people are offering. Bids are accompanied by a deposit check for 5%–10% of the purchase price, and a signed S&P agreement, which lists any conditions that apply to the offer. There is no reserve (minimum) price, although the vendor may specify a "buyer budget over" (BBO) or a guide price. A property may be advertised as "for sale by tender unless sold prior," which means it can be sold before the tender date. In a tender, the vendor is not required to accept any of the bids. But if the vendor accepts a bid, the buyer is legally bound to complete the sale, subject to the conditions in the S&P agreement.

Vendors selling by tender sometimes prefer a bid with a lower price and few conditions to a higher price and more stringent conditions. If a bid is unsuccessful, the buyer's deposit is returned and he is under no further obligation to the vendor.

In a sale by auction, the vendor's agent advertises the sale and provides an auctioneer. The vendor works with the agent to set a confidential reserve price, below which the home will not be sold. Like a tender sale, offers can be accepted beforehand, preempting the auction. Sales by auction are unconditional and, once the hammer falls, the highest bidder over the reserve price is obliged to buy the home. As a result, it is essential that buyers have arranged financing and conducted due diligence on the property, including a title search and Land Information Memorandum report, before they bid.

When the bids have reached the reserve price, the auctioneer will announce that the property is "on the market." If the bidding has stopped short of the reserve price, the auctioneer will ask the vendor for instructions. The vendor can then agree to accept the last bid, even if it does not meet the reserve price. Or the property can be "passed in," which means that the auction is concluded without a sale. In some auctions, the vendor can bid. This is a way of driving the price higher and can be indicated by the auctioneer saying, "the bid is with me."[3]

The buyer is expected to pay a deposit at the end of the auction. Settlement is usually four to six weeks after the auction.[4]

United Kingdom
The buyer identifies a property that he would like to purchase. The agent asks how the buyer will finance the purchase and whether he owns a home that will need to be sold. After one or more viewings, the buyer makes an offer through the estate agent.

When the offer is accepted, the estate agent prepares a memorandum of sale that includes the contract details. The buyer retains a solicitor or licensed conveyancer (a lawyer who is trained in property law but is not qualified as a solicitor or barrister), who establishes the vendor's title to the property and lists any encumbrances or other issues affecting the property.

If a mortgage is needed, the lender conducts a home inspection, called a survey in the United Kingdom, and an appraisal of the property, which is paid for by the buyer. The buyer may commission a separate appraisal and survey to ensure that there are no defects, like leaking pipes, that need repair.

In England, a buyer is not committed to a sale until contracts are exchanged. Different rules apply in Scotland.

Until contracts have been exchanged, the buyer does not have to purchase the property. The buyer can lower their offer to reflect defects found in the survey or abandon the purchase entirely. Likewise, the vendor does not have to sell the home to the buyer until contracts have been exchanged. The process is different in Scotland, where a vendor must provide written, legally binding acceptance of a successful bid. It usually takes about nine weeks from acceptance of the offer to exchange of contracts.

When contracts are exchanged, the buyer pays the vendor a deposit, typically 10% of the purchase price. The sale is now legally binding and the buyer loses his deposit if he abandons the purchase. If the vendor cancels the sale, the vendor returns the buyer's deposit and must compensate the buyer for any losses incurred.

The contracts state an agreed completion date when the buyer gets the keys to the home and the vendor receives the balance of the purchase price.[5]

United States
The following information is for New Jersey. Other states follow a similar pattern.

When a buyer has found a suitable home, he makes a written offer to purchase. It is not mandatory, but most buyers retain a lawyer to help them prepare the offer and the contract of sale, to negotiate with the vendor and agent on their behalf, to assist with the mortgage application and to attend the closing.

The offer includes the buyer and seller's names; the total price, including the initial deposit (also known as earnest money) and the amount to be paid when the contract of sale is executed; the property's address; any fixtures, fittings or appliances that will be included in the sale; all deadline dates; any contract riders; and any contingencies, such as the home passing an inspection or the buyer obtaining financing.

When the buyer makes the offer to purchase, he pays a deposit into an escrow account, where the funds are held until the sale is completed and then released to the vendor. If the vendor rejects the offer, the deposit is normally returned to the buyer. The escrow account is managed by an escrow agent who is named in the contract.

In some cases, an offer to purchase is not used and the buyer and seller proceed directly to the contract of sale, which is a legally binding agreement. It includes all of the terms and conditions agreed by the buyer and vendor in the offer to purchase, if one was used. In New Jersey, if the real estate agent prepares the contract of sale, it must include an attorney review clause, which gives the buyer and seller three business days from the date the contract is signed to have it reviewed by a lawyer. The lawyer can propose amendments to the contract or have it declared null and void.

Between the contract signing and completion, the buyer will need to arrange a home inspection, a title search to prove that the vendor has the right to sell the home and ensure there are no outstanding liens, title insurance to protect against any previous title defects, homeowners insurance, a survey of the property, radon testing and a flood search. If the home gets drinking water from a well or uses a septic tank, both must be tested. Some homes will also need to be tested for termites.[6]

Buyers should investigate whether there are convicted sex offenders in the area. Under Megan's Law, New Jersey county prosecutors determine whether and how to notify the public of sex offenders living in a neighborhood. Buyers can also check with the municipal clerk's office for proposed construction projects, nearby toxic waste sites or other nuisances that could affect a home's value. Vendors and agents are not required to voluntarily disclose if a property is stigmatized, such as being the site of a violent death. But if a buyer asks, the vendor and agent are obliged to disclose any such information of which they are aware.[7]

Before the closing, the buyer's lawyer or real estate agent will request a copy of the settlement statement, which is also known as an HUD-1, from the title company. The HUD-1 tells the buyer how much money he will need at the closing and explains how those funds will be dispersed. Typically, these costs must be paid by certified check or a cashier's check.

Within 24 hours of the closing, the buyer conducts a walk-through of the home. This is a final opportunity to check that the vendor has made any repairs that were agreed in the contract of sale; that all fixtures, fittings and appliances are accounted for and working; and that the home is intact. The buyer should bring any discrepancies to the attention of his agent and lawyer.

Usually, the buyer, the seller, the real estate agents, the lawyers, the title clerk and a mortgage company representative attend the closing, which can occur at the office of the lawyer, real estate agent or title insurance company.

At the closing, the buyer signs the mortgage and purchase documents and the title of the property is transferred to the buyer. The title and mortgage are recorded at the county clerk's office and the buyer receives the keys to his new home.

HOME INSPECTIONS

A home inspection is sensible wherever you buy a property. It's particularly smart when you are buying in a place where you do not speak the language or are unfamiliar with local customs and building standards.

A home inspection describes a building's current state and gives you important clues about future costs, like replacing a roof or a furnace in a single-family home. For condominiums, the inspector's report will cover the inside of the unit, while responsibility for common areas and facilities, like the lobby, roof and foundations, is shared among all owners. As a result, some condo buyers skip the inspection, believing that their liabilities are limited to less-expensive problems. This can be an expensive mistake. In Vancouver, for example, some buyers of leaky condominiums received special assessments of C$200,000 ($181,000).[1]

For condos, the inspector's report should be read in conjunction with the management or owners' committee's reports and accounts, which will outline work that is planned for the building's common areas and the funds that have been set aside for these projects. The management or owners' committee will often post notices or erect displays, with photos, material samples, schedules and other information, in the building's lobby that explain proposed or pending improvement projects.

Where to start

Before you hire an inspector, evaluate the home yourself. Start in the basement, where many expensive problems, like cracked foundations, can be found. Look for water leaks, scorch marks near electrical installations, windows and doors that do not open and close properly and damage to the roof. A ball bearing or marble can quickly highlight floors that are not level. Research common local concerns, such as radon in Ireland. Do an Internet search for the name of the condo, resort, development and builder to find media coverage of construction and design problems.

Bad smells can indicate a range of issues, including sewer or septic tank problems. They can also indicate the presence of mold, which may be visible or be related to condensation inside the walls.

Your visual check can also reveal unauthorized renovations, like walls that have been removed or balconies that have been enclosed. These renovations can create a safety hazard and a financial liability because you could be responsible for correcting the alteration or reinstating the home to its original condition—even if you did not make the changes. An architect can help you determine whether renovations have been made according to the building code and registered with the city, if required.

In some markets, like Hong Kong, home inspectors are uncommon. Many people gut apartments after they buy them, making an inspection less important. In developing countries—where construction quality and maintenance are variable and where lead paint and other hazardous materials are used—a home inspection can literally be a lifesaver. Furthermore, you may not be able to arrange a proper inspection of an inexpensive, deeply discounted or foreclosed home. As a result, it makes sense to learn basic inspection skills.

Hiring an inspector

If the home passes your review, ask friends, coworkers and acquaintances for the names of inspectors who they have used in the past. Exercise caution with inspectors who are recommended by the selling agent, as the inspector and agent may have a relationship that could influence how the inspection results are presented.

Home inspections start at about $200 and escalate quickly depending on the market and the size and complexity of the property. It takes about two hours to inspect a small home and one hour for a condo. Large dwellings and properties with complications, like outbuildings, take longer.

The inspector should be a specialist, not someone who does home inspections as a sideline. Hire an experienced inspector with a reputation for being thorough. They should carry professional indemnity insurance, also known as errors and omissions insurance, and be accredited with the International Association of Certified Home Inspectors (www.nachi.org) or a local trade or professional body, such as the Chambre Syndicale des Experts Immobiliers de France (http://cseif-com.micrologiciel.com). Some countries have national standards, like New Zealand's NZS 4206:2005 Residential Property Inspection. If you are buying something unusual, like a heritage home, ensure the inspector has relevant expertise. Check with your local consumer protection organization or Better Business Bureau to see if complaints have been lodged against the inspector.

You may need to hire an architect to determine if previous owners have made unauthorized or unsafe alterations.

Ask for a sample inspection report to ensure it is thorough and to see how the information is presented. Photos, diagrams and lots of detail will be helpful when you are negotiating with the vendor, estimating the cost of repairs and hiring tradespeople.

The inspection

Before the inspection, coordinate with the homeowner to ensure the gas, water and electricity are turned on and that the inspector has access to the entire home, including the basement, attic, closets and crawlspaces. The inspection should be conducted during daylight hours and, if possible, you should be present during the inspection. This will allow you to gauge the inspector's thoroughness and ask questions. If parts of the home are obscured by snow, ask the inspector how these elements will be evaluated.

The inspection will typically cover about 500 items, starting with the building's structural integrity, as well as mechanical systems, including electricity, plumbing and heating, ventilating and air-conditioning. The building's envelope, such as the windows, doors, exterior walls and roof, will be checked, as will the interior finishes, like paint and wallpaper. The inspector will also look at the walkway and driveway and the garage and pool if they are part of the home.

You can also hire specialists to check things like noise from nearby roads or airports, soil toxicology and other issues. Energy audits, which are mandatory for vendors in Austin, Texas, and other U.S. cities, start at around $100. In some countries, like France, tests for asbestos and other hazards are mandatory.[2] See the "Risk Factors" chapter for details.

It's important to have realistic expectations about the property and its condition. A century-old home will have more problems than a decade-old one. It's also helpful to avoid becoming too emotionally invested in a property. Few homes are literally unique, and the time, cost and stress of repairing large problems can be substantial.

The report

The inspector's report will list the address of the home, the name of the inspector, the date and time of the inspection, the scope of the inspection, a list of items that were not checked and reasons why they were omitted, an overall conclusion about the property's condition, a list of specific problems that need to be addressed and recommendations for additional inspections by a seismic engineer, electrician or plumber, if necessary. Photos and video footage may also be included.

When the report is completed, ask for clarification if anything is unclear. You may also ask for help interpreting the results from an engineer or architect. A report on Vancouver's leaking condominiums by the Canada Mortgage and Housing Corporation found that "...written comments by an inspector may appear benign but closer examination by a person knowledgeable about building envelope failure would reveal ominous warnings couched in soft language."[3]

Review the "Risk Factors" chapter so you understand the implications of problems that the inspector discovers. It can be helpful to ask the inspector open-ended questions about the home's condition, like, "What are the three biggest problems with this home?" or even, "Would you buy this home?" Be extremely cautious if the vendor or the agent tries to downplay the need for an inspection or dismisses issues that the inspector discovers.

When you have the inspector's report, you will have four options:

▲ Ask the vendor to fix any defects as a condition of the sale*

▲ Negotiate a discount to cover the cost of the repairs

▲ Accept the price and defects and buy the property "as is"

▲ Abandon the transaction

Each home and set of circumstances is different, but given the complexities of managing a cross-border renovation, the first and last options are often best.

---

* This requires a clear written description of what needs to be fixed, a schedule, information about the expected standard of materials and workmanship and a method for resolving disputes if the work is unsatisfactory.

LAND SURVEYS

If you are buying a home that includes land, an accurate, up-to-date survey is a useful resource. A survey comprises a map and a written description of the property and is prepared by a licensed or registered surveyor. The survey provides four important kinds of information:

- The size of a parcel of land

- The parcel's location in relation to neighboring parcels, roads and geographical features

- The location of buildings, fences and other improvements relative to the property's boundaries

- The property's physical features, such as creeks and rivers

Practical applications

A survey has several practical applications. First, it confirms that you are buying what you think you are buying. The property's legal boundaries may differ from those suggested by fences, hedges and other markers. Sites that border a field or vacant lot are especially prone to confusion.

Second, a survey will reveal defects. For example, part of your home may be built on a neighbor's land. Or the home may encroach on an easement—which gives an electrical company access to power lines above or under your property, for example—or a setback that specifies the minimum distance between your home and the street. Problems like these are best avoided because they can be expensive to fix.

If you are building a new house, adding an extension to your home or installing a pool or deck, a survey can ensure that you comply with setbacks and easements.

A survey can also be helpful for avoiding and resolving boundary disputes with your neighbors and ensuring that you are paying the correct amount of property taxes. A survey may be required by a lender, a title insurance company or the local authority that issues building permits.

Finally, a survey is useful when you sell your home because it gives prospective buyers confidence that the property is not affected by any of the issues described above.

Arranging a survey

A survey may be available from a local government office. A recent survey may be sufficient, but very old surveys may not reflect power lines and other recent additions or the cumulative effects of erosion or earthquakes. Some nations, such as Denmark, have hundreds of years of map data, are completely surveyed and maintain a digital cadastral map and parcel register.[1] In Greece, only about 7% of the land is properly surveyed and the details of most property transactions are handwritten in ledgers.[2]

Surveys typically start at about $300.[3] The actual price will be determined by many factors, including the size and location of the property, the level of detail required, whether the land is overgrown with vegetation, the shape of the parcel (rectangular parcels are cheaper), the topography and the season (surveys in winter are more expensive). Surveyors will prepare free quotations, but they need a copy of your deed to do so.

Title insurance should be viewed as a complement to—not a replacement for—a survey. Title insurance policies usually include an exemption for problems that would have been discovered by an accurate survey or inspection of the property.[4] Furthermore, buying a problem-free home is preferable to making insurance claims and filing lawsuits.

Measuring up

A survey is unnecessary if you are buying a condominium or co-op. However, there is no universally agreed way to measure a home's floor area. Until recently, elevator lobbies and clubhouses were counted in the gross floor area of Hong Kong apartments. In Australia, outdoor car parking spaces have been included, while swimming pools have been counted in Spain. In Japan, on the other hand, apartments are measured halfway into the outside wall.

Unlike the length of a foot, there is no global standard for measuring the size of a home.

In 2013, 20 global associations in the real estate industry agreed to establish the International Property Measurement Standards Coalition. The coalition's goal is to create a global standard for measuring land, building and floor area.[5]

RENOVATIONS

Like custom-building a home, cross-border renovations are not for the faint of heart. All of the things that make owning a home in a second country challenging—communication and differing laws, customs and standards—are amplified with a renovation project. Carefully consider the costs in time, money and frustration before starting an international renovation. You may conclude that buying a new home or one that has already been refurbished makes more sense than renovating an existing one.

Communication

Renovation projects rarely go according to plan. Problems can be caused by the unexpected and unforeseen, like extreme weather or hidden structural flaws, or by a client changing a room layout or color scheme after work has begun.

Successfully managing these challenges requires clear communication among everyone concerned: the contractor, the subcontractors, the designer or architect and the client. Without that communication and a healthy degree of trust, a minor alteration can snowball into a major problem that derails your budget and your schedule.

The burden of communication rests with the homeowner, who will pay for and live with the final results. The communication process starts with knowing what you want; changes at the planning stage cost less than after the project has begun. When you have defined the project, including the scope of work, budget, timetable, standards for material and workmanship and penalties and bonuses (if any), ensure the entire team understands your intentions. Use pictures, videos, paint chips, fabric swatches and local-language translations to ensure that you are clear. Taking a proactive approach increases your odds of success.

Effective communication must be matched with reasonable expectations. Good work takes time and costs money, and you are more likely to get museum-quality carpentry in a major city like New York or London than in a small town. In developing countries, it can be wise to use vernacular designs, which are based on local needs and traditions and domestically sourced materials, rather than trying to create something new that may be beyond the skills of local craftsmen.

Disputes are common in home renovation projects as well as large commercial developments and civil engineering works. Almost anything is preferable to a dispute that leads to an abandoned project or a multinational lawsuit. Being patient, flexible and reasonable and paying your bills on time are often a good starting point, especially if you are working with good suppliers.

Who to hire

If you renovate, hire people and companies with a proven track record for delivering quality work. If possible, use suppliers who have experience serving nonlocal customers and check their references and professional credentials (see the Architects, designers and builders section in the "Useful information" chapter). Solid English skills are a plus, as are a willingness and ability to use Skype, email and other tools to facilitate long-distance communication. Inexperienced people or companies charging rock-bottom prices may cost more in the end, if they fail to get all of the necessary permits and permissions or use substandard materials that must be repaired or replaced.

If you live in a different country and the project is large, hire a local architect or contractor to supervise and report on the work and an independent engineer to conduct a final, pre-handover inspection. You will still need to supervise the project, however, so include time and budget for site visits.

If you are renovating something special, for example, a heritage home, get professional advice and use a qualified contractor. The same holds true for a leaky condo in New Zealand or a home with lead paint or asbestos in the United States.

Finally, ensure that all of the team members have professional and public liability insurance and that the laborers and tradespeople are covered by workers' compensation insurance.

International considerations

If you are conducting a large renovation, ask the contractor to create an owner's manual for your home. This can include the model and serial numbers, warranty information and owner's manuals for all of the appliances; wiring diagrams and blueprints; construction permits, inspection certificates and related documents; and information about building materials like tile, timber and fabric that you may need to match or replace in future. English translations of operating manuals for unusual or infrequently used systems can also be included.

Adding home automation equipment that will let you monitor security and manage the heating, ventilating and air-conditioning system may also be worth considering, especially for vacation homes that are used sporadically.

Some renovations are better investments than others, with returns influenced by the strength of the housing market, demographic trends and local tastes. For example, research conducted in 2014 by *Remodeling* magazine showed that replacing a main entryway door with a steel model recouped over 96% of the cost. A sun room addition, on the other hand, yielded less than 52%. These figures were averages for the United States and there were significant variations at the regional and city levels.

A family homestead in Ireland

For Jim and Sally Thompson, owning a 500-acre (202 hectare) estate in the Republic of Ireland was the fulfillment of a dream. "Having lived in Hong Kong for 35 years and in Japan for 15 years before that, I've developed a great appreciation for space," says Jim, who is the founder and chairman of the Crown Worldwide Group of companies. "The estate presented an opportunity to have the open space and a large home that I never had during my time in Asia."

Through genealogical research, Jim discovered that his father's family had emigrated to the United States from County Waterford in the 1800s. That inspired a trip to Ireland, during which they found the estate. Jim and Sally plan to use the property as a second home that they, their children and their grandchildren can enjoy for years to come.

Jim and Sally Thompson's home is near the village of Stradbally in Ireland.

The Thompsons bought the estate, which is near the village of Stradbally, using a Hong Kong company for €7.5 million ($10.4 million) in cash, inclusive of closing costs. The purchase took seven weeks, from an initial offer in August 2012 to completion in October. Jim felt that the price was attractive, even with an anticipated €2 million–€3 million in renovation costs.

The estate includes a two-story, 12,000-square-foot (1,115-square-meter) Georgian house that was built around 1750, although there has been a home on the site since 1604. In addition to the main house, there are five cottages of various sizes.

The main house is a listed property, which means that government approval is required before it can be modified. Jim and Sally had no difficulty obtaining permission to install a new kitchen and underfloor heating, or finding a contractor for the project, which will be completed in the summer of 2014. Jim notes that the local tradesmen were enthusiastic about working on the historic home. And despite Stradbally's small population, the Thompsons were pleasantly surprised by the warmth of the welcome they received. "Since my great-grandparents were married in the village, I wasn't considered a complete outsider," Jim says.

"Designing a house like this is time-consuming, but has turned out to be a labor of love and quite a lot of fun," observes Sally, who says the project has only encountered a few difficulties. For example, the roof tiles were not available locally and had to be purchased in Spain. The home electronics, appliances and heating units were also imported. In addition, the mobile phone coverage and Internet service are not quite as reliable as they would like. Jim also notes the value-added tax, which ranges from 13.5% to 23%, is high, but that the tax can be reduced by buying the home through an Irish company.

If you are thinking of buying a home abroad, Jim suggests that you gain a thorough understanding of the local property laws and retain a knowledgeable lawyer to advise on the transaction.

He also recommends budgeting for the cost of operating and maintaining a new home. "The estate can generate a fair amount of income through land rentals and the sale of lumber and other crops, but this would not cover all of the running costs. Many people might not accept this, but I did," says Jim.

NEW HOMES

New versus Old
163

Buying Off the Plan
167

Custom-built Homes
177

NEW VERSUS OLD

For some people, there is a special thrill that comes with owning a brand-new home. The distinctive "new home" smell, coupled with the combination of features, fixtures, layout and decor that you want is uniquely satisfying. In addition to the emotional benefits, there are several other advantages to buying a new home.

Why buy a new home?

Homes require regular maintenance, such as landscaping and painting, as well as less frequent, big-ticket expenditures, like replacing roofs and furnaces. Maintenance and repairs typically represent 1%–3% of a home's value per year, with the actual amount depending on the type of dwelling, local environmental conditions and whether the home has high-maintenance features, such as a swimming pool.

New homes cost less to maintain. An asphalt-shingled roof should last 25 years, for example, while furnaces have a lifespan of 15–25 years.[1] The major systems in a new home are normally covered by a warranty, so you will have several years before you need to budget for repairing or replacing them.

Energy efficiency is another advantage. A home built in 2013 is about 30% more energy efficient than one built five years earlier. People living in hot, humid parts of the United States who own an Energy Star–certified home save about $700 per year on utility costs.[2]

You can retrofit double- or triple-glazed windows and add insulation to an older home. But these items are usually more effective and cheaper if they are installed during the initial construction.

In some markets, new homes last longer than older models. For example, Japanese houses were built on the "one generation, one home" principle and typically demolished after 30 years. In 2008, the Japanese government began promoting ultra-long-life houses that could be renovated and upgraded.

New houses have the features—such as open floor plans, high ceilings and large windows—that modern buyers want, while new condominiums use smart, high-speed elevators and advanced anti-seismic technology in earthquake-prone locations. They may also be built around a marina, golf course or other recreational facility.

New homes are built to the latest fire and safety codes and are unlikely to contain hazards, such as asbestos, polybutylene water pipes, lead paint or defective drywall. In addition to causing health and safety problems for residents, these materials can make it difficult to sell or rent your home. They can also be very expensive to fix.

Finally, developers normally resolve any outstanding title issues with a new subdivision or condominium before the individual houses or units are sold. However, as thousands of expatriates who bought and lost illegally built homes in Spain discovered, this process is not foolproof. Before you buy, conduct due diligence on the home and the builder and decide whether you have confidence in the local legal system.

Pre-owned homes, like this century-old example in Ottawa's Glebe neighborhood, have higher maintenance costs than new models.

Old attractions

Compared with pre-owned homes, new models have some drawbacks. New homes generally cost more than older ones and in many cities, vintage houses are built with materials, attention to detail and design elements that are considered extravagant today. Older developments also have mature landscaping and parks and established infrastructure—schools, shopping, hospitals and public transportation. They offer a sense of community that is often lacking in new developments.

New homes have modern features, such as home theaters and carbon monoxide detectors. But not all building trends are welcomed by homeowners. In a 2010 survey conducted for the Royal Institute of British Architects, 31% of respondents said they would not consider buying a house built in the previous decade. The main reasons cited were rooms that were too small (60%), lack of style (46%) and too little outdoor space (45%).

Finally, the choice between an older or a newer home will be influenced by your city's history, demographics and economic growth. For instance, there are no old homes in Shenzhen, China, a city that grew from 30,000 people in 1979 to 13 million in 2012.[3] Similarly, in 2013 less than 1% of the homes for sale in the U.S. sunbelt cities of Phoenix and Las Vegas were built before 1940.[4]

Warranties

All new homes have defects ranging from inconveniences like cracked plaster and sticky doors to structural flaws that can leave a dwelling uninhabitable. Big problems occur more frequently in developing economies, where corruption is more common and building inspectors are less rigorous. In the United States, a new home is about as likely to experience significant structural damage as it is to be involved in a major fire.[5]

New home warranties differ by country and by state or province. For example, in the Netherlands, they are voluntary. In China and Japan, home warranties are mandated by the government. New home warranties are mandatory in Alberta, British Columbia, Ontario and Quebec, but are voluntary in other Canadian provinces.

New home warranties also vary in the things they cover. In general, roofs, foundations, plumbing and wiring and other structural elements are covered. Items such as appliances that are supplied with the home are normally covered by the manufacturer's warranty. In France, the *Garantie de livraison à prix délai convenus* protects consumers against the builder becoming insolvent and ensures that the house will be delivered according to the agreed price and schedule.[6] Homes can also be covered against events such as water leakage.

Warranties exist between builders and developers and between developers and homeowners. They are provided by private companies; by nonprofit corporations, like Ontario's Tarion Corporation; or by governments, such as NSW Self Insurance Corporation in New South Wales, Australia.

The duration of the warranty's coverage will vary depending on the country and the component.

Warranties are a desirable form of consumer protection, but they shouldn't replace your due diligence. Buying a home from a company with a reputation for quality design and construction is preferable to living in a defective dwelling and being embroiled in time-consuming disputes or expensive lawsuits.

Your warranty is only as good as the company that provides it, so chose an insurer with a solid track record. Make a point of reading the terms and conditions. Many homeowners are dissatisfied with their warranty policies, but this is often because they don't know what is covered, the duration of the coverage or how repairs will be carried out until they have a claim.

Ensure the warranty covers soil movement. Foundation-related problems represent more than three-quarters of all warranty claims in the United States, and soil movement—settling, heaving or moving laterally—is a leading cause of damage. One expert claims that having a geotechnical inspection of the soil under the home will cut the chances of a structural issue in half.

BUYING OFF THE PLAN

An off the plan purchase occurs when a developer sells units in a condominium or homes in a subdivision before the dwellings are built. Off the plan sales can occur with a vacant lot or while construction is underway. Technically, the developer is selling property that does not exist: the subdivision may not get planning approval or the condominium may not receive a certificate of occupancy. Pre-completion sales demonstrate that the project is viable and allow developers to borrow money from banks and other lenders.

When buying off the plan, you view a show suite, an architectural model, a video or a brochure and floor plans, and then sign a contract and pay a deposit. The contract includes a description of your property, a schedule for interim payments (if applicable), as well as a completion date, when you will make the final payment or arrange a mortgage and take possession of the home. The deposit is typically 5%–10% of the purchase price, although it can be as high as 60% in exceptionally buoyant markets.

In an off the plan sale, the developer uses your deposit to fund the project's construction and marketing costs. As a result, you are gambling that the developer has the managerial skill and financial and technical resources to complete the project, on time, on budget and according to plan.

Off the plan purchases offer several benefits:

▲ Steep discounts, particularly on the first units sold

▲ The ability to lock in prices

▲ The possibility of selling the property at a profit before completion if the market is rising

▲ A new home that will cost less to maintain and operate than a pre-owned dwelling

▲ Your choice of fittings and finishes

- ▲ Modern amenities such as bike lockers and pet spas where residents can wash their dogs

- ▲ Incentives, such as rental guarantees, furniture packages and rebates of taxes and legal fees

- ▲ Potential savings on stamp duty and other taxes

With an off the plan purchase, there is always a risk that the developer will go bankrupt and leave the project half finished.

Risks

These benefits are offset by risks, including the possibility that the developer could go bankrupt, leaving the project unfinished. Depending on where the home is located, you could lose your entire deposit—or you could receive pennies on the dollar from a receiver several years after the project was supposed to be delivered. Even if your deposit is returned in full, you will have lost the returns that your money would have generated if it had been invested elsewhere.

You can minimize these risks by confirming that the developer is a legitimate company with the financial capacity to fulfill its contractual obligations. Start by checking the company's website, which will give you basic information, like the developer's name and stock ticker symbol, that you can use to search for general news on Google and for financial information on Reuters and Bloomberg.

Defective construction is another potential risk, one that can even affect projects by large, successful companies. In February 2014, Japan's largest developer, Mitsubishi Estate, announced that it would seek damages from Kajima Corporation because drain pipes were improperly installed in a project called Parkhouse Gran Minami Aoyama. The construction flaws were so serious that completion of the Tokyo condominiums, some of which were priced at ¥350 million ($3.4 million), will be delayed for at least a year. The building may need to be demolished.[1]

If your home is completed successfully, you could still be stuck with the consequences of failed nearby developments. The U.S.–based Lincoln Institute estimates that in 2012, nearly 30,000 subdivision lots—or about one-fifth of the approved land—were vacant in five Colorado counties. The incomplete developments consume natural resources, reduce property values, and cause fiscal problems because they require road maintenance, infrastructure and emergency services coverage, without contributing to the local tax base. Similar problems occurred in Arizona and Idaho.[2]

Completion dates are a common source of problems. Projects are often delayed and contracts are written to give developers flexibility if they encounter problems. On the other hand, buyers usually have a short period of time to pay the outstanding balance when the project is complete.

This highlights another issue. When they are available, pre-approved mortgages are typically valid for one to six months, but off the plan completion dates can be a year or more in the future. As a result, you could find yourself unable to arrange financing when the completion date approaches. Or if the market drops, you could have to contribute the difference between the lender's new, lower valuation and the home's contract price. For example, if the contract price is $400,000 but the market value has fallen to $370,000 at the completion date, the lender will base your mortgage on $370,000, but you will still pay the developer $400,000. Furthermore, it is common for a lender to value your new home at 5%–10% less than the contract price, and you will need to make up this difference.

Pre-approved mortgages can also run into trouble if your bank exits the market or changes its lending policies, your mortgage exceeds the bank's aggregate lending limit for a project or your financial situation changes between the initial application and the completion date.

Contracts and commitments

Off the plan contracts are long, complex and written in legalese. A signed contract cannot be changed, so ensure you understand your rights and responsibilities, including the remedies that are available if delivery is delayed and the penalties you face if you are unable to arrange financing or unwilling to complete the purchase. Contracts usually favor the developer, so get legal advice from your lawyer—not one recommended by the vendor—before signing anything.

Developers' marketing teams are skilled at maximizing a project's appeal. Videos and other sales materials emphasize the development's strengths and minimize its weaknesses, and there is a fine line between artistic license and fraud. For example:

▲ Hong Kong developers have been caught using undersized furniture and glass interior walls to make their show suites appear larger.

▲ One London developer issued a news release saying that a project was "a short walk from the luxury shopping available at Harrods," when the department store was actually 50 minutes away.[3]

▲ It's not unusual for developers to omit information about a project's proximity to undesirable neighbors, such as highways and social housing, and there is often a big gap between the "artist's impression" of the development and its final appearance.

If you buy, retain the developer's marketing materials and take photos of show suites and architectural models. Note room sizes, the specifications of supplied appliances, building materials and finishes, as well as lobbies and parking. This information will be useful if there is a difference between what the developer promises and what is actually delivered.

Check the contract to see how much latitude the developer has to alter the project, for example by adding floors, changing room or lot sizes, substituting materials or finishes, reducing the size of public areas or eliminating swimming pools and other amenities. Ensure that the management fees are competitive and the house rules do not prohibit pets or contain any unreasonable restrictions.

Contracts typically include a clause that allows the developer to cancel the agreement and return your deposit if the project does not receive planning permission or is not financially viable. Normally, both the developer and buyer can cancel the contract if there has been a long delay in finishing the project. Some unscrupulous developers have dragged out completion so they could take advantage of rising prices. When the contract expired, the developer offered the property to existing buyers at higher prices.[4]

Visit the project site, preferably at different times of the day and on weekends and weekdays, to see what the area is like and to gauge levels of noise and sunshine. If the project is built on a brownfield site, confirm that it has been properly remediated. Investigate the neighbors, too. You don't want to live next to a polluting factory or a noisy freeway.

Ensure the developer is financially solvent and has a history of delivering quality work. If possible, visit the company's earlier projects to see how they have aged.

Check with the local regulator to ensure that the developer is licensed and in good standing. In Malaysia, for example, the Ministry of Urban Wellbeing, Housing and Local Government maintains a website with a directories of blacklisted developers as well as late and abandoned housing projects (www.kpkt.gov.my).

Cross-border issues

In addition to the above, there are some items to which cross-border buyers should pay particular attention. For example, if you are buying a home in one country and the contract is signed in a second country, you need to determine which nation's laws and regulations apply. This can affect things like cooling-off periods and disclosure requirements, as well as your legal options if there are problems.

The relationship between the local salesperson or agency and the developer is also important. The salesperson could be employed directly by the developer, work for an affiliated local company or be employed by an unrelated real estate agency. This relationship will influence everything from who receives your deposit to the salesperson's ability to make legally binding commitments on behalf of the developer. The fact that a project is sold by a global real estate agency does not guarantee that the developer is solvent or competent.

Developers spend a lot of money marketing projects overseas. The cost of function rooms in five-star hotels, champagne and canapes, sales commissions, brochures and videos and incentives such as free legal services and rental guarantees are all added to your home's selling price. As a result, you may get a more attractive price by visiting the target city. You will also get a better idea of the alternatives—other off the plan developments, newly finished dwellings and pre-owned homes—and you will be in a better position to evaluate different neighborhoods and their proximity to schools, shopping and transportation. That said, some projects in London are now launched in Hong Kong, Singapore and Shanghai, and sell out before they are offered for sale in the United Kingdom.

Overseas ownership can cause problems when most of the dwellings in a development are purchased as investments and rented to tenants. There is often a rush to rent units when the building is finished, which can depress rents. Unlike owner-occupiers, investors are less likely to care about the local community and the building's maintenance and upkeep.

In markets such as London, Hong Kong and Singapore, there is growing concern among governments and community activists about properties that are bought by overseas investors and left empty. Critics say so-called "buy-to-leave" investors inflate prices without providing homes for local people or paying taxes. High-profile examples include the multimillion-pound One Hyde Park apartments in London, three-quarters of which were reported to be unoccupied in September 2013.[5] Overseas owners are an attractive source of tax revenue, and effective April 1, 2013, a premium of up to 50% of the council tax became payable on U.K. property that has been left unoccupied and unfurnished for two years or more.[6] In March 2014, the London Borough of Islington proposed a fine of up to £60,000 ($100,000) for homes that were not occupied "regularly throughout the year."[7]

Overseas buyers should be cautious when making progress payments to a developer. If possible, payments should be made to an escrow company that only releases the money to the developer when agreed project milestones are met. You can confirm the project's status with a site visit, or by hiring an architect or quantity surveyor to check the developer's work. In addition, title to the land should be transferred from the developer to the buyer when the first or second payment is made. These two measures protect your interests if the developer goes bankrupt. Small developers are unlikely to agree to either the escrow company or title transfer because they will be using your cash to fund the project and the title as collateral for a loan.

In addition, as Rene Philippe Dubout notes in his book *How to Purchase Real Estate Offshore Safely: The Case of Thailand* there are special dangers in dealing with small, first-time developers. Many of these companies are run by recently arrived expatriates who are passionate, but have limited experience and cash. Compared to large developers, whose projects and marketing staff are slick and impersonal, the novices are charming and earnest. Unfortunately, inexperience and under-capitalization means their projects are much more likely to fail than those built by their larger competitors.

That said, large companies are not immune to problems. For example, there is the In Tempo development in Benidorm, Spain, which *El Pais* described as, "a symbol of incompetence."[8] Originally scheduled to open in 2009 and advertised as Europe's tallest residential building, In Tempo was still under construction at the end of 2013. Since work began in 2007, 13 workers were injured when a freight elevator collapsed, the builder and the bank financing the project declared bankruptcy and Intempo's architects resigned. Only a third of the project's 269 homes have been sold, with the remainder reportedly available at a discount.[9]

Paul Stocker's condominium in Phuket, Thailand, is a short walk from Bang Tao Beach.

 A condo in Phuket

Paul Stocker wasn't looking for a holiday home. But when an investment adviser suggested an off the plan purchase in Phuket, Thailand, Stocker saw an opportunity. "I'd been traveling to Phuket since 1989 and the price was very attractive," says the London native, who lived in Bangkok from 1989 to 1992 and now resides in Hong Kong.

In 2005, Stocker paid 4.2 million baht (about $106,000, at the time) in cash for a condominium that is a five-minute walk from Bang Tao Beach and a 30-minute drive from Phuket International Airport. The 120-square-meter home has two bedrooms, two bathrooms, a kitchen and a balcony, and is one of 54 units in a four-story complex that features a gym, a swimming pool, a clubhouse and a restaurant. The complex has cable TV and WiFi. Water is delivered by tanker truck and the complex has a septic tank.

The condo came with a European-style kitchen and major appliances. The developers offered a furniture package, but Stocker wanted distinctive decor. He bought some furniture in Phuket and had several pieces custom-made from his own designs and from photos that he had clipped from magazines.

Stocker had a lawyer in Bangkok review the transaction before he signed the sale and purchase agreement. He says the lawyer wasn't very engaged and treated the process as a formality. "It felt like a rubber stamp."

The complex was developed by two men from London, one of whom was a professional builder and the other Stocker describes as, "a ducker and diver." The pair recruited a foreman from London to oversee the construction process. Stocker was delighted when he took possession of his unit in the spring of 2005. "The size, layout and construction quality all exceeded my expectations. It seemed like I got a steal."

The complex is managed by the local arm of a global property company. Stocker pays a management fee of 42,000 baht ($1,300) per quarter, which includes a contribution to the reserve fund. A second firm arranges short-term rentals of the condos and provides housekeeping services.

In Thailand, foreigners are not allowed to own land. Stocker owns his unit, and a share of a company that bought the leasehold rights to the land under the complex. That company is 49% owned by Stocker and the other condo owners, with the remaining 51% held by three Thai nominees. The land is leased for 30 years, with two 30-year extension options. Because the land is tied to the buildings, it has value but is an illiquid asset.

Things went well until 2009, when the owners learned that the developer had used the land under the building as security for a $300,000 loan. The outstanding loan made it all but impossible for the owners to sell their units. "One of the other owners was a retired lawyer, who reviewed the situation," notes Stocker. "We quickly saw that we had two choices: we could sue the developers or we could pay off the loan."

Suing the developers would have taken years and had a limited likelihood of success, so each of the owners agreed to make 15 payments of 12,000 baht to discharge the loan. "We were lucky," observes Stocker. "The lender was a Thai-Chinese man who was sympathetic to our dilemma. He worked with us to reach a solution and didn't charge us interest on the loan."

Despite these problems, Stocker is happy with the condo, which he uses three or four times a year. Friends also use the unit three or four times a year, which helps to defray the management fees. While he could generate income through the rental program, Stocker likes being able to visit Phuket when the urge strikes him. "And I don't have to worry about my friends trashing the place," he says.

Stocker's advice to potential buyers is simple. Research the market and pay attention to market liquidity. "We were lucky," he says. "But not everyone is."

CUSTOM-BUILT HOMES

Like most things in this book, building a home is complex activity in its own right, and is even more complicated when you cross a border. Planning and building a custom home can easily take two years—longer in developing countries or those with invasive bureaucracies—and cost millions of dollars. The results, however, can be spectacular.

An architect is central to this process. In addition to planning and designing your home, an architect can arrange bids, negotiate with contractors and suppliers and supervise the construction process. An architect can also help you achieve your environmental goals, make the most of an unusual building site, overcome drainage problems and ensure your home complies with zoning and other regulations.

Defining the project

Building a custom home starts with a budget, which will include land, design and construction, furniture and appliances, taxes, insurance, maintenance and contingencies. A realistic budget will prevent you from running out of money halfway through the project or building something that you cannot afford to occupy.

Next, decide what you want. This includes physical and functional requirements, such as the home's overall size, the number of bathrooms and bedrooms, and your storage and parking needs. Consider your hobbies and interests, and whether you want a home office, a gourmet kitchen, a garden or basement or space to entertain guests. Think about the future, especially if you plan to have children or if your kids will be moving out. List your aesthetic preferences: do you want a modern or traditional design? Finally, address environmental issues, such as rainwater collection or the use of solar power. These factors may also influence your choice of a site.

Understanding your needs, wants and preferences will help you find an architect whose style and experience are compatible with your vision. This process will also form the basis for the brief that you will give the architect.

Hiring an architect

When you have defined your priorities, start looking for an architect. The International Union of Architects (www.uia-architectes.org) will direct you to your national architectural association. Sites like Architizer (http://architizer.com) may also be helpful.

Assemble a short list of candidates whose style and approach are consistent with your own and contact them. Describe your project, goals, schedule and budget. If the firm is interested and has the capacity to work on your project, arrange a meeting. Talking to three to five firms will give you a sense of what is possible without consuming too much time.

A meeting will let you review the firm's technical credentials, design philosophy and attitude toward customer service. Ensure the firm has professional liability insurance. Meet the architect who will design your home—not just the salesperson—so you can gauge the chemistry between you. Good chemistry is vital because you and the architect will spend a lot of time together and it will not be pleasant or productive if you dislike or distrust each other. Ask for references, talk to previous clients and visit the architect's finished projects. Smart architects interview their clients, so don't be surprised if she asks to visit your building site or your home. As part of the selection process, you may ask the architect to prepare preliminary sketches for which you will be charged a fee.

Ask how the architect charges for her work. This can be a percentage of the total building cost (excluding land) or on a lump-sum, hourly or square-meter basis.

After you have selected an architect, notify her and the unsuccessful candidates as soon as possible. The winning architect will ask you to sign a contract that will specify the schedule and the services she will provide. Depending on how the contract is structured, you will make several payments over the life of the project. Typically, there is a small initial payment for preliminary work, several larger ones as the project progresses and a small, final payment when minor defects and outstanding issues are resolved.

The brief

A well-organized, unambiguous brief is the foundation of a successful project. Use words, sketches, pictures from books and magazines, websites, videos, paint samples, fabric swatches and anything else that conveys your goals and intentions. The more detail, the better.

Producing an effective brief takes time and effort. But with a clear brief, the architect will understand what you want and achieve your goals more quickly and efficiently. Creating the brief will help you clarify your thinking and may uncover gaps between your and your spouse's preferences. These differences are best resolved early in the design process before changes become expensive.

In addition to your functional requirements and aesthetic preferences, tell the architect what features you consider essential and which ones are negotiable. If you are unsure about something, say so. Don't forget to give the architect creative "breathing space," so she can use her training and skill to turn your vision into a home you can both be proud of.

Working with contractors and architects

After you retain an architect, you engage a general contractor—who hires specialist subcontractors, such as glaziers, masons and plumbers—to execute the architect's plans. You can oversee the construction process or hire a third party to fill this role.

There are also options, known as "design-build," where the architect and contractor jointly design and build the project. Either the architect or the contractor can lead the project, with the other party playing a secondary role. For example in a contractor-led model, the architect could be an employee or a subcontractor of the contractor, or the contractor and architect could form a joint venture company.

Many architects test the boundaries of construction technology, like Frank Gehry's design for the Guggenheim Museum in Bilbao, Spain. Contractors—who must implement architects' ideas, make a profit and stay in business—tend to be more practically oriented. It is not unusual for this difference to result in conflicts between architects and contractors that can end up in court.

If you have a home custom-built, hire an independent inspector to review the construction process just before the foundation is poured, when the framing is completed but before drywall and insulation are installed, and again when the home is finished. These checks will catch many issues before they become expensive, difficult-to-solve problems.

Alternatives

There are alternatives for people who want a distinctive home but prefer not to hire an architect. These approaches are complicated, time consuming and require hands-on involvement.

For example, you can buy complete building plans and hire a contractor to erect the house for you. A variety of customizable designs are available, some of which are free. If you have the time and are looking for an adventure, you can design and build your own home. See the "Build it yourself" section in the "Information Sources" chapter for more information.

Green buildings

Environmentally friendly homes have joined the mainstream. The price of green products like photovoltaic cells continues to drop, while their efficiency and reliability increases. At the same time, architects are responding to growing public awareness of climate change as well as the financial benefits that can accompany green homes.

Environmentally friendly designs optimize the home's relationship with the building site to maximize sunlight and natural cooling. They also reduce energy consumption, conserve water, minimize construction waste and incorporate environmentally friendly materials, including recycled components, products from renewable sources and locally sourced items. These steps create improved indoor air quality and lower operating costs without sacrificing aesthetic values.

While conventional designs benefit from this trend, cutting-edge passive homes are setting new standards for energy efficiency. Passive houses are sealed to prevent warm air from escaping in winter and cool air from leaking out in summer. Triple-glazed windows are used, as are mechanical ventilation systems and up to 45 centimeters of thermal insulation. These features add tens of thousands of dollars to the construction cost, but proponents say they can cut a home's energy consumption by 50% or more.[1]

The lack of global standards is one of the challenges of building across borders. For example, the Green Building Council of Australia operates Green Star (www.gbca.org.au), the German Sustainable Building Council has the DGNB System (www.dgnb-system.de) and the Japan Green Build Council has CASBEE (www.ibec.or.jp/CASBEE), to name just three. Many countries are interested in exporting their national standards to create business opportunities for their manufacturers and consultants.

There are also competing rating systems in the same country. For example, LEED is championed by the U.S. Green Building Council (www.usgbc.org), while the Green Globes program is operated by the Green Building Initiative (www.thegbi.org). There are also organizations like the American High-Performance Buildings Coalition (www.betterbuildingstandards.com), which are supported by trade groups from the lumber, plastics, HVAC and other industries.

Home automation

Home automation systems that manage entertainment; heating, ventilating and air conditioning; appliances and security are available as commercial products and as open-source projects. Some systems can be programmed and controlled with smartphones and personal and tablet computers, letting you monitor your home's front door while you are at the office or dim the lights in your living room without leaving the sofa. Some systems also track energy usage.

This technology promises a number of advantages. By scheduling appliances like clothes dryers and dishwashers for off-peak hours, homeowners save money on their electricity bills and utilities can better manage their generating capacity. Video monitoring systems have already helped police identify burglars. Sensors and timers, meanwhile, ensure that homes are lit, heated and cooled when they are occupied and save energy when they are empty.

Unfortunately, home automation faces several challenges. First, for home automation to deliver its full potential, your appliances, electronics and computers must share information seamlessly. At present, there are several competing communications standards and some products will not "talk" to each other. This is also keeping manufacturers out of the market, as they wait for a single standard to emerge.

Second, connecting your home to the Internet creates a security risk. In 2013, products ranging from baby monitors to high-tech toilets were hacked.[2] To protect yourself, you will need to ensure that the software in your home automation systems is kept up to date, that passwords are changed from their default settings and that adequate firewalls and other security systems are in place.

The third problem is privacy. Home automation systems produce vast quantities of data, and this information can be analyzed to track a family's activities, preferences and habits. Smart electricity meters—which are being tested in Hong Kong, installed throughout the United States and will be mandatory in the United Kingdom by 2019[3]—transmit detailed information about consumers' usage patterns to utility companies. In Australia, one utility was found to be sharing data from smart meters with government bodies, debt collectors and other companies.[4] In a post-Snowden world, the privacy and data-retention policies of product and service providers takes on a new importance.

 A beachfront retreat in Sri Lanka

Broadcast journalist Teymoor Nabili's initial attraction to Sri Lanka was practical: foreigners could own freehold property and the island offered excellent value. "Compared with Bali and Phuket, it had rock-bottom prices," notes Singapore-based Nabili, "But in time, Sri Lanka really grew on us."

Teymoor Nabili's home in Sri Lanka is on a three-acre beachfront plot.

Nabili's home is located two hours south of Colombo, on a three-acre beachfront plot. In 2004, he paid $200,000 for the land, which included a small house that was subsequently demolished.

Nabili bought the property while he was living in Kuala Lumpur, Malaysia. He found the plot through an agent he discovered online. The agent, a foreigner based in Sri Lanka, had researched the property and come to an agreement to represent the owners.

The regulations have changed several times since Nabili purchased his property. Starting in 1963, foreign buyers were subject to a 100% transfer tax, which was repealed in 2002 and then reinstated in 2004. Nabili had the good fortune to buy while the tax was canceled and freehold ownership was allowed. On January 1, 2013, foreigners were prohibited from buying freehold. They may now acquire a 99-year lease, subject to a 100% tax on the property's value.[5]

Before completing the purchase, Nabili hired a surveyor to confirm the property's boundaries. He also retained a lawyer to ensure that he received clear title to the land. This task was complicated by the 2004 tsunami, which killed more than 30,000 people and destroyed many public records.

He hired a Kuala Lumpur–based architect to create a modern home that incorporated local design elements and materials and had a small carbon footprint. The three-bedroom, 250-square-meter house is bright and airy, with a grass roof and stunning sea views. The home, which is built into a nearby hill and incorporates a garden into its open-plan design, took nearly two years to complete.

Along the way, Nabili overcame several obstacles. For instance, the home wasn't a conventional Sri Lankan design and there weren't many builders with international experience in the area. As a result, the contractor didn't always grasp the architect's intentions and the necessary tools and equipment were sometimes unavailable. Nabili had no trouble buying a flat-screen television and sanitary ware in Colombo, but notes that imported items are subject to duties.

To keep the project on track, Nabili flew the architect in from Malaysia and hired a Colombo-based architect to visit the job site once a week. "I'm not sure the visits happened on schedule," observes Nabili, "and when the architect wasn't around, the contractor would sometimes revert to his usual way of doing things, even if it wasn't in the plan."

Nabili's home is 500 meters from the main road, where the nearest power lines are located. Cellular telephone service is available in the area, but it was not fast enough to provide usable Internet access, so he had a phone line run in from the road. Piped water was available nearby, but he had to install a septic tank. The contractor handled all of these elements.

Building a home in a close-knit community also posed challenges. "Suppliers can become proprietorial, and everyone knows everyone else's business. It's not like a big anonymous city where you can change suppliers easily. People take it personally, and you have to manage relationships."

Work on the home is now finished and all that remains is minor landscaping and the construction of a fence. Nabili found a property manager—a British man who worked as a banker in Hong Kong before relocating to Sri Lanka—and opened a non-resident rupee account (NRRA) with the Colombo branch of a global retail bank. He can transfer money from his Singapore bank account to the NRRA over the Internet.

Nabili is optimistic about Sri Lanka's tourism potential and is now renting the home out. A new highway has improved access to the area and there is a growing foreign presence. This includes his immediate neighbors, one of whom is an Englishman who has lived there for decades. The other is an American who relaxes in Sri Lanka when he is not teaching English in the Middle East.

In 2013, the family enjoyed two holidays in Sri Lanka and Nabili thinks they will continue to visit at that rate, drawn by the sunshine, beaches and food. "Our local supermarket doesn't stock premium Italian olive oil," he says. "But we eat very well. There is fresh food everywhere, with everything from regular farmers' markets to fishermen selling their catch on the side of the road."

MONEY

Paying for Your Home
189

Mortgages
197

Insurance
213

Tax
219

PAYING FOR YOUR HOME

When buying a home across borders, you have three basic payment options: cash, an offshore mortgage or a mortgage in the country where your home is located.

Cash

Paying cash is the simplest way to buy a home. In competitive markets, it can give you an advantage in terms of speed and certainty over buyers who need a lender's approval.

Typically, you will use a telegraphic transfer to send funds from a bank account in your home country to a bank account in the country where you are buying a home. Depending on the country, the deposit or final payment can be made to your lawyer, the vendor's lawyer, the notary or real estate agent handling the transaction or directly to the vendor or developer. Funds can also be wired to your bank account in the target country.

In some places, such as Japan and Brazil,[1] you will need a resident's card (called a *gaikokujin toroku shomeisho* in Japan and a *Registro Nacional de Estrangeiros* in Brazil) to open a bank account. To obtain a resident's card, you may have to be fingerprinted, register with the local tax system and disclose a significant amount of personal information, including the sources of your income. Other places, like France, allow tourists with a *visa de long séjour* (long-stay visa) to open a bank account.[2] As noted in the "Risk Factors" chapter, the Foreign Account Tax Compliance Act (FATCA) has made it difficult for Americans to obtain financial services in many countries.

Even if you transfer your payment to an intermediary, you will probably need a bank account to pay utilities, taxes and other bills. One way to avoid this problem is to hire a local management company to collect rents and pay your expenses. You can then pay the management company or have them remit the proceeds to you via telegraphic transfer.

If you are transferring money to an intermediary, make certain that you are paying the right person, that they have the legal right to represent the vendor, that the recipient is legitimate and that all of the payment details, such as the company name and bank account number, are correct. Once money has been transferred abroad, there is very little you can do if you have been defrauded.

Banks are generally the easiest way to transfer money, but not always the fastest or cheapest. Depending on the origin and destination countries, you may be able to use a financial services company that offers more competitive transfer fees and exchange rates. On a large transaction, you can save thousands of dollars, so it's worth shopping around. Ensure that the company is licensed and legitimate.

Investigate the foreign exchange regulations for the countries where your transfer originates and terminates. Some nations, such as China, have capital controls that limit the amount of money that can be transferred in or out each year. Others, like Japan, require you to notify the authorities for transfers over a specified limit. Failure to observe these regulations can result in fines and other penalties, or make it impossible to repatriate funds from the sale of your home.

Offshore mortgages

It is difficult to arrange a mortgage from a lender that does not have a presence in the same country as your new home. Without a local license and personnel, lenders have trouble valuing your home, servicing your mortgage and foreclosing if you default.

If you do obtain an offshore mortgage, you may be required to make a larger down payment, pay a higher interest rate or pledge additional collateral.

One way to avoid this is to take out a mortgage on your primary residence and use the proceeds to purchase a second home abroad. Wealthy buyers may be able to arrange financing through a private bank.

Onshore mortgages

Many lenders will provide mortgages to nonresidents. It becomes progressively easier (and often cheaper) to obtain a mortgage if you are a legal resident of the country, a legal resident married to a national of that country, a permanent resident or a naturalized citizen.

Your current bank is one of the best places to start the search for a mortgage. Ask if they have a branch, a subsidiary, a joint venture or an affiliate in the market where you plan to buy. For instance, many Canadian banks are active in the United States and Hong Kong–based lenders operate in Mainland China.

If your bank can't help, contact a global retail bank that has a branch in your target market. Banks such as HSBC and Citibank understand the needs of international clients and provide application forms, background information and services in English. Global banks are often more customer-oriented than their local competitors and can sometimes link your bank account in your home country with your mortgage account.

However, global banks' interest rates may be higher than those of domestic banks and, where a local bank may have thousands of branches and automated teller machines, a global bank may only have a handful of outlets and offer a restricted range of services.

Next, investigate domestic banks and lenders in your target market. They will have superior local knowledge and may offer more competitive terms. However, they will be used to serving domestic clients and their products may not suit someone who doesn't speak the language or have a local credit history.

Ask your real estate agent, developer and friends and neighbors for recommendations. They may have a relationship with a lender that is worth exploring.

A mortgage broker, either in your home country or target market, can help you find funding, particularly if your situation is complex or unusual. Brokers have relationships with a range of financial institutions and use this expertise to match your circumstances to a lender that is likely to accept your application and offer a competitive financing package. The broker will tailor your application to the lender, ensuring that you have all the necessary documents and that your paperwork is presented correctly. For their services, brokers typically charge an application fee as well as a percentage of the mortgage amount. Ask for client references and examples of mortgages the broker has arranged from different lenders to gauge the breadth of his contacts and experience.

Brokers can be useful for people with complicated needs, like foreign diplomats. Banks often refuse to lend to diplomats, fearing that they will default on the loan and invoke their diplomatic immunity, which exempts them from local laws.

In many countries, there are trade organizations for mortgage lenders and their regulators. Operating at the supranational, national and state level, these bodies can be a good source of information on a variety of topics. Examples include the Council of Mortgage Lenders (www.cml.org.uk) in the United Kingdom, the American Association of Residential Mortgage Regulators (www.aarmr.org) in the United States and the International Union for Housing Finance (www.housingfinance.org).

Other sources of funds

If you are a permanent resident, naturalized citizen or are married to a national, investigate incentive programs for home buyers. For example, the U.K. government's "Help to Buy" scheme lets people make a 5% down payment, take a 20% equity loan from the government and borrow the remaining 75% from a bank.[3]

Many countries, including China and Singapore, have compulsory saving programs that are funded by contributions from employers and employees. Participants can use the money that accumulates in these funds to buy a home and to pay for related expenses, such as renovations. They can also obtain low-interest loans from the fund. These programs are often available to foreigners who are permanent residents.

Repatriating your funds

If you are thinking of buying a home abroad, consider how you will dispose of it. For example, if you plan to sell the home and repatriate the proceeds, research the foreign exchange regulations for both the source and destination countries. When you repatriate the money, you may have to prove that the funds entered the country legally, produce contracts for your purchase and sale of the home, and demonstrate that all local taxes have been paid.

The transfer may be subject to limits or to other restrictions. Countries that have a history of capital controls—for example, Argentina, Cuba and Venezuela—require special planning.

In addition to being a financial burden, taxes can slow the repatriation process. When a foreigner sells a home in Canada, the vendor's lawyer is required to retain 25%–50% of the sale proceeds until Canadian authorities confirm that all outstanding taxes have been paid.[4] This can take six to eight weeks.

The cost of buying a home includes many miscellaneous expenses, such as those associated with registering the sale with the local government.

Closing costs

When you buy a home, there are a variety of additional costs that can add thousands of dollars to the final price. These examples are from the United States. Many of these items are discussed at length elsewhere in the book.

- ▲ Application fees. Charged for processing your mortgage paperwork

- ▲ Appraisal fee. Charged for an independent appraisal of your new home

- ▲ Commitment fee. Charged to guarantee your interest rate

- ▲ Courier fee. Charged for transporting documents

- ▲ Credit report fee. Charged for obtaining your credit history

- ▲ Discount points. Charged for obtaining a lower interest rate on your mortgage

- ▲ Escrow fee. Charged by an escrow company for holding your funds

- ▲ Fire insurance. Normally required by the lender as a condition of the mortgage

- ▲ Flood insurance. Sometimes required by the lender as a condition of the mortgage

- ▲ Government filing fees. Charged for registering your loan and title documents

- ▲ Inspection fee. Charged for a home inspector to examine your new home

- ▲ Lawyer fees. Charged for conveyancing and advice

- ▲ Mortgage insurance. Often required by the mortgage lender when the buyer has a small down payment

- Mortgage insurance application fee. Charged for processing your insurance application

- Notary fee. Charged for notarizing your deed

- Origination points. Charged by a lender or broker for arranging your mortgage

- Property transfer tax. Charged for registering the property in your name

- Sales tax. Can be charged by local, state and federal governments

- Survey fee. Charged for a land survey of your new home

- Tax service fee. Charged for verifying your property tax account status

- Title insurance. Sometimes required by the mortgage lender

- Wire transfer fee. Charged for sending money to an escrow company

MORTGAGES

A mortgage is a generic term for a loan secured by real property, such as land, a house or a condominium. A mortgage is also an encumbrance on the property, like an easement (for more information on encumbrances, see the "Ownership and property rights" chapter).

Mortgage basics

The terms used to describe mortgages vary in different countries, but all mortgages include the following elements.

- A property that is being financed

- A mortgage document, which includes a promissory note stating the terms under which the borrower will repay the lender and a lien giving the lender an interest in the property

- A borrower, also known as a mortgagor

- A lender, also called a mortgagee

- Principal, which is the money borrowed by the mortgagor

- Interest, which the mortgagor pays to the lender for the use of the principal

- The right of foreclosure or repossession by the lender, if the borrower fails to observe the terms of the loan

- Completion, which is the date that the mortgage begins

- Redemption, which is the date that the mortgage ends, the interest and principal have been repaid to the lender and the lender's interest in the property ends

Mortgages are complex, and it's important that you understand the agreement and your responsibilities, particularly with exotic mortgages and if multiple cultures and languages are involved. If anything in the mortgage agreement is unclear, ask for more information.

A typical, conventional mortgage has an amortization period of 30 years and a down payment of 10%–30%. Monthly repayments are split between interest and principal, with interest making up a greater proportion of earlier payments and principal comprising more of later ones.

Borrowers have many choices in the way that their mortgage is structured. These options are influenced by national laws and customs, and there are advantages and disadvantages to each choice.

Fixed and adjustable rates

Interest rates can be constant for the entire mortgage term, called a fixed-rate mortgage (FRM), or change at certain times. Long-term FRMs, which are common in the United States and France, protect borrowers from future interest rate increases, but generally come with a higher interest rate than short-term FRMs or adjustable-rate mortgages (ARMs). Short- to medium-term FRMs are common in Canada, Denmark, Germany, the Netherlands and Switzerland.

The interest rate for ARMs is set by the lender for all borrowers at the lender's discretion, or it can track a reference, such as the U.S. federal funds rate or the London Interbank Offered Rate (LIBOR). The interest rate for an ARM can be adjusted daily, weekly, monthly, quarterly, or annually. ARMs in France, Denmark and other countries include caps that limit interest rate increases.

The popularity of FRMs and ARMs varies according to market conditions and local regulations. In 2009, for instance, ARMs comprised more than 90% of the mortgages in Australia, Ireland, South Korea and Spain.[1] Many Canadians envy their American neighbors' access to 30-year, low-interest FRMs, which are unavailable in Canada.[2]

Some mortgages have a fixed interest rate for an initial period. The interest rate is then reset one or more times over the mortgage term, or the mortgage becomes an ARM. Convertible mortgages let the borrower switch between an FRM and an ARM, or between an ARM and an FRM.

Interest rates for mortgages can be compounded daily, yearly or semi-annually.

Term and amortization

The mortgage term is the length of time you commit to the interest rate, the lender and the mortgage's terms and conditions. Mortgage terms start at one year and extend to multigenerational loans, in which the borrower's children or next of kin assume the mortgage when the original borrower dies. Multigenerational mortgages became popular in Japan in the 1990s and can still be found in Japan, Sweden and other countries.[3] Switzerland, meanwhile, has "infinite" mortgages, which are multigenerational loans with no maturity date.[4]

The mortgage term can match or differ from the mortgage amortization period, which is the length of time it will take you to pay off the mortgage. For example, in a 30-year, fixed-rate mortgage, both the term and amortization period are 30 years. But you could also have a one-year or a five-year FRM with a 30-year amortization period. You would need 30 one-year mortgages or six five-year mortgages, respectively, to pay off the home.

Repayment

Mortgages are typically repaid on a monthly basis, but you can sometimes save money by making biweekly payments. Instead of making 12 monthly payments per year, you divide the monthly payment in half and make 26 payments, one every two weeks. For example, if your monthly mortgage payment is $2,000, you make 26 biweekly payments of $1,000. This way, you repay $26,000 each year instead of $24,000, saving on interest and redeeming the mortgage sooner.

With some ARMs, the repayment amount increases when interest rates rise and falls when rates decrease. With others, the repayment amount remains constant and the number of payments increases or decreases to accommodate interest rate fluctuations.

In many countries, you will be charged a fee if you pay off your mortgage ahead of schedule. In Hong Kong, for example, lenders typically charge 3% of the outstanding balance if you redeem a mortgage within the first year, 2% in the second and 1% in the third. After three years, there is no prepayment penalty.

Your mortgage repayment comprises interest and principal. In some countries, like the United States and Canada, it also includes premiums for homeowners insurance and local property taxes. This is known as PITI, for principal, interest, taxes and insurance. Mortgage insurance premiums and homeowner associations' fees may also be included. The lender holds these funds in an escrow account and pays the bills on your behalf when they are due.

Down payments

Before the 2008 subprime crisis, you could borrow 120%—or more—of a property's value, which was often enough to cover your closing and moving costs. Now, you usually need to make a cash down payment representing 5%–50% of the property's value. Income and recreational properties, second and subsequent homes, and purchases by nonresidents normally require larger down payments than primary residences bought by local, first-time buyers.

The loan-to-value ratio (LTV) is the relationship between the down payment and the mortgage. For instance, if you make a 30% down payment and take out a mortgage for the balance, you have a 70% LTV. Low LTVs are safer for lenders than high ones, because the lender is less likely to lose money if you default on the mortgage. The maximum LTV is determined by local laws and regulations, by market conditions and by the lender's policies.

Mortgages sometimes contain a clause specifying that if the loan-to-value ratio exceeds a specific threshold, the borrower must make up the difference. For example, if the maximum LTV is 80% and a fall in the price of your home means the outstanding mortgage represents 85% of the home's value, you have to send the lender a check for 5%. This clause is common in markets where prices are expected to fall and with multicurrency mortgages where exchange rate movements can erode a borrower's equity.

If you obtain a mortgage with a high LTV, the lender may require you to buy mortgage insurance. Canada, Hong Kong and the Netherlands have government-backed mortgage insurers. Elsewhere, mortgage insurance is provided by the private sector.

Valuations

Lenders provide mortgages based on the value of the property. But one property can have several values. For example, there is an appraised value for tax purposes, the price that the last buyer paid for the home, a replacement cost and a value derived from the property's ability to generate rental income. Depending on the home, neighborhood and market, these figures can vary wildly.

When you take out a mortgage, the lender will estimate the home's value. The lender may have the home valued by an independent appraiser and send you the bill. Lenders tend to be conservative, and there is usually a gap between the price you agree to pay for a home and the lender's valuation. You can sometimes contest an inaccurate valuation.

Mortgage variations

Before the subprime crisis, borrowers in the United States had a wide range of mortgage choices.[5] In 2010, the Dodd-Frank Wall Street Reform and Consumer Protection Act banned or restricted the use of prepayment penalties, balloon payments and interest-only mortgages. Other countries introduced similar changes. Maximum LTVs were cut, mortgage terms were shortened, loan-to-income criteria were tightened and it became more difficult to obtain interest-only mortgages.

Despite these changes, lenders continue to create mortgages to meet different needs, including those relating to borrowers' financial circumstances, religion and life stage. Here are some examples.

Balloon
Balloon mortgages feature a small monthly payment that is applied to the interest and the principal and one large payment at the end of the mortgage term. For example, the borrower may pay $1,000 per

month for five years, and make a final installment (known as a balloon payment) of $500,000 at the end of the mortgage.

Buy-to-let
Common in the United Kingdom, buy-to-let mortgages are designed for small landlords who purchase a home with the intention of renting it out. These mortgages are available to expatriates and locals through retail banks and specialist lenders. They are an alternative to conventional mortgages, which usually include a clause requiring that the owner—not a tenant—occupy the dwelling.

Flexible
Flexible mortgages let borrowers underpay, take payment holidays, overpay and borrow against the mortgage without taking a second mortgage. There are annual limits on the number of missed payments and unpaid interest is capitalized into the loan balance. Flexible mortgages are available in Australia, Canada, France, Germany, the Netherlands, Spain and the United Kingdom.

Interest-only
In the U.K. and many European countries, buyers can take out interest-only mortgages, in which only the interest is repaid during the mortgage term. The principal is repaid in a lump sum at the end of the mortgage, often after the borrower sells the home. Interest-only mortgages typically have a maximum LTV of 65% and are often bundled with savings or investment products.

Multicurrency
Available in many jurisdictions, these mortgages let you borrow in a currency with a lower interest rate than the currency you used to buy your home, or one that is appreciating against your purchase currency. For example, in the early 2010s people buying homes in China took out U.S. dollar mortgages, which offered a lower interest rate than renminbi-denominated loans plus currency appreciation as the dollar strengthened against its Chinese counterpart. Multicurrency mortgages based on the Swiss franc and euro have also been popular in transition countries in Central and Eastern Europe, such as Hungary, Latvia and Poland.

Offset
Offset mortgages deduct the credit balance in a borrower's bank account from the outstanding mortgage. For example, if the mortgage balance is $200,000 and the borrower's credit balance is $50,000, interest is only charged on $150,000. ARMs and FRMs are available as offset mortgages.

Recourse and nonrecourse
In a nonrecourse mortgage, if you default and the lender forecloses, you are not personally liable for the difference between the amount the lender recovers after disposing of the property and the outstanding balance of your mortgage. With a recourse mortgage, on the other hand, if you owe $500,000, but after foreclosing and selling your home the lender only recovers $400,000, the lender can pursue you for the $100,000 shortfall. Because they carry more risk for the lender, nonrecourse mortgages usually have a lower maximum LTV.

In the United States, 11 states are regarded as being nonrecourse for residential mortgages. In Belgium, Germany, France and the Netherlands, the duration of a debtor's liability is unlimited. In Spain, it is 15 years.

Reverse
Reverse mortgages are designed for older people who have accumulated equity in their homes. Under the most common type of reverse mortgage, a lender gives the homeowner a lump sum, a series of installments or both, based of the value of their home. The lender is repaid when the loan matures, typically when the borrower or borrowers die. Reverse mortgages are a form of equity release and are available in many countries, including China and the United States

Sharia-compliant
In Islam, earning or charging interest is forbidden. There are three ways to structure a mortgage that complies with this restriction. Using *Ijara,* the lender buys the home for the customer and then leases it back to them. At the end of the lease, the lender transfers the title of the home to the customer. With *Musharaka*, the lender and buyer jointly purchase the home and the customer gradually buys out the lender's share. In *Murabaha,* the lender purchases the property and

then sells it on to the buyer for a profit. The buyer makes fixed monthly payments to the lender, based on the higher price.[6]

Reverse mortgages are designed for homeowners over 55 years of age who have accumulated equity in their property.

Applying for a mortgage

While there are national and regional variations, most mortgage applications follow this pattern:

▲ The borrower signs a preliminary sale and purchase (S&P) agreement, a subscription agreement for an off the plan purchase or an S&P agreement for the property and makes the necessary down payment.

▲ The borrower completes the lender's application form.

▲ The borrower gathers the documents listed below and submits them to the lender.

▲ The borrower pays an application fee to the lender. The borrower may also pay a fee to have the home appraised, as well as various charges for setting up and administering the mortgage.

▲ The lender reviews the documents, values the property and processes the application.

▲ The lender approves or rejects the application, or asks for additional information. If the application is rejected, the lender may make a counteroffer.

▲ The lender arranges insurance on the property. (In some countries, the borrower may need to take out insurance before applying for the mortgage.)

▲ The mortgage contract is signed.

▲ The mortgage is registered as a lien against the property.

▲ The lender releases the funds borrowed through the mortgage.

▲ The borrower begins repaying the mortgage.

▲ After several years, the borrower makes the final payment and the mortgage is redeemed.

Credit checks

When you apply for a mortgage, the lender will gauge your ability to repay the loan. One way they do this is by contacting a credit bureau, which maintains a record of your identity; address; residential and employment histories; credit card balances and payment history; car, student and consumer loans; mortgages and other data. Some bureaus gather positive information, while others only collect negative data, such as defaults and late payments.

The results of your credit report will influence the interest rate you pay, the size of your down payment and whether or not your loan is approved. Check your credit report for errors and omissions, and have any problems fixed before you apply for the loan. You can obtain a copy of your file free of charge or for a nominal fee.

The credit reporting industry is fragmented. There are single-country, government-run bureaus, like the National Credit Information Database that is operated by the People's Bank of China. Large companies, such as TransUnion (www.transunion.com), Experian (www.experian.com) and Equifax (www.equifax.com), operate bureaus in multiple markets. In Singapore, Japan and elsewhere, local bankers' associations run credit bureaus. Mature markets like the United States are served by multiple, sophisticated bureaus, while many developing countries have limited coverage. As a result of the industry's fragmented nature, the credit rating that you have carefully maintained at home may count for very little in another country.

In addition to checking your credit history, lenders will use different formulas to determine your creditworthiness. For example, in the United States lenders typically expect your debt-to-income ratio (monthly debt repayments divided by pretax monthly income) to be less than 36%. Your total housing costs, including insurance and property taxes, should be less than 28% of your pretax monthly income.

Pre-approval

A conversation with a lender or mortgage broker can be a useful reality check for prospective homeowners. "Ideally, this should be done in advance of buyers even looking at properties, so that they they know their real budget, including closing costs," notes Jennifer Kay Chan, a Toronto-based real estate agent.

Lenders will often provide "approval in principle" or "indicative approval" for a mortgage in exchange for background information on you and your target property. This approval is not binding on the lender, but it does give you an idea of what mortgage products are available and how much you can borrow. You can also formally apply to the lender and get pre-approved for a mortgage. A pre-approved mortgage comes with a time limit and is binding on the lender.

Approval in principal and pre-approval give the buyer and the vendor confidence that the sale will be completed, and pre-approval can speed up the closing process.

In parts of the United States, a more advanced form of pre-approval, called "pre-underwriting," is available. Taking place between the offer and the contract, pre-underwriting uses a more thorough credit check to give the buyer greater certainty that the mortgage will be granted. Pre-underwriting is most common in the suburbs, where a home's value is easier to predict, and is intended to reduce the advantage that cash buyers have in competitive markets.[7]

Some lenders charge a fee for providing approval in principle, pre-approval and pre-underwriting services.

Supporting documents

Here is a list of the information and documents that lenders typically request with your application. You may not need everything on this list, but some lenders may request additional items. You should expect to sign a release form authorizing the lender to request additional information from the organizations that issued your documents.

Identification
▲ Passport and/or identity card for you and your spouse

▲ Marriage certificate or divorce decree

▲ Proof that you have to right to reside in the country where you are buying

▲ Proof of residency, such as a utility or property tax bill

▲ Business registration certificate if you are buying through a company

▲ Your name, address, phone and fax numbers and email address, and those of your real estate agent, banker and lawyer

Financial
▲ Proof that you have paid the deposit on your new home

▲ Employment contract, listing your salary

▲ Most recent tax return

▲ Audited financial statements and proof of ownership if you are self-employed or buying through a company

▲ Bank and brokerage account statements

▲ Schedule of repayments for other mortgaged property you own

▲ Information about any outstanding debts, such as credit cards or car and student loans

▲ Proof of ownership of other assets, such as stocks, bonds, mutual funds, businesses and property

▲ Other sources of income, such as gifts, commissions and royalties

▲ Information about anything else that affects or could affect your financial status, such as a past bankruptcy or pending lawsuit

Property
▲ Sale and purchase agreement

▲ Land transfer certificate

▲ Certificate of occupancy

▲ A legal description of the property

▲ Project details and specifications and a copy of the building certificate, if you are buying off the plan

Insurance
▲ Proof of fire insurance, including the insurer's name, policy number and insured amount

- Proof of earthquake insurance, including the insurer's name, policy number and insured amount

- Proof of life insurance, including the insurer's name, policy number and insured amount, if the insurance is not provided by the lender

Timing

Processing time for a mortgage application depends on the size of the loan, your relationship with the lender, how busy the lender is, local government policies, the complexities of your particular application and many other factors.

Some lenders realize that processing time is a selling point. In March 2014, for example, Commonwealth Bank of Australia's Website said "It is possible for us to provide a decision on your loan in as little as 60 minutes, if the factors above are favorable." That is a best-case scenario and loan applications typically take 30–90 days to process. In a developing country, it can take significantly longer.

Restrictions and requirements

A lender will appraise your home before issuing a mortgage and insist that you have fire insurance. Other common requirements and restrictions include:

- Aggregate age. In Hong Kong, bank policies limit the sum of the building's age and the mortgage tenor to 60 or 70 years.

- Applicant's age. In generally, you must be 18 years old. Some banks will lend to people who are 70.

- Application fee. Lenders and brokers may charge a fee when you apply for a mortgage.

- Building age. In China, for example, it is difficult to obtain a mortgage for a home that is more than 15 years old.

▲ Construction and location. Lenders often have lower LTVs for wooden homes and property outside big cities (which can be difficult to value) and on reclaimed land.

▲ Guarantor. The guarantor can be a person, or a company providing this service for a fee.

▲ Life insurance and a physical examination. In Japan, these are standard requirements.

▲ Minimum loan size. Some lenders have high minimum loan sizes because underwriting costs for large and small loans are similar, but small loans are much less profitable.

▲ Residency. You may need to be legally resident in the country before you can apply for a mortgage.

In Hong Kong, banks encourage the sale of new homes by limiting the sum of the building's age and the mortgage tenor to 60 or 70 years.

Improving your odds

Ultimately, the success or failure of your mortgage application will hinge on your income and debt load, the home's appraised value and the LTV ratio. However, there are things that you can do to improve your odds and, in some cases, get more attractive terms.

- ▲ Become a permanent resident. Meeting the government's permanent residency requirements tells the lender you are a person of good character and suggests that you plan on staying in the country.

- ▲ Speak the language. Fluency in the local language makes it easier for the bank to serve you and allays concerns that you will not understand and comply with the mortgage agreement.

- ▲ Have ties to the community. A local spouse, family living in the country and participation in community activities suggest that you will stay for the long term and are a good risk.

- ▲ Exude stability. Banks like borrowers who have worked for the same employer for a long time. Entrepreneurs and commissioned salespeople can be seen as poor risks because their incomes are more volatile than those of salaried employees.

- ▲ Get your paperwork in order. You'll save time and make it easier for the lender to approve your application if you have all of the documents they need, translated and notarized as appropriate.

- ▲ Be conventional. You are more likely to get a mortgage for a new condominium in the city center than a loft conversion in a working-class neighborhood.

- ▲ Use introductions. A referral from your real estate agent, developer, employer, spouse or a friend or neighbor can open doors that would otherwise remain shut.

- ▲ Make the numbers work. Ensure your LTV, debt-to-income ratio, mortgage amount and term are within the ranges specified by the bank and local regulations. A large down payment also works in your favor.

▲ Leave some wiggle room. Add 7%–10% to the purchase price for closing costs and incidentals, and don't forget to budget for repairs and maintenance. Buying a little less than you can afford is sensible.

If your mortgage application is rejected, there are several things that you can do.

▲ Ask why. In many places, lenders are required to explain their decision and you may have overlooked something that is easy to fix.

▲ Try another lender. Your application may have fallen afoul of the lender's internal policies. For example, they may have already filled their loan quota for a new development. Another lender may approve the same loan application.

▲ Reduce your principal. If the application is rejected because your income is too low, ask for a smaller loan.

▲ Fix your credit rating. If you haven't already done so, ensure your credit record is current and correct. If the record is accurate, get help from a counselor to improve your score.

INSURANCE

Owning a property exposes you to a variety of risks, many of which can be managed with insurance.

Fire, public liability and homeowners insurance are available nearly everywhere, but other products, like flood insurance, are not. Developed countries generally offer a greater range of more sophisticated products than developing nations, but many countries have quirks with respect to what kinds of losses are covered.

You can buy some coverage, like health insurance, in your home country. This will give you access to English-speaking customer service staff and the potential to save money by having all of your insurance with one company. You can also save money by arranging some forms of international coverage—automobile insurance, for example—as a rider to an existing policy in your home country. However, many forms of insurance must be purchased locally.

If you are insuring a holiday home that will be vacant for months at a time or student quarters that will be empty between terms, watch out for reporting deadlines. If you don't report damages promptly, your claim may be rejected.

When you buy insurance, you will deal with an agent, who represents one insurance company. Or you can use a broker, who represents you and helps you find the best offering from a range of insurers. A knowledgeable broker can also help you compare disparate policies and balance the sum insured against the deductible so that the coverage makes economic sense.

Finally, pay particular attention to the losses that are excluded from the policy. For example, the high cost of American medical care means that many international health care policies cover hospitalization everywhere, except the United States.

Here are some of the common types of insurance needed by international property buyers.

All risks

All risk insurance covers all losses, except those that are specifically excluded in the policy. It is in contrast to named perils coverage, which applies only to losses from causes that are specifically listed in the policy. Because it is inclusive, all risk insurance is usually expensive.

Domestic helper

If you employ domestic helpers, you may be required to insure them against injury and death. This is the law in Hong Kong and Singapore, among other places.

In addition to damaging homes, earthquakes affect public utilities. Subsidence left this sewer manhole exposed after the Great East Japan Earthquake in 2011.

Earthquake

The availability of earthquake insurance varies widely. In Turkey, for instance, it is mandatory: you cannot get a mortgage or connect your home to the gas, water or electricity supply without earthquake insurance.[1] In Italy, where coverage rates are low, the government recently introduced legislation to make earthquake insurance available throughout the county.[2] In Japan, earthquake coverage can only be purchased as a rider, also called an endorsement, on your fire insurance policy.

Earthquakes cause massive economic losses, so your insurer must have the resources to pay multiple, large claims. Not all policies cover losses caused by subsequent events, such as fires, floods, explosions and tsunamis. In the United States, earthquake shocks that are more than 72 hours apart are treated as separate claims.[3]

Fire

As its name suggests, fire insurance covers the structure of a home against damage caused by fire. Riders can be added to a fire insurance policy to cover losses due to earthquakes, storms, burst pipes, landslides, subsidence and similar risks. In general, you need fire insurance to obtain a mortgage. If you live in a condominium, the building's master policy may provide sufficient fire insurance coverage for your mortgage lender.

Flood

Flood insurance covers overland flooding, which occurs when water enters a dwelling after a river, stream or lake overflows and covers normally dry land. Burst pipes and overflowing sewers are typically covered by fire insurance, not flood insurance.

In Canada, flood insurance is not available. In the United States, it is subsidized by a federal government program that has accumulated debts of over $20 billion. In 2013, the program was amended, resulting in large premium increases for more than a million homeowners.[4]

Health

If you belong to a national health insurance program in your home country, check to see if you are covered while you are living overseas. Where international coverage is provided, there may be a time limit. As a legal resident, some countries will let you join their national health care program. You can also buy health insurance from a private company. If your second home is in a country with limited medical services, you may want to buy a policy that includes repatriation for medical emergencies.

Homeowners

Homeowners insurance is a package policy that covers damage to the structure of the home and related buildings such as garages, the contents of the home, the cost of temporary accommodation if the home damaged or destroyed and personal liability insurance. Tenants insurance is similar to homeowners insurance, but does not cover the structure of the building.

Landlord

Landlord insurance protects owners from damage caused by tenants, including theft and vandalism. Typically, landlord insurance covers public liability, damage from burst pipes and lost rental revenue due to fires, storms and other risks. Some policies include legal and travel expenses.

If you are renting your vacation home on a short-term basis through an online vacation rental site, you can offer third-party insurance. For example, www.vacationprotection.com charges $49 for $1,500 of coverage, and you can insist that renters buy the coverage as a part of the rental.

Latent defect

Latent defect insurance covers inherent flaws in the design, workmanship or materials of a new building that only become apparent after the structure is completed. Latent defect insurance can be useful in places where there is no new-home warranty program or where there are concerns about the contractor's or the developer's ability to honor warranty claims.[5]

Life

In Japan, many lenders will not issue a mortgage unless you pass a physical examination and enroll in a group life insurance plan, with the lender named as the beneficiary. In the United States, this product is known as *mortgage life insurance* and can be purchased voluntarily.

Mortgage

In many countries, mortgage insurance is mandatory when you make a smaller than-normal down payment. In Canada, for example, it is required for down payments of less than 20% of the purchase price. Mortgage insurance protects the lender against the risk of the borrower defaulting.

Professional liability

Professional liability insurance is bought by people and companies that provide specialist services to protect them from negligence lawsuits. It is also known as professional indemnity and errors and omissions insurance.

If you suffer a loss because a supplier made a mistake—for example, you bought a home that an inspector incorrectly reported was free of asbestos—professional liability insurance increases the likelihood that you could sue the inspector and successfully collect damages.

In addition to home inspectors, professional liability insurance is purchased by accountants, appraisers, architects, contractors, engineers, lawyers, notaries public and real estate agents. In some professions and jurisdictions, service providers are required by law to have professional liability insurance.

Public liability

Public liability insurance covers claims from damage to property and bodily injury, except those arising from the ownership of automobiles and aircraft. Public liability insurance is usually included in a homeowners policy and is particularly important during renovations, when accidents often happen.

Title

Title insurance protects a buyer if there is a defect in a property's title, like a lien, that was not discovered when he purchased the property. For information on title insurance, see the "Ownership and Property Rights" chapter.

Travel

If you plan on visiting your holiday home frequently, travel insurance may be a worthwhile investment. Travel insurance protects you against losses from canceled or interrupted trips, lost luggage and the default of a carrier or tour operator.

Workers' compensation

In many countries, there is a legal requirement that tradespeople and laborers who are building, repairing or renovating your home are covered by workers' compensation insurance, which covers them against occupational injury. Normally, this is provided by the company that employs the workers, but it may be your responsibility.

TAX

Tax law is notoriously complicated, but it is an area where research and careful planning can pay large dividends.

Getting started

In general, it is better to obtain advice *before* taking action — buying, renting, renovating or selling a home—than afterward. That way, you can ensure that you comply with the law and minimize your tax bill.

Where tax law is complex, international tax law is even more convoluted. You may need assistance from lawyers and accountants in both your home and second countries. Getting accurate information is essential, so educate yourself about common issues, ask prospective advisers questions and check their references and credentials.

When you have found suitable advisers, start by asking these questions:

▲ Can I arrange this expenditure or investment to make it tax deductible?

▲ Can I time the receipt of rental or sale income to reduce my tax bill?

▲ Can my expenditure or investment be structured to qualify for tax credits?

▲ Are there tax treaties between my home and second countries?

▲ What documentation is required?

▲ Are there any other strategies or approaches that I should be considering?

Acquisition

Broadly speaking, property taxes can be grouped into four categories: acquisition, occupation and ownership, income and disposal.

Acquisition taxes are incurred when you buy a property. They can be paid when you settle your lawyer's fees at the end of the transaction, as they are in Hong Kong, or a few months later, as they are in Japan.

When you purchase land, it may be tax-exempt or taxed at a different rate than buildings. Residential, commercial and industrial properties are often treated differently for tax purposes, and large or expensive homes are frequently taxed at a higher rate than modest dwellings, as they are in China. You may be charged both provincial and federal sales taxes, as is the case for new homes in parts of Canada. Sales tax may apply to associated costs, like brokerage fees. Some countries charge a transfer tax when you acquire a home, and you may be liable for stamp tax on sale and purchase agreements as well as rental contracts. Governments also assess surtaxes, which are taxes on taxes, to pay for things ranging from schools to rural development.

Shanghai is one of two Chinese cities that introduced a property tax on a trial basis in 2011.

Governments use taxes to encourage and discourage certain behaviors. For example, from January 2013 foreigners buying a residential property in Singapore pay a 15% additional buyer's stamp duty (ABSD). Permanent residents of Singapore pay a 5% ABSD on the purchase of their first residential property and 10% on their second property. Singaporean citizens pay 7% ABSD on the purchase of their second residential property and 10% on subsequent ones. The ABSD is charged on top of stamp duty of 1% on the first S$180,000 ($143,000); 2% on the next S$180,000 and 3% on the remainder.[1]

Occupation and ownership

National, state and local governments charge homeowners a variety of occupation and ownership taxes. For example:

- China does not have a national property tax, although Shanghai and Chongqing introduced local property taxes on a trial basis in 2011.

- Costa Rica has an annual luxury tax that is levied on homes valued at more than $200,000.

- In Denmark, owners pay 1% of the value of their property for the first DKK 3.04 million ($563,000) and 3% for anything above that amount.[2]

- France has two property taxes: *taxe d'habitation*, which is paid by the occupier, regardless of whether they own the property, and *taxe foncière*, which is paid by the owner.

- Spain has an "imputed income tax" that is payable regardless of whether the home produces rental revenue.[3]

- In Whistler, a Canadian ski resort, owners of designated "resort lands" must join Tourism Whistler and pay annual fees to support the resort's marketing programs.[4]

Many property taxes are based on an assessed value. Typically, this reflects the sale and rental values for similar properties in the area, the home's age, size, condition and location; and amenities in the neighborhood, such as transportation. In Japan, property taxes are based on four separate appraised values, each calculated on a different calendar and formula.

You may not have to pay the amount shown on your property tax bill. Mistakes occur, assessments can be appealed and deductions and exemptions are often available. By understanding how property taxes are calculated, you can avoid homes that come with a large tax liability. You can also renovate or remodel a property in a way that improves its appeal without increasing your tax bill.

In most places, property taxes pay for roads and police and fire departments. Taxes may also fund garbage collection and schools, which are paid for separately elsewhere.

Property taxes can be influenced by a jurisdiction's overall financial health, by demographic trends like the need for new schools and by political factors, such as the amalgamation of several towns into a single city.

The immobility of real estate makes it a tempting tax target for governments. In a 2014 policy paper, the International Monetary Fund notes that there is "considerable scope to exploit this tax more fully," particularly in developing countries where property tax yields are about half the level of those in developed countries.[5]

Income

Income taxes apply if you are renting your property out. The amount of tax you pay and the way it is calculated will be affected by how much money you earn, by your residency status and by whether the property is owned by you or by a company.

If you earn income from your property, you may be required to file a tax return in the country where the property is located. You can file the return yourself or have a representative, such as your property manager or accountant, file it for you. Many expenses incurred in generating the rental income can be deducted from the gross rent.

If you are a nonresident, your rental income may be subject to a withholding tax. In Canada, for instance, the withholding tax is currently 25% of the gross rental income.[6] While residents are generally exempt from withholding taxes, they are usually taxed on their worldwide income.

This can make your residency status an important tax planning consideration. Some jurisdictions use a simple formula, like the number of days that you are in the country, to determine your status. For example, you are considered a U.S. resident for tax purposes if you are physically present in the United States on at least 31 days during the current year and 183 days during the three-year period that includes the current year and the two years immediately before that.[7]

Other nations base your residency status on your connections to the country. Canada, for instance, determines residency on a case-by-case basis by considering whether you have a home, dependents, bank accounts and social ties to the country.

Many nations maintain bilateral or multilateral tax treaties that prevent you from being taxed twice on the same income by your country of residence and by the jurisdiction where your income-producing home is located. This is a particular benefit to U.S. citizens, who are taxed on their worldwide income, regardless of where they live. For information about tax treaties, see your national tax agency's website.

Disposal

When you sell your property, you may be subject to capital gains tax, which is charged on the difference between the price you paid for the property and the amount you received when you sold it. Many countries, including Australia, the United Kingdom and the United States, offer an exemption from capital gains tax when your sell your primary residence. Often, you must live in the home for a minimum period to qualify for this exemption. If you are buying and selling homes regularly, you may have to pay income tax instead of capital gains tax.

Transferring large amounts of money across international borders can trigger taxes and reporting requirements. If you are emigrating from a country like Canada, money you take with you may be subject to an exit tax.

Investments in environmentally friendly technologies, like the photovoltaic cells on the roof of this factory, often qualify for tax credits.

Exemptions, credits and deductions

There are many exemptions and deductions that can be legally used to minimize your tax liabilities throughout the life of a property. This is an area where a knowledgeable accountant can pay for his services.

If you are earning income from your property, ask about the following basic deductions: property taxes, depreciation, maintenance (including repairs, pool service, electricity, gas and telephone), management fees, travel, legal expenses, interest, advertising and insurance.

You may be exempt from tax or eligible for a reduced rate by virtue of your age or marital status. Improvements that save energy, like adding insulation or solar panels, or that make the home accessible to the disabled, like wheelchair ramps, can also have tax advantages.

In some countries—including Austria, Belgium, Denmark, Finland, Greece, Ireland, Italy, the Netherlands, Norway, Portugal, South Korea, Spain, Sweden, Switzerland, Taiwan and the United States—interest paid on a residential mortgage is tax deductible.[8] In certain circumstances, American citizens can claim mortgage interest on homes outside the United States. See Internal Revenue Service publication 936 for details (www.irs.gov/pub/irs-pdf/p936.pdf).

Using an onshore or offshore company to buy, hold and rent out your property can provide tax advantages in some circumstances. For example, many of the costs associated with operating the company and the property can be written off against rental income. However, this advantage must be weighed against the cost of establishing and running a company, including annual business licenses and bookkeeping and audit fees.

If a company owns a property, it is sometimes possible to sell the company, rather than the property. This can result in a significant tax savings, but the buyer must be confident that the company has no hidden liabilities.

Some jurisdictions, such as the United Kingdom, are using taxes to discourage the use of companies to hold real estate that is not being used for commercial purposes. In 2012, the U.K. introduced the annual tax on enveloped dwellings (ATED), which includes a 15% stamp duty, an annual tax of £15,000–£140,000 ($25,000–$235,000) and the imposition of capital gains taxes for nonresident entities. The ATED will come into full effect by 2016.[9]

Tax evasion versus tax avoidance

Tax evasion involves under-reporting your rental income, overstating your expenses, claiming personal expenditures as business costs and similar schemes. Tax avoidance is legitimately arranging your affairs to reduce the amount of tax you pay. Tax avoidance is good business. Tax evasion is illegal and, with the help of the Internet and social media, cash-strapped governments are vigorously pursuing tax evaders.

There are varying degrees of tax avoidance. By using simple techniques, like claiming available tax credits and timing your property purchases and sales to minimize capital gains taxes, you can save a great deal of money. There are more aggressive techniques that can save you even more money, but these schemes often attract the attention of the authorities, who may use you as a test case. In general, elaborate strategies make sense for large transactions and portfolios, and you need to balance the money you save with the time, effort, cost and stress needed to execute the strategy.

RESOURCES

Property Buyer's Checklist
231

Information Sources
239

PROPERTY BUYER'S CHECKLIST

The following items will not apply in every market or to every type of property.

Building and land

▲ Does the home have **aluminum** or **knob-and-tube wiring?**

▲ Are there **archaeological artifacts** on the land?

▲ Has an **asbestos** survey been conducted?

▲ Does the **builder** or building have a reputation for quality problems?

▲ Does the home comply with applicable **building codes?**

▲ How much are the **condominium** fees?

▲ Has a **death, rape, suicide** or **violent crime** occurred in the dwelling?

▲ Has Chinese-made **drywall** been installed?

▲ Are there any **easements** or rights of way on the property?

▲ What **facilities**—storage rooms, swimming pools or tennis courts—are included?

▲ Are there any hidden **fees** for parking, facilities, ground rent, etc.?

▲ Has a home **inspection** been performed?

▲ Is **lead paint** used in the home?

▲ Has **marijuana** been grown in the home?

- ▲ Have **methamphetamines** been manufactured in the home?
- ▲ Is the building populated by **owner-occupiers** or tenants?
- ▲ Is **parking** available?
- ▲ Is **polybutylene** or **galvanized steel pipe** installed?
- ▲ Has the home been tested for **radon**?
- ▲ Does the building suffer from **sick building syndrome**?
- ▲ Is the land affected by **subsidence**?
- ▲ Has a land **survey** been conducted?
- ▲ How much are the property **taxes**?
- ▲ Has the home been inspected for **termites** and other pests?
- ▲ Has **urea formaldehyde foam insulation (UFFI)** been installed?
- ▲ Are there many **vacancies** in the building?
- ▲ Does the home comply with local **zoning** regulations?

City and neighborhood

- ▲ Is the neighborhood built on a **brownfield** site or other source of soil pollution?
- ▲ Is the neighborhood near an **earthquake** fault?
- ▲ Are properties in the area being **expropriated**?
- ▲ Is the home in a **floodplain**?
- ▲ Does the climate or vegetation pose a **forest fire** risk?
- ▲ Are the local, state and national **governments** solvent and stable?

- Is **infrastructure** being built (or demolished) nearby?

- Is the home in a **landslide** zone?

- Is the **neighborhood** stable, decaying or being gentrified?

- Does the area receive normal **services**: ambulance, broadband Internet, cable TV, electricity, fire, gas, police, public transportation, mail, restaurants, schools, sewerage, shopping, telephone and water?

- Is the area at risk from **tsunamis** or storm surges?

- Are **undesirable neighbors** nearby: cemeteries, expressways, factories, incinerators, nuclear power plants, prisons or red-light districts?

- Is the tap **water** safe to drink?

- Is the area prone to dangerous **weather**, such as typhoons, hurricanes or tornadoes?

Developers

- Does the developer's name match the name of the **bank account** holder?

- How long has the developer been in **business?**

- Does the developer have a history of **complaints** with the local consumer protection authority?

- Does the salesperson's **email** account (e.g., salesperson@developername.com) match the company's web address (www.developername.com)?

- Is the developer **financially sound?**

- ▲ Is there anything **incongruous** or **odd** about the developer, salesperson, building site, contract documents, marketing materials, etc.?

- ▲ Is the developer facing **lawsuits** from unpaid suppliers and unhappy customers?

- ▲ What is the developer's legal **name** and registered address?

- ▲ How many **projects** has the developer completed in the city where you plan to buy?

- ▲ Is the **salesperson** authorized to represent the developer?

Income property

- ▲ Is there a local **accountant** who will prepare and file taxes for you?

- ▲ What tax and legal **documents** do I need to maintain?

- ▲ What is your **exit** strategy?

- ▲ What **expenses** are tax deductible?

- ▲ How much is the management company's monthly **fee**?

- ▲ What is the tenant's payment **history**?

- ▲ How will I receive rental **income**?

- ▲ Are tenants charged **"key money?"**

- ▲ How much time remains on the tenant's **lease**?

- ▲ How much does the management company charge to **recruit** tenants?

- ▲ How does the management company **report** its activities?

- ▲ What legal **rights** do the landlord and tenant enjoy?

- ▲ What tenant **services** does the management company provide?

- ▲ What **taxes** and **license fees** apply?

- ▲ Is there a **tax treaty** between your country of residence and the one where the property is located?

- ▲ Is the property **tenanted**?

- ▲ Under what circumstances can the lease be **terminated?**

- ▲ Does the tenant or the owner pay **utilities** and **other expenses?**

- ▲ What is the expected **yield** or **capitalization** rate?

Money

- ▲ Can foreigners open a local **bank account**?

- ▲ Are **capital gains** taxable in your country of residence or the country where the home is located?

- ▲ Are there **foreign exchange** controls in the country where the property is or where you are domiciled?

- ▲ What **insurance** coverage—earthquake, fire, flood, homeowners, public liability—is available?

- ▲ Are **mortgages** available to foreign buyers?

- ▲ What documents do you need to **repatriate** money?

- ▲ Do **withholding taxes** apply to rental income or sale proceeds?

- ▲ Is your **will** recognized in the country where the home is located and your country of domicile?

Off the plan purchases

- ▲ Are your deposit and progress payments protected if the developer goes **bankrupt?**

- ▲ Has the developer built other projects in this **city** or **country**?

- ▲ Does the developer have a record of **completing** projects on time and on budget?

- ▲ Could I save money by buying **directly** from the developer in the country where the home is located?

- ▲ What is the **payment** schedule?

- ▲ Does the developer have all of the **permits** and **permissions?**

- ▲ When will you take **possession** of your home?

- ▲ Have the developer's **previous projects** aged well, or are they falling apart?

- ▲ What legal **remedies** apply if the developer changes the project's scope or fails to deliver the project on time?

- ▲ Is **social housing** included in the development?

Recreational property

- ▲ How far is the nearest **international airport?**

- ▲ Does the resort's **management** have a good reputation?

- ▲ Is your **medical insurance** effective in this country?

- ▲ What **off-season** activities are available?

- ▲ Does the resort or complex provide **rental** services for owners?

- ▲ Can the property be **rented** when you are not there?

Retirement property

▲ Is a national **health care** service available?

▲ Can you collect a **pension** from your home country?

▲ Are **nursing** and home-care services available?

▲ After how many days does your **residency** trigger tax consequences?

▲ Does the property include **universal design**?

▲ Is a retirement **visa** program available?

Suppliers

▲ Is the supplier **accredited** with the appropriate local and international professional bodies?

▲ How much does the supplier **charge**?

▲ Have you checked for **complaints** against the supplier with the local consumer protection authority?

▲ Is the supplier **experienced** with your type of property?

▲ Does the supplier have professional indemnity **insurance**?

▲ Does the supplier have experience with **international transactions**?

▲ Have you confirmed that the supplier is **representing** you and not another party?

▲ What **warranties** apply to the supplier's services?

Title and transaction

▲ Are the condominium fees or utilities in **arrears**?

- ▲ What are the estimated **closing costs?**
- ▲ In what **court** or arbitration venue will disputes be resolved?
- ▲ What penalties apply if the vendor or the buyer **delays** or fails to complete the transaction?
- ▲ Are there any liens or **encumbrances** on the property?
- ▲ How much "**earnest money**" is payable?
- ▲ What decorations and **equipment** are included in the sale?
- ▲ Is an **escrow** service available?
- ▲ Are there sufficient funds in the condominium or co-op's bank account to cover future **expenses?**
- ▲ Are there restrictions on **foreign** ownership?
- ▲ When is the **handover** date?
- ▲ Has a **lawyer** reviewed the sale and purchase agreement?
- ▲ Is the **price** consistent with the market valuation?
- ▲ Are there any local **quirks** that might affect the transaction?
- ▲ Is the condominium or co-op planning major repairs or **renovations?**
- ▲ Have major **repairs** been deferred?
- ▲ Has a **title** search been conducted?
- ▲ Is the **vendor** the registered owner of the property?
- ▲ Is this property included in your **will?**

INFORMATION SOURCES

This chapter features resources to help you buy and own a home. The entries are arranged alphabetically and, unless otherwise noted, are in English and have global applicability. Web addresses are generally for the main page.

International bodies representing several disciplines and professions are included. These associations' Websites are a good place to start if you are hiring a service provider. For example, if you were looking for legal advice in Auckland, you could start at the International Bar Association's Website, which has links to the New Zealand Law Society's site, which, in turn, has a "find a lawyer" service where you can sort lawyers by language, location and practice area.

The inclusion or omission of a company should not be taken as a recommendation that you use or avoid them. Government and supranational organizations with an interest in housing and real estate are included, and technical resources are available for buyers seeking detailed information. Many of the national sites in this section offer information with global applicability.

Finally, things change quickly. Consider this information a starting point, not the last word.

A

Air pollution

Air-pollution maps for cities in Asia and elsewhere are available at http://aqicn.org/map. A near real-time map showing global wind currents can be found at http://earth.nullschool.net.

Appraisal services

The International Valuation Standards Council is a trade body for the appraisal industry. The council has 74 members from 54 countries (www.ivsc.org).

Architects, designers and builders

The International Federation of Interior Architects/Designers represents 270,000 designers, educators and stakeholders in 110 countries and territories (www.ifiworld.org).

The International Housing Association (IHA) represents home builders from 20 countries. Information about the IHA can be found in the community section of the National Association of Home Builders' Website (www.nahb.org).

The International Real Estate Federation (FIABCI) is an umbrella organization with chapters in 48 countries. FIABCI represents appraisers, architects, brokers, consultants, developers, insurers, property managers, lawyers and urban planners (www.fiabci.org).

The International Union of Architects is a global federation of national associations of architects with practitioners in 124 countries and territories (www.uia-architectes.org).

Build it yourself

Hometta (www.hometta.com) and Houseplans (www.houseplans.com) sell professionally designed building plans for single-family homes.

Paperhouses is a group of architects offering free downloads of home blueprints. Similar to the open-source software movement, Paperhouses' network includes partners who can customize designs to meet users' needs and local conditions (www.paperhouses.co).

The U.K.–based National Self Build Association offer a range of reports, videos, technical information and other resources for people who are building their own homes (www.nasba.org.uk).

Several organizations in the United States offer courses for people interested in learning to build a home: Rocky Mountain Workshops (www.rockymountainworkshops.com), the Shelter Institute (www.shelterinstitute.com) and the Yestermorrow Design/Build School (www.yestermorrow.org).

C

Consumer protection

The Business Anti-Corruption Portal provides practical information to help small and medium-sized businesses avoid corruption. Run by the governments of Austria, Denmark, Germany, the Netherlands, Norway, Sweden and the United Kingdom, the multilingual site has information on 64 countries (www.business-anti-corruption.com).

Consumers International is a federation of consumer groups with more than 240 member organizations in 120 countries (www.consumersinternational.org).

The International Consumer Protection and Enforcement Network (ICPEN) comprises government agencies from more than 50 countries. ICPEN has an interest in cross-border commercial activities affecting consumers (http://icpen.org).

E

Earthquakes

The United States Geological Survey provides background on earthquakes (http://earthquake.usgs.gov).

Energy conservation

The U.S. Department of Energy, along with NC State University and other organizations, operates the Database of State Incentives for Renewables and Efficiency, a comprehensive source of city, state and federal information about energy efficiency in the United States (www.dsireusa.org).

The Green Home Guide is produced by the nonprofit U.S. Green Building Council (USGBC) (http://greenhomeguide.com). The Regreen Program, which is a partnership between the American Society of Interior Designers Foundation and the USGBC, offers residential remodeling guidelines and related resources (www.regreenprogram.org).

The Passive House Institute is an independent research body in Germany that champions the development of energy-efficient sealed homes (http://passiv.de). Similar goals are pursued in the United States by the Passive House Institute US (www.passivehouse.us).

The Pretty Good House movement incorporates ideas from passive house designs, with a focus on using local materials, minimizing embedded energy and finding the optimum balance between expenditures and gains (www.greenbuildingadvisor.com).

The World Green Building Council is a network of national green building councils in more than 90 countries (www.worldgbc.org).

Environmental resources

The United States Environmental Protection Agency (EPA) has information about indoor air quality, volatile organic compounds and other environmental issues (www.epa.gov).

The EPA also has a site where you can enter a ZIP code and search the agency's databases to learn more about environmental conditions in your community (www.epa.gov/epahome/whereyoulive.htm).

The World Health Organization offers background information and data about environmental health issues (www.who.int/topics/environmental_health).

F

Financing

The following banks—or their subsidiaries—offer mortgages in multiple countries. Banks regularly enter and abandon markets, and mergers and acquisitions are common, so use this list as a starting point. The banks are listed by the location of their headquarters.

Africa
▲ FirstRand Group (www.firstrand.co.za)

▲ Standard Bank (www.standardbank.com)

Asia
▲ Agricultural Bank of China (www.abchina.com)

▲ Bank of China (www.boc.cn)

▲ Bank of Communications (www.bankcomm.com)

▲ Bank of Taiwan (www.bot.com.tw)

▲ China CITIC Bank International (www.cncbinternational.com)

▲ China Construction Bank (www.ccb.com)

▲ CIMB Group (www.cimbbank.com)

▲ DBS (www.dbs.com)

▲ Hana Bank (www.hanabank.com)

▲ Industrial and Commercial Bank of China (www.icbcasia.com)

▲ Korea Exchange Bank (www.keb.co.kr)

▲ Maybank (www.maybank.com)

▲ Mitsubishi UFJ Financial Group (www.mufg.jp)

- ▲ OCBC Bank (www.ocbc.com)
- ▲ Public Bank (www.publicbank.com.my)
- ▲ Shinhan Bank (www.shinhan.com)
- ▲ United Overseas Bank (www.uobgroup.com)
- ▲ Woori Bank (www.wooribank.com)

Australia and New Zealand
- ▲ Australia and New Zealand Banking Group (www.anz.com)
- ▲ Commonwealth Bank (www.commbank.com.au)
- ▲ National Australia Bank (www.nab.com.au)
- ▲ Westpac (www.westpac.com.au)

Europe
- ▲ Banco Santander (www.santander.com)
- ▲ Barclays (www.barclays.com)
- ▲ BBVA (www.bbva.com)
- ▲ BNP Paribas (www.bnpparibas.com)
- ▲ Commerzbank (www.commerzbank.com)
- ▲ Crédit Agricole (www.credit-agricole.com)
- ▲ Danske Bank (www.danskebank.com)
- ▲ Deutsche Bank (www.db.com)
- ▲ DZ Bank Group (www.dzbank.com)
- ▲ HSBC (www.hsbc.com)

- ▲ ING Group (www.ing.com)

- ▲ Intesa Sanpaolo (www.intesasanpaolo.com)

- ▲ Landesbank Baden-Württemberg (www.lbbw.de)

- ▲ Nordea (www.nordea.com)

- ▲ Rabobank (www.rabobank.com)

- ▲ Royal Bank of Scotland (www.rbs.com)

- ▲ Sberbank of Russia (www.sberbank.ru)

- ▲ Société Générale (www.societegenerale.com)

- ▲ Standard Chartered Bank (www.standardchartered.com)

- ▲ UBS (www.ubs.com)

- ▲ UniCredit (www.unicreditgroup.eu)

North America
- ▲ Bank of Montreal (www.bmo.com)

- ▲ Bank of Nova Scotia (www.scotiabank.com)

- ▲ Canadian Imperial Bank of Commerce (www.cibc.com)

- ▲ Citibank (www.citibank.com)

- ▲ Royal Bank of Canada (www.rbc.com)

- ▲ Toronto-Dominion Bank (www.td.com)

South America
- ▲ Itaú Unibanco (www.itau.com)

- ▲ Banco do Brasil (www.bb.com.br)

Fire

The U.S. Fire Administration has tips for preventing and surviving residential fires, including information for children, the elderly and people with disabilities (www.usfa.fema.gov).

Your nearest fire station will provide information about local codes and regulations.

For sale by owner (FSBO) listings

The following sites list FSBO properties. Some sites cover multiple countries and offer non-English language versions.

Canada
- Canada4SaleByOwner (www.canada4salebyowner.com)
- The For Sale By Owner Canada Network (www.forsalebyownercanada.com)
- The For Sale By Owner Depot (www.forsalebyowner.ca)
- PropertyGuys (www.propertyguys.com)
- PropertySold (www.propertysold.ca)

Europe
- Entreparticuliers (www.entreparticuliers.com)
- Free House Agent (www.freehouseagent.com)
- SeLoger (www.seloger.com)

United Kingdom
- Homes on Sale (www.homesonsale.co.uk)
- The Little House Company (www.thelittlehousecompany.com)
- MyPropertyForSale (www.mypropertyforsale.co.uk)

▲ Tepilo (www.tepilo.com)

▲ Usforhomes (www.usforhomes.com)

United States
▲ ByOwner (www.byowner.com)

▲ ForSaleByOwner (www.forsalebyowner.com)

▲ HomesByOwner (www.homesbyowner.com)

▲ Owners (www.owners.com)

▲ US Realty (www.usrealty.com)

Government debt

Carmen Reinhart and Kenneth Rogoff, authors of *This Time Is Different: Eight Centuries of Financial Folly,* maintain an online database about sovereign defaults, financial crises and inflation rates that can be browsed by country or event (www.reinhartandrogoff.com).

Credit rating agencies, including Fitch (www.fitchratings.com), Moody's (www.moodys.com) and Standard & Poor's (www.standardandpoors.com) provide assessments of national, state and local debt. These three organizations, which also rate corporate debt issued, have a 95% share of the ratings market.

Heritage and conservation

The International Council on Monuments and Sites is a body for conservation professionals, including architects, town planners and archaeologists. The council has national groups in more than 110 countries that publish papers and hold conservation-related events (www.icomos.org).

The Society for the Protection of Ancient Buildings is a U.K.-based charity dedicated to maintaining and repairing old and interesting buildings. The society's online bookstore has publications for homeowners and building professionals (www.spab.org.uk).

The Society of Architectural Historians is a U.S.-based body that promotes the study and conservation of architecture and urbanism worldwide. The society has partner organizations around the world (www.sah.org).

Home automation

Automation companies such as Crestron (www.crestron.com) and Lutron (www.lutron.com) have been joined in the home automation market by computer hardware and software firms including Apple (www.apple.com), Google (www.google.com), Intel (www.intel.com), Microsoft (www.microsoft.com) and a growing number of start-ups, such as Nest Labs (www.nest.com), which makes smart thermostats and smoke detectors. Amazon, meanwhile, has opened a home automation store (www.amazon.com).

Home inspection

The International Association of Certified Home Inspectors is a trade group for home inspectors. It has members around the world (www.nachi.org).

The association maintains a database showing the life expectancy of home components, ranging from doors and windows to swimming pools and furnaces (www.nachi.org/life-expectancy.htm).

Infestation

The National Pest Management Association's Website includes information about insects and other household pests, as well as links to exterminators around the world (www.pestworld.org).

The University of Florida's Entomology and Nematology Department has detailed information about termites and other insects (http://entomology.ifas.ufl.edu).

Insurance

The U.S.-based Insurance Information Institute offers an exhaustive glossary of insurance terms and other resources (www.iii.org).

The International Association of Insurance Supervisors (IAIS) represents regulators in about 140 countries. The association's Website includes links to national regulators' sites (www.iaisweb.org).

In July 2013, the IAIS published a list of global systemically important insurers, which are the world's largest insurance companies. Of the nine companies on the list, the following offer property and casualty insurance and are a good starting point for home insurance.

▲ Allianz (www.allianz.com)

▲ American International Group (www.aig.com)

▲ Assicurazioni Generali (www.generali.com)

▲ Aviva (www.aviva.com)

▲ AXA (www.axa.com)

▲ MetLife (www.metlife.com)

▲ Ping An Insurance (www.pingan.com)

- Prudential plc (www.prudential.co.uk)

International brands

Appliances and electronics

- Bang & Olufsen; audiovisual equipment (www.bang-olufsen.com)

- Bosch; appliances (www.bosch.com)

- Carrier; heating, ventilation and air-conditioning systems (www.carrier.com)

- Crestron; lighting and home automation systems (www.crestron.com)

- Electrolux; appliances (www.electrolux.com)

- Fisher & Paykel; appliances (www.fisherpaykel.com)

- Fujitsu; air-conditioning systems (www.fujitsu.com)

- Haier; appliances (www.haier.net)

- Hitachi; audiovisual equipment and appliances (www.hitachi.com)

- Leviton; lighting and home automation systems (www.leviton.com)

- LG; audiovisual equipment and air-conditioning systems (www.lg.com)

- Lutron; lighting and home automation systems (www.lutron.com)

- Miele; appliances (www.miele.com)

- Mitsubishi Electric; audiovisual equipment and appliances (www.mitsubishielectric.com)

- Panasonic; audiovisual equipment and appliances (www.panasonic.com)

▲ Philips; audiovisual equipment and appliances (www.philips.com)

▲ Samsung; audiovisual equipment and appliances (www.samsung.com)

▲ Sharp; audiovisual equipment and appliances (www.sharp-world.com)

▲ Siemens; appliances, lighting and home automation systems (www.siemens.com)

▲ Smeg; appliances (www.smeg.com)

▲ Sony; audiovisual equipment (www.sony.com)

▲ Toshiba; audiovisual equipment (www.toshiba.com)

Bathrooms and Kitchens
▲ American Standard; sanitary ware (www.americanstandard.com)

▲ Blum; kitchen systems (www.blum.com)

▲ Boffi; kitchens and bathrooms (www.boffi.com)

▲ Bulthaup; kitchen systems (www.bulthaup.com)

▲ Duravit; sanitary ware (www.duravit.com)

▲ Gaggenau; kitchens and appliances (www.gaggenau.com)

▲ Hansgrohe; plumbing (www.hansgrohe.com)

▲ Kohler; sanitary ware (www.kohler.com)

▲ Leicht; kitchens (www.leicht.com)

▲ Moen; plumbing and sanitary ware (www.moen.com)

▲ Poggen Pohl; kitchens and appliances (www.poggenpohl.com)

- ▲ Snaidero; kitchens (www.snaidero.com)
- ▲ Sub-Zero/Wolf; kitchen appliances (www.subzero-wolf.com)
- ▲ Toto; sanitary ware (www.toto.com)
- ▲ Valcucine; kitchens (www.valcucine.com)
- ▲ Viking; appliances (www.vikingrange.com)

Floor and window coverings
- ▲ Armstrong; floor coverings (www.armstrong.com)
- ▲ Hunter Douglas; window coverings (www.hunterdouglas.com)

Furniture
- ▲ Armani Casa; furniture and accessories (www.armanicasa.com)
- ▲ Cassina; Le Corbusier and Frank Lloyd Wright furniture (www.cassina.com)
- ▲ Conran; furniture and accessories (www.conranshop.co.uk)
- ▲ Herman Miller; Eames and Aeron chairs (www.hermanmiller.com)
- ▲ Ikea; furniture and accessories (www.ikea.com)
- ▲ Ralph Lauren; furniture and accessories (www.ralphlauren.com)
- ▲ Roche Bobois; furniture (www.roche-bobois.com)
- ▲ Versace; furniture and accessories (www.versace.com)

L

Law

The Association of Real Estate License Law Officials operates a Website where consumers can check the credentials of real estate lawyers in 45 jurisdictions in Canada and the U.S. (www.arello.com).

Findlaw includes general legal information about U.S. and U.K. law, a section about real estate law and a "find a lawyer" service (www.findlaw.com).

The International Bar Association (IBA) is a professional organization comprising more than 50,000 legal practitioners and 200 law societies and bar associations. The IBA's Website includes links to national associations around the world, many of which have local directories (www.ibanet.org).

Many national law societies, including those of New Zealand (www.lawsociety.org.nz) and South Africa (www.lssa.org.za), publish guides to buying and selling a home. Written for consumers, these guides are a good place to learn about standard sale and purchase terms and procedures.

The International Union of Notaries operates a Website with links to national and regional notaries' associations (www.uinl.com).

Mondaq provides commentary on legal, regulatory and financial topics from leading law and accounting firms. This free service lets you subscribe to updates, which can be filtered by topic and region. There are also comparative legal guides to various countries (www.mondaq.com).

Nolo is a legal publisher specializing in do-it-yourself law in the United States. Nolo's Website includes calculators and other resources, as well as a dictionary that explains common legal concepts in plain English (www.nolo.com).

M

Maps

The David Rumsey Map Collection includes more than 49,000 historical maps and resources like aerial photos from around the world. The collection can provide useful clues about how a neighborhood or city has changed over time (www.davidrumsey.com).

Map services by Google (http://maps.google.com) and Microsoft (www.bing.com/maps) offer street-level images that can be helpful if you are investigating a neighborhood. Maps that organizations such as the National Geographic Society and the United States Geological Survey have produced using Google software are available at http://maps.google.com/gallery.

There is a growing amount of data available in interactive map format. For example:

▲ London property prices and related information are mapped at Illustreets (http://illustreets.co.uk). The National Library of Scotland and David Rumsey have overlaid a map of London from 1896 on Google maps, allowing you to see the location of homes, factories and public buildings (http://maps.nls.uk/geo/explore).

▲ For New York City, Vizynary (http://datawovn.com) offers an interactive map of property prices, Propertyshark (www.propertyshark.com) has a map of toxic sites and the city government (www.nyc.gov) operates a portal with neighborhood rat inspection data.

▲ For the Netherlands, the Waag Society has a map of nearly 10 million buildings color coded by their construction date (http://dev.citysdk.waag.org/buildings). You can also track the position of buses and trains in real time on a Google map (http://ovzoeker.nl).

▲ The Council on Foreign Relations operates a map showing global outbreaks of vaccine-preventable diseases, including measles, mumps, polio, rubella and whooping cough (www.cfr.org/interactives/GH_Vaccine_Map).

Media

Mainstream media
The outlets listed below publish or broadcast in English, cover international real estate and related news and operate Websites that are free, unless otherwise indicated. Many sites offer really simple syndication (RSS) subscriptions.

Bloomberg is a global financial wire service that is a good source of business and economic data (www.bloomberg.com).

The Economist is a weekly publication covering general and business news. Large sections of content are free, although full access requires a subscription. *The Economist* also publishes a quarterly Index of global house prices (www.cconomist.com).

The Financial Times is a London-based, global business newspaper. The weekend edition includes a global real estate section called House & Home. Much of the paper and its archives are free or free with registration (www.ft.com).

The New York Times (www.nytimes.com) and its international edition (www.inyt.com) cover business and general news and report on residential real estate around the world.

Reuters is a global wire service that covers general and business news (www.reuters.com).

The Wall Street Journal is a U.S.-based, global business newspaper. Sections of the newspaper and its archive are free, while full access requires a subscription (www.wsj.com).

Yahoo! News compiles stories from wire services, including Reuters, Agence France-Presse and the Associated Press (http://news.yahoo.com).

Following the local media in a city where you plan to purchase a home is an excellent way to learn about trends, problems and opportunities that could affect the value of your investment. A quick Google search will provide the names and URLs of local media outlets.

Social media

There are hundreds of social media outlets covering property, including Globaledge (www.globaledge.co.uk), Nubricks (www.nubricks.com), Property Magazine International (www.property-magazine.eu), Real Estate Japan (www.realestate.co.jp), World Property Channel (www.worldpropertychannel.com) and Zillow Blog (www.zillowblog.com).

Nuclear power

Information about the global nuclear industry is available from the industry's trade body, the World Nuclear Association. The association's Website includes links to national nuclear power groups and other resources (www.world-nuclear.org).

The NTI Nuclear Materials Security Index is an international survey of countries with nuclear materials that is conducted by the Nuclear Threat Initiative and the Economist Intelligence Unit. The index rates control and accounting procedures, response capabilities, on-site physical protection and other factors (www.ntiindex.org).

The Nuclear Information and Resource Service (www.nirs.org) and World Information Service on Energy (www.wiseinternational.org) are global antinuclear organizations.

Safecast is a sensor network for collecting and sharing radiation measurements. Safecast started in Japan after the Fukushima disaster in 2011 and now operates globally (www.safecast.org).

Property management

The Association of Residential Managing Agents is a trade group for residential property managers in England and Wales. The association's Website offers training and related information (http://arma.org.uk). In the United Kingdom, the Institute of Residential Property Management offers a professional qualification for property managers (www.irpm.org.uk).

The Building Owners and Managers Association International (BOMA) is a federation of building owners in the United States and 14 other countries. BOMA's focus is on commercial buildings, but its Website also includes information of interest to owners of residential real estate (www.boma.org).

The Institute of Real Estate Management is a trade association for property managers. Based in the United States and with affiliates in 13 countries, the institute offers accreditation, education and resources (www.1rem.org).

The National Apartment Association is a trade group for owners, managers and developers of multifamily housing. The association operates in the United States and Canada and offers information for people who are managing their own rental property (www.naahq.org).

R

Real estate agencies

The following companies have offices or franchises in multiple markets.

- ▲ CBRE (www.cbrc.com)
- ▲ Century 21 (www.century21global.com)
- ▲ Chesterton Humberts (www.chestertonhumberts.com)
- ▲ Christie's (www.christiesrealestate.com)
- ▲ Coldwell Banker (www.coldwellbanker.com)
- ▲ Colliers International (www.colliers.com)

- Cushman & Wakefield (www.cushmanwakefield.com)
- DTZ (www.dtz.com)
- Engel and Voelkers (www.engelvoelkers.com)
- ERA (www.era.com)
- Hamptons (www.hamptons.co.uk)
- Knight Frank (www.knightfrank.com)
- RE/MAX (http://global.remax.com)
- Savills (www.savills.com)
- Sotheby's (www.sothebysrealty.com)
- Vigers (www.vigers.com)

Real estate agents' associations

The International Consortium of Real Estate Associations is an association of national real estate groups (www.worldproperties.com).

Many countries have national organizations for real estate agents, such as the Fédération Nationale de l'Immobilier in France (www.fnaim.fr, French only), the National Association of Realtors–India (www.narindia.com) and the National Federation of Property Professionals in the United Kingdom (www.nfopp.co.uk).

National associations exist to promote the real estate industry and advance the interests of their members. Many associations engage in political lobbying and have a code of ethics to which members are expected to adhere. They also compile statistics and produce research reports.

Real estate listings

To find international property listings, start with the real estate agencies and the media sites listed above.

No property site offers comprehensive global listings—all have strengths in some countries and weaknesses in others. That said, Global Property Guide (www.globalpropertyguide.com), World Estate (www.world-estate.com) and World Properties (www.worldproperties.com) are worth a look.

An Internet search for "country name" or "city name" and "real estate listings" will provide information about local developers, Internet listing sites and real estate agents.

Buyers in the United States have access to some of the most advanced online services, including Redfin (www.redfin.com), Trulia (www.trulia.com) and Zillow (www.zillow.com).

Renovations

Toolbase.org is a Website maintained by the National Association of Home Builders in the United States. While the site is written for an American audience, it has useful links and information about renovations, building and construction techniques, energy efficiency, universal design and other topics (www.toolbase.org).

Research and statistics

Aggregator, crowd-sourced and data-mining services
City-Data has data about property prices, crime rates, income levels and many other topics for cities in Canada and the United States (www.city-data.com).

CrimeReports provides information about crime rates in neighborhoods in Canada, the United Kingdom and the United States (www.crimereports.com).

Foursquare offers an app and crowd-sourced reviews—mainly of restaurants and bars—in 20 countries. While Foursquare won't directly help you find a home, it will give you a sense of what's going on in your neighborhood (http://foursquare.com).

Numbeo is a crowd-sourced database covering the cost of living, housing and other information in more than 4,400 cities worldwide (www.numbeo.com).

Yelp offers an app and crowd-sourced reviews of restaurants, shops, bars, parks, museums and more in over 20 countries (www.yelp.com).

Financial institutions
Financial institutions produce research that usually falls into two categories: macroeconomic analysis and reports on property developers as investment targets. You may need to be a client to obtain these reports.

- ▲ AllianceBernstein (www.alliancebernstein.com)

- ▲ Barclays Bank (www.barclays.com)

- ▲ BNY Mellon (www.bnymellon.com)

- ▲ Citibank (www.citibank.com)

- ▲ CLSA (www.clsa.com)

- ▲ Credit Suisse (www.credit-suisse.com)

- ▲ Goldman Sachs (www.gs.com)

- ▲ HSBC (www.hsbc.com)

- ▲ J.P. Morgan (www.jpmorgan.com)

- ▲ Merrill Lynch (www.ml.com)

- ▲ Morgan Stanley (www.ms.com)

- ▲ PIMCO (www.pimco.com)

▲ Royal Bank of Scotland (www.rbs.com)

▲ Standard Chartered Bank (www.standardchartered.com)

▲ UBS (www.ubs.com)

Institutes and others
Credit rating agencies, including Fitch (www.fitchratings.com), Moody's (www.moodys.com) and Standard & Poor's (www.standardandpoors.com) provide a range of research and data.

The Economist Intelligence Unit produces a range of paid and free research (www.eiu.com).

Eurostat is operated by the European Commission and provides housing statistics and other information (http://epp.eurostat.ec.europa.eu).

The Lincoln Institute of Land Policy publishes books, reports and other materials about the use, regulation and taxation of land (www.lincolninst.edu).

McKinsey & Company is a management consultancy that produces articles and research on a range of property related topics (www.mckinsey.com).

National, state and local governments as well as trade associations for real estate agents, developers, lenders and other groups produce a range of statistics and data.

The Urban Land Institute is a U.S.-based nonprofit organization that conducts research and publishes materials on real estate-related topics around the world (www.uli.org).

The World Bank publishes research and statistics on economic, social and environmental issues (www.worldbank.org).

Real estate agencies
Many of the real estate agencies listed above produce research material. While much of the material is written for investors and corporate

end-users, it can be a good source of information about market conditions and emerging trends. Some sites require registration.

S

Software

Architecture and design

Design software comes in three variations. The first is professional computer-aided design (CAD) software, like the packages sold by Autodesk (http://autodesk.com). This software is powerful and has a steep learning curve, which may be hard to justify if you are only involved in one or two projects. Autodesk also offers software rental plans, free viewers and mobile apps, and a free Web-based program called Homestyler (www.homestyler.com) that lets you create floor plans in two and three dimensions.

Second is consumer-oriented software from IMSI/Design (www.imsidesign.com), Punch! Software (www.punchsoftware.com) and others. Software in this category is less expensive, less sophisticated and easier to learn than professional products. Android and iOS versions are available for use on tablets.

Third, is free software like Sketchup, a versatile, three-dimensional modeling package. A basic version of Sketchup is free for computers using the Windows or Mac operating systems. A professional version and video tutorials are also available (www.sketchup.com).

Floorplanner is a Web-based design tool that lets you create two- and three-dimensional room layouts and home designs (www.floorplanner.com). The basic program is free; a premium, paid service provides extra functionality. Ikea offers online design tools that may be useful if you are planning to use that company's furniture (www.ikea.com).

Decoration

The Internet is a useful source of tools for generating color schemes. Paint manufacturers such as Dow Chemical operate sites with tools to help you choose a color theme (www.paintquality.com). Intended primarily for Web designers, Colorotate includes useful tools for understanding and working with color (www.colorotate.com). Pinterest can be useful for inspiration and for keeping your plans organized (www.pinterest.com).

Kuler lets you build color schemes and send color information to other Adobe products, such as Illustrator, InDesign and Photoshop (http://kuler.adobe.com). Colr.org is similar to Kuler, but easier to use (www.colr.org).

Colorjive lets you upload a photo of a room and virtually "paint" it. A premium version, which allows you to store images online, is also available (http://colorjive.com).

The myhomeideas blog has a calculator that lets you enter the dimensions of a room and determine how much paint, carpet or tile you'll need (www.myhomeideas.com/project-calculator).

Zillow Digs lets you see decoration ideas sorted by room, color scheme, price range and popularity among other users (www.zillow.com/digs).

Surveying

The Cadastral Template Website offers profiles of the land surveying systems in more than 40 countries (www.cadastraltemplate.org).

The International Federation of Surveyors is a global trade association. The federation's Website includes links to national surveying organizations around the world (www.fig.net).

T

Tax

Large accounting firms, including Deloitte (www.deloitte.com), Ernst & Young (www.ey.com), Grant Thornton (www.grantthornton.com), KPMG (www.kpmg.com) and PricewaterhouseCoopers (www.pwc.com), produce free real estate guides and bulletins containing useful information about local tax and accounting issues. These firms also produce tax guides for expatriates.

The International Federation of Accountants is a global professional organization. The federation's Website includes links to associations in 129 countries and territories (www.ifac.org).

National governments in your origin and destination countries can be a useful starting point. For example, the Spanish government provides tax information in English at www.agenciatributaria.gob.es. The British government, meanwhile, offers tax and other information for U.K. nationals living in Spain at www.gov.uk/living-in-spain.

Timeshare

The American Resort Development Association is the timeshare industry's trade association in the United States (www.arda.org).

The Resort Development Organization is the timeshare industry's trade body in the United Kingdom (www.rdo.org).

The Timeshare Users Group is an online forum for people who own timeshare units (www.tug2.net).

The U.S. Federal Trade Commission offers information for consumers about buying and selling timeshares and vacation plans (www.consumer.ftc.gov).

Title

The American Land Title Association is the national trade group for the title insurance industry in the United States. The association's Website includes information for consumers and a directory of title insurance companies (www.alta.org).

Translation

Google Translate lets you enter a word, a paragraph or an entire Website, which it then translates. While the site is no substitute for a professional translator, it will give you a general idea of the original text's meaning. It's fast, free and integrated with Google's Chrome browser (www.translate.google.com).

The International Federation of Translators represents more than 100 professional associations, which, in turn, represent some 80,000 translators in 55 countries (www.fit-ift.org).

U

Universal design

Buildings that incorporate universal design are aesthetically pleasing and usable by the greatest number of people possible, regardless of their age or ability.

The Center for Universal Design at NC State University's College of Design has information for people who are building or renovating a home, including floor plans, checklists and design suggestions (www.ncsu.edu/ncsu/design/cud). *A Practical Guide to Universal Home Design* is available from the Iowa Program for Assistive Technology (www.iowaat.org/udbooklet).

W

Water

The World Health Organization offers detailed biological and chemical information about drinking water (www.who.int/water_sanitation_health).

Weather

Tropical Storm Risk combines the efforts of the British Meteorological Office and several insurance and reinsurance companies to map and predict the progress of storms worldwide (www.tropicalstormrisk.com).

The U.S.–based Cooperative Institute for Meteorological Satellite Studies offers a similar service (http://cimss.ssec.wisc.edu/tropic2).

The World Meteorological Organization (WMO) is a United Nations agency. The WMO's Website includes links to member organizations around the world (www.wmo.int).

NOTES

Where to Buy?

1. "New Research from Oxford Quantifies the Impacts of 'Safe Haven' Investing on London House Prices," University of Oxford, January 13, 2014.
2. Alois Stutzer and Bruno Frey, "Stress that Doesn't Pay Off: The Commuting Paradox," IZA Discussion Paper No. 1278, September 2004.
3. Jane E. Brody, "Commuting's Hidden Cost," Well, October 28, 2013.
4. "Michelin Guide Tokyo Yokohama Shonan 2014: 6 New Two Stars and 15 New One Stars Restaurants!," Michelin.com, December 3, 2013.
5. Allison Berry and Randy Carpenter, "Walkability and the Risk of Mortgage Default," Community Builders, March 25, 2014.

Why Buy Abroad?

1. Grace Wong Bucchianeri, "The American Dream or The American Delusion? The Private and External Benefits of Homeownership," Knowledge@Wharton, June 2, 2009.
2. Naoki Nakazato, Ulrich Schimmack and Shigehiro Oishi, "Effect of Changes in Living Conditions on Well-Being: A Prospective Top-Down Bottom-Up Model," Social Indicators Research, January 1, 2011, 115–35.
3. "Research Backs Pay-per-Use Spending," *Chicago Tribune*, July 18, 2003.
4. "Holiday Homes Arson Anniversary," BBC, December 12, 2009.
5. Nichola Saminather, "Australia Gold Coast Homes at 50% Below 2010 Lure Buyers," Bloomberg, September 5, 2013.
6. Paul Supawanich, "Why Ridesharing is a Way Bigger Deal for Suburban Seniors than Urban Millennials," The Atlantic Cities, April 23, 2014.
7. "Moving to Maputo," *The Economist*, June 18, 2013.
8. "Fort McMurray, Alberta, Labour Market Information," Regional Municipality of Wood Buffalo, October 30, 2013.
9. Sanat Vallikappen and Pooja Thakur, "Yangon More Expensive Than NYC Sparking Boom: Real Estate," Bloomberg, July 30, 2013.
10. Lynne O'Donnell, "Subsidies Prop up Kabul's Property Market as Troops Prepare to Withdraw," *South China Morning Post*, November 20, 2013.
11. Liau Y-Sing and Yumi Teso, "Cheaper Diving Lures Singaporeans as Ringgit at 1998 Low," Bloomberg, September 5, 2013.

12. Daren Blomquist, "Zombie Foreclosures: The Vacant Dead," RealtyTrac, March 12, 2014.

13. "Madrid's 300,000 Vacant Homes Spawn Black Market in Lodging," *South China Morning Post*, February 24, 2014.

14. Frank Ford, April Hirsh and Kathryn Clover, "The Role of Investors in the One-to-Three Family REO Market: The Case of Cleveland," Joint Center for Housing Studies, Harvard University, 2013, 8–9.

15. Richard Florida, "Why Gayborhoods Matter," The Atlantic Cities, February 13, 2014.

16. Christian L. Wright, "Stepping in for Foreign Apartment Owners," *The New York Times*, March 7, 2014.

17. "Lumping It," *The Economist*, February 15, 2014.

18. Roseann Lake, "All the Shengnu Ladies," Salon, March 12, 2012.

Agents

1. G.M. Filisko, "Understanding Real Estate Representation," Houselogic, 2013.

2. "Cuba Expands List of Allowed Private Sector Jobs," FRANCE 24, September 26, 2013.

3. Ola Jingryd, "Impartial Legal Counsel in Real Estate Conveyances: The Swedish Broker and the Latin Notary," Building and Real Estate Economics, School of Architecture and the Built Environment, Royal Institute of Technology, 2012.

4. Harold W. Elder, Edward A. Baryla and Leonard V. Zumpano, "Buyer Brokers: Do They Make a Difference? Their Influence on Selling Price and Search Duration," *Real Estate Economics* 28, no. 2, 2000, 337–62.

5. Garth Turner, "The Trouble with BRAs," Greater Fool, November 13, 2011.

6. Steven D. Levitt and Chad Syverson, "Market Distortions When Agents Are Better Informed: The Value of Information in Real Estate Transactions," National Bureau of Economic Research, January 2005.

7. Dan Ariely, *Predictably Irrational: The Hidden Forces That Shape Our Decisions,* HarperCollins, 2009, 8.

8. Graham Norwood, "Sold on the Idea?," *Financial Times*, May 19, 2012.

9. "Home Buying and Selling: A Market Study," Office of Fair Trading, February 2010, 220.

10. B. Douglas Bernheim and Jonathan Meer, "How Much Value Do Real Estate Brokers Add? A Case Study," Stanford Institute for Economic Policy Research, 2007.

11. Igal Hendel, Aviv Nevo and François Ortalo-Magné, "The Relative Performance of Real Estate Marketing Platforms: MLS versus FSBOMadison.com," The Center for the Study of Industrial Organization at Northwestern University, 2007.

Ownership and Property Rights

1. *The American Bar Association Guide to Home Ownership*, American Bar Association, 2013.
2. R.A. Simons and Ron Throupe, "Debundling Property Rights for Contaminated Properties: Valuing the Opportunity Cost of the Right to Sell, Using Cumulative Options," *International Real Estate Review* 15, no. 2, 2012, 235.
3. "Legislation & Policy: Mineral Ownership," British Geological Survey, 2013.
4. Paula Eales and Christopher Page, "Manorial Rights—Register Them Or Risk Losing Them!," Mondaq/Charles Russell LLP, July 16, 2013.
5. Michelle Conlin and Brian Grow, "Special Report: U.S. Builders Hoard Mineral Rights Under New Homes," Reuters, October 9, 2013.
6. "Shoreline Management Plans—Sea Level Rise & Coastal Erosion," The Crown Estate, January 18, 2010, 1–2.
7. "Myths: Public Ownership of the Oceans," Marine Conservation Agreements, The Nature Conservancy, 2013.
8. "Land Management Bureau—FAQs," Department of Environment and Natural Resources, Government of the Philippines, July 31, 2013.
9. "Crown Land Administration Division—Private Moorage Crown Land Tenure Program," Ministry of Forests, Lands and Natural Resource Operations, Province of British Columbia, January 25, 2013.
10. Angus Evers, "House Rules: Property Law and Riverside Homes," *Financial Times*, December 10, 2013.
11. Julian Hattem, "EPA Looks to Clarify Regulations on Streams," The Hill, September 17, 2013.
12. "Torrens Title System," The State of Victoria, July 12, 2013.
13. Shaun Watchie Perry, "Outline of the Torrens Act," Law Trends & News, August 2005.
14. "Title Insurance: A Comprehensive Overview," American Land Title Association, April 26, 2005.
15. David Lazarus, "Title Fees Are Hard to Swallow When Refinancing Mortgage," *Los Angeles Times*, September 16, 2011.
16. "Registering Property," *Doing Business*, The World Bank Group, 2013.

Negotiating

1. Jim Thomas, *Negotiate to Win: The 21 Rules for Successful Negotiating,* HarperBusiness, 2006, 240.

2. Jeswald W. Salacuse, "Negotiating: The Top Ten Ways That Culture Can Affect Your Negotiation," *Ivey Business Journal,* October 2004.

3. Richard D. Lewis, *When Cultures Collide: Leading across Cultures: A Major New Edition of the Global Guide,* Nicholas Brealey International, 2005, 169.

Demographics

1. "Datagraphic: Snapshot of Urban Western Europe in 2020," Euromonitor International, January 9, 2014.

2. Noboru Hashizume, "The Population Issue of Rural Regions in Japan," Policy Research Institute, Ministry of Agriculture, Forestry and Fisheries, Government of Japan, 2005, 4.

3. "Population Ages 65 and above (% of Total)," The World Bank, 2014.

4. "China's Gender Imbalance Alleviated but Still Grave," Xinhua News Agency, January 22, 2013.

5. "World Population Prospects, The 2012 Revision, Highlights and Advance Tables," United Nations Department of Economic and Social Affairs, 2013.

6. "Global Aging Index," Oxford Institute of Aging, 2013.

7. *Aging in the Twenty-First Century: A Celebration and A Challenge,* United Nations Population Fund, 2012, 13.

8. "Africa and Asia to Lead Urban Population Growth in the next Four Decades," Department of Economic and Social Affairs, United Nations, April 5, 2012.

9. Kaid Benfield, "Ten Things Planners Need to Know about Demographics and the Future Real Estate Market," Switchboard, Natural Resources Defense Council, January 30, 2014.

10. Matt Phillips, "Could Cupertino Go Bust Like Detroit?," The Atlantic Cities, February 5, 2014.

11. Katharine Q. Seelye, "Detroit Population Down 25 Percent, Census Finds," *The New York Times,* March 22, 2011.

12. Nathan Bomey and John Gallagher, "How Detroit Went Broke: The Answers May Surprise You—and Don't Blame Coleman Young," *Detroit Free Press,* September 15, 2013.

13. Steve Pardo, "Detroit Plans Mass Water Shutoffs over $260M in Delinquent Bills," *The Detroit News*, March 21, 2014.
14. Chastity Pratt Dawsey, "Detroit Public Schools' Scores Improve, but Still at Bottom on Nation's Report Card; Poverty a Factor," *Detroit Free Press*, December 19, 2013.
15. Corey Williams, "Detroit Crime, Including Homicides, Drops in 2013," Associated Press/ABC News, January 2, 2014.
16. Christine Ferretti, "Task Force to Compile Database in Detroit Blight Fight," *The Detroit News*, November 25, 2013.
17. Sarah Goodyear, "A 140-Acre Forest Is About to Materialize in the Middle of Detroit," The Atlantic Cities, October 25, 2013.
18. Aaron Smith, "Detroit Is Going Dark," CNNMoney, July 19, 2013.
19. Chris Christoff, "Abandoned Dogs Roam Detroit in Packs as Humans Dwindle," Bloomberg, August 21, 2013.
20. Laura Berman, "Death (certificates) Took Holiday in Wake of Bankruptcy Filing," *The Detroit News*, August 29, 2013.

Risk Factors

1. Sandra McCulloch, "B.C. Had No Authority to Make Oak Bay Homeowner Pay for Archeological Digs, Court Rules," *The Vancouver Sun*, June 5, 2013.
2. Christopher Reynolds, "Ancient Musqueam Burial Ground in Marpole to Remain Free of Development," *The Vancouver Sun*, September 30, 2012.
3. Kamila Hinkson, "400 Year Old Skeleton of Aboriginal Woman Found in Sarnia Backyard Costs Couple $5,000," *The Toronto Star*, June 15, 2013.
4. "Public Health Assessment, Libby Asbestos Site, Libby, Lincoln County, Montana," Agency for Toxic Substances and Disease Registry, United States Government, May 15, 2003.
5. Maryn McKenna, "Censorship Doesn't Just Stifle Speech—It Can Spread Disease," Wired, August 21, 2013.
6. Nick Madigan, "South Florida Faces Ominous Prospects from Rising Waters," *The New York Times*, November 10, 2013.
7. Mark Weisleder, "To Avoid a Lawsuit It is Best to Let Buyers Know Whether a Death Has Occurred on the Property," *The Toronto Star*, February 15, 2013.
8. Herbert J. Cohen, "Did the Seller Die in the House?," Realtor.com, 2013.
9. "History of Blackheath," Lewisham Council, 2013.

10. Andrew Osborn, "British Experts Say They Have Found London's Lost Black Death Graves," Reuters, March 30, 2014.
11. Sophie Yu, "Built on Ignorance," *South China Morning Post*, July 16, 2011.
12. "Leaky Condo Crisis Far from Over," *The Vancouver Sun*, July 9, 2008.
13. Sarah Lyall, "In Ruined Apartments, Symbol of Ireland's Fall," *The New York Times*, September 3, 2012.
14. Paul Melia, "Council Has Paid out €3m Dealing with Priory Hall Fallout," Independent.ie, August 6, 2013.
15. "The Boom in Binational Divorces: Money in Misery," *The Economist*, February 5, 2009.
16. Michael Glenn Easter, "Are You Living in a Former Meth Lab?," scientificamerican.com, April 29, 2010.
17. "Iran, Pakistan, Other South Asian Countries Seeing Rise in Meth-Production Labs," *The Plain Dealer*, May 19, 2012.
18. "Extent of Corruption in Countries Around the World Tied to Earthquake Fatalities," University of Colorado Boulder, January 12, 2011.
19. Claire Berlinski, "1 Million Dead in 30 Seconds," *City Journal*, Summer 2011.
20. "Report on the 2010 Chilean Earthquake and Tsunami Response," The American Red Cross Multi-Disciplinary Team, March 18, 2011.
21. "How Would Your Home Stand Up?," Natural Resources Canada, December 30, 2002.
22. Steve Stecklow, Babak Dehghanpisheh and Yeganeh Torbati, "Assets of the Ayatollah 1. Land Grab," Reuters, November 11, 2013.
23. Dominic Adams, "Lost in the Flames: More than 1,600 Arsons Scar Flint's Landscape," *The Flint Journal*, March 25, 2013.
24. "Which Coastal Cities Are at Highest Risk of Damaging Floods? New Study Crunches the Numbers," World Bank Group, August 19, 2013.
25. "The 'Foreign Exchange Trap' Shakes Up Real Estate in Argentina and Uruguay," Knowledge@Wharton, October 17, 2012.
26. "Nigeria Property Boom Offers Rewards If You Know What You're Doing," *South China Morning Post*, September 18, 2013.
27. Steven Malanga, "The Indebted States of America," *City Journal*, Summer 2013.
28. Russ Banham, "Cities on the Brink," *CFO Magazine*, October 2013.
29. Henry Sanderson, "China Auditor Finds Irregularities in $1.7 Trillion Local Government Debt," Bloomberg, June 27, 2011.

30. Graeme Wearden, "Greece and Portugal Boost Eurozone," *The Guardian*, April 23, 2014.
31. Liz Alderman and Landon Thomas Jr, "Taking a Risk, Investors Snap Up Once-Shunned Greek Debt," *The New York Times*, April 10, 2014.
32. "All-Transactions House Price Index for New York (NYSTHPI), Quarterly, Not Seasonally Adjusted, 1975-01-01 to 2013-04-01," Federal Reserve Bank of St. Louis, September 2, 2013.
33. "CONPLAN 3551-09," United States Northern Command, United States Government, August 13, 2009, 5.
34. Jonel Aleccia, "Measles Outbreak Tied to Texas Megachurch Sickens 21," NBC News, August 27, 2013.
35. Adam Forman, "Caution Ahead: Overdue Investments for New York's Aging Infrastructure," Center for an Urban Future, March 2014.
36. Emily Badger, "The Map that Reveals 5,900 Natural Gas Leaks Under Washington, D.C.," *The Atlantic Cities*, January 17, 2014.
37. Joanna M. Foster, "Methane Is Popping Up All Over Boston," Green Blog, November 20, 2012.
38. James West, "How Dangerous Are the Gas Pipes Under Your City?," *The Atlantic Cities*, March 21, 2014.
39. Robert B. Jackson, "Natural Gas Pipeline Leaks Across Washington, D.C.," Environmental Science & Technology, January 16, 2014.
40. Suzanne Daley and Nicholas Kulish, "Germany Fights Population Drop," *The New York Times*, August 13, 2013.
41. Angela Che, "Airport Building Plan Set to Take Off," *South China Morning Post*, July 21, 2012.
42. "Soil Pollution Poisons More than Farmland," China.org.cn, March 10, 2011.
43. Abhay Kumar, "Lead in New Decorative Paints," IPEN, 2009.
44. Robert P. Clickner, "National Survey of Lead and Allergens in Housing, Volume I: Analysis of Lead Hazards," Prepared for the Office of Lead Hazard Control, U.S. Department of Housing and Urban Development by Westat, Inc., April 18, 2001, 7.
45. "Beetle-Free Certificate," Smith Tabata Buchanan Boyes, 2010.
46. "Chagas Disease," Centers for Disease Control and Prevention, July 19, 2013.
47. Raphaël Béra and Fiona Larcombe, "House Rules: Property Law and Tax Breaks in France," *Financial Times*, October 16, 2013.
48. "Money Laundering Awareness Handbook for Tax Examiners and Tax Auditors," OECD, 2009.

49. Charlotta Eriksson, "Cardiovascular and Metabolic Effects of Long-Term Traffic Noise Exposure," Karolinska Institutet, 2012.

50. Sarah Floud, "Exposure to Aircraft and Road Traffic Noise and Associations with Heart Disease and Stroke in Six European Countries: A Cross-Sectional Study," *Environmental Health* 12, no. 1, October 16, 2013, 89.

51. "World Nuclear Power Reactors," World Nuclear Association, April 1, 2014.

52. Shinhye Kang and Sungwoo Park, "S. Korea Issues Power Shortage Alert amid Nuclear Stoppages," Bloomberg, June 3, 2013.

53. U.S. Attorney's Office, "Former Indian Point Supervisor Charged in White Plains Federal Court with Falsifying Records to Conceal Information from the Nuclear Regulatory Commission," U.S. Department of Justice, July 23, 2013.

54. Laurence Iliff, "Mexico Weighs Opening Up Wider to Foreign Property Buyers," *The Wall Street Journal*, July 9, 2013.

55. "FIRB: Acquisitions Exempt from Approval (residential)," Foreign Investment Review Board, Government of Australia, 2013.

56. Kazi Stastna, "Real Estate Rules Don't Discriminate against Foreigners," CBC News, March 19, 2012.

57. Claudia Calleja, "Stop Treating Expats like Cash Cows" Timesofmalta.com, May 10, 2013.

58. "Canada, U.A.E. Agree to Do Away with Visitor Visas," CTV News, April 2, 2013.

59. Toluse Olorunnipa, "Flood Insurance Jumping Sevenfold Depresses U.S. Home Values," Bloomberg, October 24, 2013.

60. Charles Mackay, Martin S Fridson and Joseph de la Vega, *Extraordinary Popular Delusions and the Madness of Crowds*, John Wiley & Sons, 1996, 115.

61. Joseph Foley, "International Focus: Argentina Plans New Social Housing on Railway Land," *The Guardian*, February 1, 2013.

62. Kate Briquelet, "Upper West Side Condo Has Separate Entrances for Rich and Poor," *New York Post*, August 18, 2013.

63. Tom Rawstorne, "Apartheid UK: How a Controversial Law to Integrate Social Housing in New Developments Is Creating Mini-Ghettos," Mail Online, August 1, 2008.

64. "2013 Report Card for America's Infrastructure," The American Society of Civil Engineers, 2014.

65. Jian Xie and Fasheng Li, "Overview of the Current Situation on Brownfield Remediation and Redevelopment in China," World Bank Group, September 1, 2010, 4.

66. "China's Leading Steelmaker Halts Production in Capital to Cut Pollution," *People's Daily*, January 13, 2011.

67. Cecilia Wong and Andreas Schulze Bäing, "Brownfield Residential Redevelopment in England: What Happens to the Most Deprived Neighborhoods?," Joseph Rowntree Foundation, June 2010.

68. Kazuaki Nagata, "Tsukiji Panel Slammed during Final Meeting," *The Japan Times*, July 28, 2008.

69. Juliette Derry and Hans van der Wal, "New Zealand Building and Environment Issues: Rebuilding Triggers Contamination Worries," Mondaq/Duncan Cotterill Lawyers, October 2, 2013.

70. Alexander Nazaryan, "Love Hurts," *Newsweek*, October 18, 2013.

71. "Current Status of the Brownfields Issue in Japan Interim Report," Expert Studying Group for Countermeasures against Brownfields, Ministry of the Environment, Government of Japan, March 2007.

72. John Bacon, "Condos Collapse into Sinkhole near Disney World," *USA Today*, August 12, 2013.

73. "Country Comparison: Total Fertility Rate," The World Factbook, Central Intelligence Agency, United States Government, 2013.

74. "Formosan Subterranean Termites—Fact Sheet," BASF, April 19, 2007.

75. "The Top 10 Causes of Death," World Health Organization, July 2013.

76. "Roads Kill Map," Pulitzer Center, August 12, 2013.

77. "State Traffic Safety Information for Year 2010," National Highway Traffic Safety Administration, United States Government, 2014.

78. Cahal Milmo, "Made in Britain: The Toxic Tetraethyl Lead Used in Fuel Sold to World's Poorest," *The Independent*, January 14, 2013.

79. "Progress on Sanitation and Drinking-Water: 2013 Update," World Health Organization, 2013.

80. Jing Gong, "The Dirty Truth about Water Quality," *Caixin*, May 7, 2012.

81. "The Internment of the Japanese during World War II," Historica Foundation, 2013.

The Buying Process

1. "Guide to Buying Property in Italy," Knight Frank, 2013.

2. "The Guide to Buying and Selling Property in Italy," FIAIP, 2009.

3. "Get Smart before Buying and Selling Property," The Real Estate Agents Authority, September 2013.

4. "First Home Buyers Guide—Making an Offer," Kiwibank, 2013.

5. "Home Buying and Selling: A Market Study," Office of Fair Trading, February 2010, 221.

6. "A Guide for the First-Time Homebuyer," New Jersey Housing & Mortgage Finance Agency, November 2013.

7. "Steps to Buying a Home," New Jersey Department of Banking and Insurance, July 2013.

Home Inspections

1. "Re-Sale of Leaky Condos: Did the Buyer Know?," Canada Mortgage and Housing Corporation, December 5, 2003.

2. "Property Surveys in France," French-Property.com, 2013.

3. "Re-Sale of Leaky Condos: Did the Buyer Know?".

Land Surveys

1. "Cadastral Template," Department of Geomatics of the University of Melbourne, 2008.

2. Suzanne Daley, "Who Owns This Land? In Greece, Who Knows?," *The New York Times*, May 26, 2013.

3. "Survey—Do I Need One?," Landsurveyors.com, 2010.

4. "Survey Exception," Practical Law, 2013.

5. "RICS Joins the International Property Measurement Standards Coalition (IPMSC) at World Bank Meeting in Washington DC," Royal Institution of Chartered Surveyors, May 8, 2013.

New versus Old

1. "InterNACHI's Standard Estimated Life Expectancy Chart for Homes," International Association of Certified Home Inspectors, Inc., 2014.

2. Jay McKenzie, "Buying Green Equals Buying Smart," Realtor.com, August 20, 2013.

3. Christopher Dillon, *Landed China*, Dillon Communications Limited, 2013, 217.

4. Jed Kolko, "American Homes By Decade," *Forbes*, May 2, 2013.

5. Lew Sichelman, "New Home Warranty Can Keep Investment on Solid Footing," *Los Angeles Times*, April 5, 2013.

   6. "Our Members—AGEMI," The International Housing and Home Warranty Association, 2011.

Buying Off the Plan

   1. "Mitsubishi Estate Seeks Damages from Kajima over Botched Condo," Japan Today/Reuters, February 9, 2014.

   2. "Confronting Zombie Subdivisions," At Lincoln House, January 22, 2014.

   3. Brenda Goh, "Far East Buyers Beware in London Property Rush," Reuters, May 20, 2012.

   4. Nick Lockhart, "Buying 'Off The Plan' The Good, The Bad & The Ugly," MRD Partners, December 20, 2008.

   5. Hilary Osborne, "One Hyde Park: A Good Address, but One Doesn't Actually Live There," *The Guardian*, September 27, 2013.

   6. "Council Tax: Empty Homes Premium," Government of the United Kingdom, May 7, 2013.

   7. Robert Booth, "London Council Plans to Fine 'Buy-to-Leave' Investors," *The Guardian*, March 31, 2014.

   8. Ruben Esquitino, "Benidorm's Prized High-Rise Tower Becomes a Symbol of Incompetence," *El Pais,* July 26, 2013.

   9. Stephen Burgen, "In Tempo: Towering Testament to Madness of Spain's Construction Boom," *The Guardian*, July 17, 2013.

Custom-built Homes

   1. Sandy Keenan, "The Passive House: Sealed for Freshness," *The New York Times*, August 14, 2013.

   2. Kashmir Hill, "When 'Smart Homes' Get Hacked: I Haunted A Complete Stranger's House Via The Internet," *Forbes*, July 26, 2013.

   3. "Energy Smart Meters Are a Threat to Privacy, Says Watchdog," *The Guardian*, July 1, 2012.

   4. Vince Chadwick, "Smart Meter Data Shared Far and Wide," *The Age*, September 23, 2012.

   5. Shane Shamal, "A Guide to Foreign Investing in Sri Lanka," Mondaq/Lanka Law Firm, May 11, 2013.

Paying for Your Home

1. "Moving to Brazil," HSBC Brasil, 2013.
2. "Opening a Bank Account in France," France.fr, August 20, 2013.
3. "Affordable Home Ownership Schemes," Government of the United Kingdom, February 3, 2014.
4. "Non-Resident Property Owners," BDO Dunwoody LLP, 2008.

Mortgages

1. Michael Lea, "International Comparison of Mortgage Product Offerings," Research Institute for Housing America, 2010, 18.
2. Chris Sorensen, "Another Way Americans Get Better Deals: Cheap, Flexible, 30-Year Mortgages," *Macleans*, March 30, 2013.
3. Karolina Tagaris and Natalia Drozdiak, "Spirit of Boom-Time Mortgages Lives on in Europe," Yahoo News/Reuters, August 18, 2013.
4. Lea, "International Comparison of Mortgage Product Offerings," 26.
5. Richard Green and Susan Wachter, "The American Mortgage in Historical and International Context," *Journal of Economic Perspectives* 19, no. 4, Fall 2005, 93.
6. Huma Qureshi, "Sharia-Compliant Mortgages Are Here—and They're Not Just for Muslims," *The Guardian*, June 29, 2008.
7. Lisa Prevost, "A New Weapon for Bidding Wars," *The New York Times*, March 20, 2014.

Insurance

1. Emre Peker, "Turkey Tightens Mandatory Quake-Insurance Rules, Hurriyet Says," *BusinessWeek*, May 14, 2012.
2. Mariana Osihn, "Italy Moves on Disaster Loss Database," United Nations Office for Disaster Risk Reduction, March 25, 2013.
3. Harvey W. Rubin, *Dictionary of Insurance Terms*, Fourth edition, Barron's Educational Series, 2000, 147.
4. Toluse Olorunnipa, "Flood Insurance Jumping Sevenfold Depresses U.S. Home Values," Bloomberg, October 24, 2013.
5. "How to Buy Overseas Property Safely," Association of International Property Professionals Ltd., 2013, 41.

Tax

1. "Stamp Duty Rates and Computation," Inland Revenue Authority of Singapore, February 21, 2014.
2. "How a Levy Based on Location Values Could Be the Perfect Tax," *Financial Times*, September 27, 2013.
3. "Spanish Nonresident Tax," Advoco.es, 2013.
4. "Membership," Tourism Whistler Member Website, 2014.
5. "Fiscal Policy and Income Inequality," International Monetary Fund, January 22, 2014.
6. "Filing and Reporting Requirements," Canada Revenue Agency, Government of Canada, December 8, 2008.
7. "Substantial Presence Test," Internal Revenue Service, United States Government, February 13, 2014.
8. Steven Bourassa, Donald Haurin and Patric Hendershott, "Mortgage Interest Deductions and Homeownership: An International Survey," Swiss Finance Institute, February 9, 2012, 14.
9. "Extension of the Annual Tax on Enveloped Dwellings," Mondaq/Deloitte, March 19, 2014.

INDEX

To minimize duplication, the section headings but not the individual entries from the "Information Sources" chapter are included in this index. For example, the index entry for Microsoft refers to the company's appearance on page 82. Microsoft also appears in the Software section of "Information Sources" on page 262.

accountants, 38, 59, 217, 219, 222, 224, 234, 264
Adelaide, 20
Aldrich, Daniel, 111
Afghanistan, 54, 58, 127
aging, 79, 82
air-conditioning, 118, 157, 181
air pollution, 85, 103, 116, 120, 126–7, 239
air rights, 65
Airbnb, 28
airports, 28, 102, 109–10, 115, 148, 174, 236
Alameda County, 32
Alaska, 100, 107
Alberta, 34, 165
Algeria, 127
Ambraseys, Nicholas, 100
American Association of Residential Mortgage Regulators, 192
American High-Performance Buildings Coalition, 181
American Homes 4 Rent, 36
American Society of Civil Engineers, 110, 128
Amsterdam, 18
Andorra, 20
Ankara, 79
Antifragile, 15
Antigua and Barbuda, 42
"apartotel," 27
apostille, 62
Apple, 82
appliances, 53, 73–4, 96, 138, 142–3, 157, 159, 166, 171, 175, 177, 181–2, 250
appraisal, 55, 140, 194, 239
Arab Spring, 80

architects, 73, 146–7, 149, 155–6, 165, 173–4, 177–80, 184, 217, 240
Architizer, 178
Argentina, 53, 90, 105, 107, 193
Ariely, Dan, 52
Arizona, 31, 36, 103, 169
arsenic, 123
Art Deco, 23
artifacts, 87–9, 231
Arudou Debito, 129
asbestos, 65, 89–90, 96, 99, 113, 119, 148, 156, 164, 217, 231
Association for Real Estate Securitization, 42
Athens, 103
Atlanta, 21
Auckland, 20
auctions, 139–40
Austin, 110, 148
Australia: agents, 52; attractions and reasons to buy, 15–6, 18–9, 22, 26, 30, 39, 42; demographics, 81; laws, 57–8; new homes, 152, 166, 181–2; mortgages, 198, 202, 209, 244; property rights, 66, 69; risk factors, 88, 96, 99, 101–6, 112, 117–8, 126, 128; tax, 223
Austria, 18, 42, 225
Ayatollah Khomeini, 101
baby boomers, 39, 79
balconies, 32, 40, 146, 175
Bali, 27, 182
Bangkok, 125, 174–5
Bangladesh, 18, 81
bank accounts, 29, 33, 61, 86, 92, 114, 185, 189–91, 203, 223, 233, 235, 238
banks, 27, 29, 35, 38, 71, 87, 105, 135, 137, 167, 170, 174, 185, 190–2, 202–3, 206–12, 243

281

barristers, 58, 140,
basements, 125, 145, 148, 177
bathrooms, 29, 32, 111, 113, 174, 177, 251
beaches, 15, 20, 25, 29, 65, 68, 105, 174, 182–3, 185
bedrooms, 29, 32, 34, 48, 174, 177, 184
Beijing, 36, 85, 122, 126–7
Beirut, 20
Belarus, 81, 112
Belgium, 201, 225
Benidorm, 173
benzene, 123
Berkeley, 17
Berlin, 37, 79
Bern, 16
Bilbao, 179
Bilham, Roger, 100
Blackstone Group, 36
Bloomberg, 90, 169
Boğaziçi University, 100
Bogotá, 100
boom towns, 34
Boston, 17, 21, 104, 110
Brazil, 71, 75, 81, 112, 118, 127, 189
bridges, 110, 125
briefs (architectural), 177, 179
British Columbia, 68, 80, 87–8, 165
British Property Federation, 42
Brittany, 29
brokers, 47–8, 135, 191–2, 195, 206, 208–9, 213
brownfield sites, 122–4, 171, 232
Bucchianeri, Grace Wong, 23–4
budgets, 23, 29, 51, 135, 155–6, 159, 163, 177–8, 206, 212
Buenos Aires, 121
build it yourself, 240
Bulgaria, 81
Burundi, 80
buy-to-leave, 173
buyer's agent, 49, 53, 55, 77
cadmium, 123
Caen, 29
Cairo, 72, 100
Calgary, 20–1
California, 17, 32–3, 36, 57, 68, 82, 85, 100, 103, 106–7, 110, 118
California Institute of Technology, 17
Cambodia, 18
Cambridge, 17

Cameroon, 112
Canada: agents, 52, 54; attractions and reasons to buy, 16, 18–20, 22, 34, 37, 39, 41–2; demographics, 80–1; financing, 193, 198, 200–2; home inspections, 149; insurance, 215, 217; laws, 57–8; property rights, 64, 66, 68–9, 72; risk factors, 85, 87–9, 93, 96, 99, 104, 106, 111–2, 117, 119, 128; tax, 220, 223–4
Canada Mortgage and Housing Corporation, 149
cancer, 89, 116, 119
cannabis (marijuana), 61, 97–8, 231
Caracas, 100
carbon monoxide, 33, 165
ceilings, 89, 113, 164
cemeteries, 93–4, 233
Chagas disease, 113
Chambre Syndicale des Experts Immobiliers de France, 147
Chan, Jennifer Kay, 206
chancel repair, 113
checks, 61, 105, 136–7, 139, 143, 200
Chicago, 16–7, 21, 35, 52, 64, 127
Chichester, 88
Chile, 16, 100
China: attractions and reasons to buy, 15, 18, 26, 35–6, 39, 43; demographics, 80–1; financing, 190–2, 202–3, 206, 209; laws, 58, 60, 62; new homes, 165; property rights, 64; risk factors, 87, 90–1, 93, 95, 100, 105, 107, 109–10, 112, 114, 116–8, 121–2, 125, 127–8, 130; tax, 220–1
chromium, 123
Cialdini, Robert, 52
Citibank, 191
civil law, 57–9, 61
Clermont, 125
Cleveland, 36
climate change, 26, 91, 103, 112, 116, 180
coffee, 52
Colombia, 21
Colombo, 183–4
Colony Capital, 36
Colorado, 169
commissions, 47, 49, 51, 53–5, 73, 137, 172

common law, 57–9, 64, 69
Commonwealth Bank of Australia, 209
commuting, 15–6, 127
completion dates, 73, 137, 142, 167, 169–70
computers, 181–2
condominiums: attractions and reasons to buy, 26, 32, 34; checklists, 231, 237–8; demographics, 79; financing, 197, 211; home inspections, 145–6, 149; insurance, 215; new homes, 164, 167, 169, 174–6; pre-owned homes, 152, 156; property rights, 63–5; risk factors, 86, 88, 95, 125
"condotels," 27
Confucianism, 76
consularized documents, 62
consumer protection, 50, 106, 147, 166, 201, 233, 237, 241
contractors, 50, 73, 155–8, 177, 179–80, 184, 217
contracts: agents, 49, 54; checklists, 234; financing, 193, 205, 207, 208; insurance, 217; laws, 59–60; negotiating, 73–5; new homes, 167, 169–172, 178; pre-owned homes, 135, 137–8, 140–143; property rights, 65; risk factors, 105, 122; tax, 220
conveyancers, 58, 140
conveyancing, 29, 32, 59, 71,194
cooperatives (co-ops), 63–4, 111, 152, 238
Copenhagen, 17
CoreLogic, 35
corruption, 16, 75, 83, 92, 100, 102, 165
cost of living, 16, 21, 24
Costa Rica, 21, 221
Council of Mortgage Lenders, 192
County Waterford, 157
credit bureaus, 205–6
crime, 21–2, 38, 61, 83, 92, 94, 107, 231
Croatia, 81
Cuba, 47, 81, 193
Cupertino, 82
Cyprus, 42
Damietta, 72
Danang, 25
death, 23, 33, 61, 72, 79, 84–5, 92–4, 100, 116, 127, 143, 214, 231

Death and Life of Great American Cities, The, 102
deeds registration, 66, 68–70
defective design and construction, 92, 95–6, 106, 164, 166, 169
demographics, 79–84, 157, 165, 222
Denmark, 16, 18, 20, 81, 152, 198, 221, 225
Department of Housing and Urban Development, 112
deposits (earnest money), 55, 88, 135–42, 167–8, 171–2, 189, 208, 236, 238
designers, 52, 155–6, 240
Detroit, 73, 82–4, 107
Detroit Free Press, 84
developers, 41, 73–4, 91, 114, 121–2, 164, 166–7, 169–73, 175–6, 233
Dhaka, 100
diabetes, 115
Diaoyu Islands, 130
diesel, 127
Dillon, Christopher, 39–41, 130
distressed property, 35–6, 50, 73, 97
divorce, 15, 23, 41, 70, 72, 96–7, 207
Dodd-Frank Wall Street Reform and Consumer Protection Act, 201
Dominican Republic, 18, 127
doors, 112, 145, 148, 157, 165, 181
Dordogne, 23
Dragonair, 25
droughts, 128–9
Drug Enforcement Administration, 98
drywall, 96, 164, 180, 231
dual agency, 147–8
Dubai, 16, 36, 118
Dublin, 95
Dubner, Stephen, 51–2
Dubout, Rene Philippe, 173
Durham University, 111
earthquakes, 33, 89, 99–101, 111–2, 115, 124, 152, 164, 209, 214–5, 232, 235, 240
easements, 65, 70, 137, 151, 197, 231
Economist Intelligence Unit, 20
Economist, 97
Ecuador, 21, 31, 112
Edmonton, 37
Egypt, 72, 76, 80, 112
El Pais, 173
electricians, 86, 98, 111, 149

Electronic Frontier Foundation, 91
elevators, 63, 101, 152, 164, 173
energy audits, 148
energy conservation, 241
engineers, 98, 110, 128, 138, 148–9, 156, 217
England, 29, 32, 57–8, 66, 69, 101, 141
Environmental Protection Agency, 68, 91, 122
environmental resources, 242
environmentally friendly designs, 180–1
Equifax, 206
Erdik, Mustafa, 100
erosion, 112, 152
escrow, 33, 55, 135–6, 142, 173, 194–5, 200, 238
European Public Real Estate Association, 42
exchange-traded funds (ETFs), 42
Experian, 206
expropriation, 64, 101–2
Facebook, 91
farms, 20, 97–8, 101, 129–30
farmhouses, 28–30
fee simple, 64
fertility, 126
financing, sources of, 50, 190–2, 243
Finland, 16, 18, 20, 81, 225
fire, 33, 86, 95, 98–9, 101–3, 111, 116, 164–5, 215–6, 232, 246
Flint, 102
floods, 33, 91, 103–6, 106, 118, 143, 215, 232
Florida, 28, 31, 36, 91, 96, 118, 125
for sale by owner, 54–5, 246
Foreign Account Tax Compliance Act (FATCA), 86, 189
Foreign Corrupt Practices Act, 61
foreign exchange, 27, 104–5, 107, 109, 114, 190, 193, 235
formaldehyde, 121, 128, 232
Fort McMurray, 34
foundations, 104, 110, 119, 125, 145, 166, 180
France: attractions and reasons to buy, 20, 23, 28–30, 36; financing, 189, 198, 202–3; home inspections, 147–8; new homes, 166; risk factors, 116; tax, 221
fraud, 74, 102, 105–6, 170, 190

Freakonomics, 51–2
freedom, 16, 20
freehold, 19, 57, 63–5, 138, 182–3
Fuggerei, 121
Fukushima, 115–6
furnaces, 145, 163
furniture, 38, 120, 168, 170, 175, 177, 252
gardens, 98, 177, 184
"gayborhoods," 38
Gehry, Frank, 179
Geneva, 16, 18
gentrification, 37–8
Georgia (country), 71, 81
German Sustainable Building Council, 181
Germany, 20, 24, 75, 91, 110, 115, 120, 198, 202–3
Girona, 17
Global Alliance to Eliminate Lead Paint, 113
Going Solo: The Extraordinary Rise and Surprising Appeal of Living Alone, 81
Gold Coast, 26
golf, 25, 79, 164
Google Maps, 49
government debt, 106, 247
Great East Japan Earthquake, 101, 115, 214
Greece, 20, 42, 103, 107, 130, 152, 225
Green Building Council of Australia, 181
Green Building Initiative, 181
Grosvenor, 21
Guangdong, 35
Guangzhou, 104
gutters, 113
Haiti, 72, 100
Hanoi, 25
happiness, 18, 23–4, 28
Harrods, 170
Harvard University, 17, 36
Hawaii, 15
health care, 20, 30–1, 106, 108, 213, 216, 237
Hegelian logic, 76
HelpAge, 21
"Help to Buy" scheme, 192
Helsinki, 20
heritage and conservation, 247
Heritage Foundation, 16

HIV, 33
Ho Chi Minh City, 25
Hokkaido, 76, 129
home automation, 157, 181–2, 248
home inspections, 96, 140, 143, 145–9, 231, 248
home stagers, 52
HomeAway, 28
homeowners' associations, 32–3
Honduras, 17
Hong Kong: agents, 53; attractions and reasons to buy, 16, 18, 23, 25, 28–9, 32, 34–5, 41, 43; financing, 191, 200–1, 209–10; home inspections, 146; insurance, 214; laws, 57, 61; new homes, 170, 172, 174, 182, 185; pre-owned homes, 152, 157–8; property rights, 66, 69; risk factors, 85, 93–4, 113–4, 118–9, 121, 125, 130; tax, 220
hospitals, 27, 108, 116, 165, 213
hotels, 23, 27–8, 42, 172
Housetrip, 28
Houston, 35, 110
How to Purchase Real Estate Offshore Safely: The Case of Thailand, 173
HSBC, 191
Hungary, 108, 202
hurricanes, 112, 127, 233
hypertension, 115
Iceland, 18, 20, 89, 127
Idaho, 169
Illinois, 107
illiquidity, 19, 42, 109, 175
Imperial College of London, 100
In Tempo, 173
India, 57, 69, 81, 99, 108, 112
Indonesia, 18, 27, 79, 81, 91, 103, 112
infestations, 126, 249
Influence: The Psychology of Persuasion, 52
influenza, 108
insects, 113, 126
insulation, 89, 111, 126, 128, 163, 180–1, 225, 232
insurance: all risks, 214; domestic helper, 214; earthquake, 209, 215; fire, 136, 194, 208–9, 213, 215; flood, 104, 118, 194, 213, 215; health, 213, 216; homeowners, 143, 200, 213, 216; landlord, 216; latent defect, 216; life, 209–10, 217; mortgage, 194–5, 200–1, 217; professional liability, 178, 217; public liability, 28, 156, 217–8; title, 70–1, 136, 143, 152, 195, 218; travel, 218; workers' compensation, 156, 218
International Association of Certified Home Inspectors, 147
international brands, 250
International Living, 21
International Monetary Fund, 222
International Union for Housing Finance, 192
International Union of Architects, 178
Internet, 18, 25, 28, 90–1, 95, 145, 159, 182, 184–5, 225, 233
Iran, 69, 99, 101
Iraq, 127
Ireland, 16, 42, 95, 119, 145, 157–9, 198, 225
Islamabad, 100
Islington, Borough of, 173
Israel, 76
Istanbul, 79, 100
Italy, 17, 81, 103, 136–8, 215, 225
Jacobs, Jane, 102
Jakarta, 100, 125
Japan: agents, 48, 50, 54; attractions and reasons to buy, 20, 39–42; demographics, 79, 81–3; financing, 189–90, 199, 206, 210; insurance, 214–5, 217; laws, 58–9; negotiating, 75–6; new homes, 163, 165, 169, 181; pre-owned homes, 153, 157; property rights, 65; risk factors, 92, 100–1, 104–5, 108, 115–6, 118, 124, 129–30; tax, 220, 222
Japan Green Build Council, 181
Japan Real Estate Institute, 124
jeonse, 38–9
Johor, 35
Joint Commission International, 108
joint ownership, 72
Jones Lang LaSalle, 19
judicial scriveners, 40, 59
Kabul, 34
Kansas (state), 118, 127
Karachi, 100
Katmandu, 100
Kelo case, 101
Kentucky, 83

Kenya, 18
Keynes, John Maynard, 119
Kilpatrick, Kwame, 83
Kiribati, 72
kitchens, 29, 84, 111–2, 174–5, 177, 251
Klinenberg, Eric, 81
Kuala Lumpur, 183–4
Kwazulu-Natal, 113
land surveys, 151–3, 195, 232
landscaping, 73, 163, 165, 185
landslides, 91, 99, 111–2, 215, 233
Laos, 18
Las Vegas, 165
Latvia, 42, 81, 202
laws, 28, 33, 57–62, 64, 69, 74–5, 86–8, 90, 92, 96–7, 102, 106, 114, 117, 143, 155, 159, 172, 192, 198, 200, 214, 217, 219
lawyers, 32, 38, 55, 57–62, 67, 70, 72–3, 97, 105, 135–40, 142–3, 159, 170, 175–6, 184, 189, 193–4, 207, 217, 219–20, 238
lead, 96, 112–3, 123, 127, 146, 156, 164, 213
leasehold, 19, 63–5, 138, 175
Lebanon, 80, 112
Legal Practitioners Fidelity Fund, 105
Levitt, Steven, 51–2
Liechtenstein, 20
Lima, 100
Lincoln Institute, 169
liquefaction, 99, 101
listing services, 35, 55
Lithuania, 81
living alone, 81
loan-to-value ratio (LTV), 104, 200–3, 210–1
London: attractions and reasons to buy, 15–17, 23, 32, 37, 41; demographics, 79; new homes, 170, 172–5; pre-owned homes, 155; risk factors, 87, 94–5, 100, 110, 113, 119, 121–2, 125, 127
London Interbank Offered Rate (LIBOR), 198
Los Angeles, 17, 35, 103
Loughborough University, 16
Louisiana, 58
Love Canal, 124
Luanda, 16

Luxembourg, 20
Macau, 114, 125
Madagascar, 69
Madison, 55
Madrid, 35
maintenance, 23, 26, 29, 35, 39, 41, 50, 63, 120, 146, 163–4, 169, 172, 177, 212, 224
Malawi, 80
Malaysia, 15, 21, 35–6, 54, 69, 91, 103, 112, 171, 183–4
Maldives, 15, 58
Mali, 80
Malta, 21, 42, 118
management, 26–8, 31, 41, 68, 83, 102–3, 145, 171, 175–6, 189, 224, 234–6
Manila, 100
maps, 16, 49, 70, 104, 119, 152, 254
Maputo, 34
Massachusetts, 15, 17
Massachusetts Institute of Technology, 17
Mauritius, 16
measles, 108
media, 76, 91, 110, 116, 145, 225, 255–6
Megan's Law, 143
Meikai University, 124
Melbourne, 20, 103
Mercer, 16
mercury, 116, 123
MERS (Middle East respiratory syndrome), 90
methamphetamines, 98–9, 232
Mexico (country), 18, 21, 54, 57, 81, 103, 112, 117
Mexico City, 100, 125, 127
Miami, 23, 35, 91, 104, 113
Michelin, 17
Microsoft, 82
mineral rights, 65–7
minerals, 66, 89
mining, 66, 124
Ministry of Urban Wellbeing, Housing and Local Government, 171
Mississippi (state), 107
Missouri, 83
Mitsubishi Estate, 169
Modena, 17
mold, 55, 97–8, 120, 128, 146
Moldova, 81

Index   287

Monaco, 49
monsoons, 112
Montana, 89
Montreal, 18, 58, 127
Mortgages: adjustable rate, 198–9, 203; amortization of, 198–9; applying for, 204–12; balloon, 201–2; brokers, 135, 191, 206; buy-to-let, 37, 202; discount points, 194; documents for, 207–9; down payment, 73, 138, 190, 192, 194, 198, 200–1, 204–5, 217; fixed rate, 198–9, 203; flexible, 202; insurance, 194–5, 200–1, 217; interest-only, 201–2; multicurrency, 200, 202; multigenerational, 199; offset, 203; offshore, 189–90; prepayment of, 200–1; processing time, 219; recourse and nonrecourse, 203; rejected applications, 212; repayment of 198–200, 206, 208; restrictions on, 209–10; reverse, 203–4; Sharia-compliant, 203; term of, 198–9, 201, 203
Moscow, 16
Mozambique, 34
Mugabe, Robert, 101
Mumbai, 104
Munich Re, 91
Myanmar, 18, 34, 80, 108, 127
N'Djamena, 16
Nabili, Teymoor, 182–5
Nagoya, 104
Nakazato, Naoki, 24
National Aeronautics and Space Administration (NASA), 104, 112
National Association of Real Estate Investment Trusts, 42
National Cancer Institute, 116
National Credit Information Database, 206
National Geographic, 15
natural gas, 33, 110, 116
Naypyidaw, 80
Nebraska, 127
negotiating, 49, 53–4, 60–1, 65, 73–7, 114, 139, 142, 147, 149, 177, 179
Nelson, Arthur C., 82
Netherlands, 16, 18, 20, 118, 165, 198, 201–3, 225
Nevada, 31, 36
New Delhi, 100

New Haven, 17
New Jersey, 142–4
New London, 101
New Mexico, 103, 107
New Orleans, 104
New South Wales, 88, 105, 166
Michigan, 83, 102
New York City: attractions and reasons to buy, 16, 17, 22–3, 28, 35, 38, 41; demographics, 83; pre-owned homes, 155; property rights, 63; risk factors, 94, 104, 107, 110, 113, 119, 121–2, 125
New York (state), 15, 107, 118
New York Times, 82, 90
New Zealand: agents, 54; attractions and reasons to buy, 16, 20, 39; home inspections, 147; laws, 57–8; pre-owned homes, 136, 138–40, 156; property rights, 69, 71; risk factors, 99, 100, 117, 124
Newbury, 36
Nicaragua, 18
Niger, 80–1
Nigeria, 80–1, 105, 112
noise, 110, 114–5, 127, 148, 171
Normandy, 28–9
North Korea, 34, 99, 127
Northwestern University, 55
Norway, 16, 18, 20, 71, 81, 225
Norwich, 29
NSW Self Insurance Corporation, 166
nuclear power, 115–7, 223, 256
Oaktree Capital Group, 36
obesity, 115
Ohio, 23, 36, 107
oil, 34, 66–7, 116, 124
Oishi, Shigehiro, 24
Oklahoma, 127
One Hyde Park, 173
Ontario, 117, 165–6
Oregon, 68
Organization for Economic Cooperation and Development (OECD), 15, 21
Osaka, 104, 125
Oskamp, Erik, 39
owners' committees, 63, 145
Oxford, 17, 36
paint, 39, 96, 112–3, 120, 130, 146, 148, 155–6, 163–4, 179, 231
Pakistan, 81, 99, 103, 108

Palo Alto, 17
Panama, 21
Panday, Mark and Alicia, 28–30
Paraguay, 112
Pasadena, 17
passive houses, 181
passports, 18, 32, 42–3, 117
pensions, 30, 35, 39, 83, 94, 107, 237
People's Bank of China, 26
permanent residents, 117, 191–2, 211, 221
permits, 28, 68, 75, 152, 156–7, 236
Perth, 20
Peru, 18, 112
pesticides, 120, 123, 129
Petley, David, 111
Philippines, 18, 67–8, 79, 100, 103, 108, 112, 117, 127
Phoenix, 110, 165
Phuket, 174–6, 182
pipe, 96, 119, 140, 169, 215–6; galvanized steel, 106, 232; polybutylene (PB), 96, 106, 164, 232
Pittsburgh, 21
plumbers, 149, 179
Poland, 202
police, 64, 79, 92, 97–8, 182, 222, 233
polio, 108
polychlorinated biphenyls (PCBs), 123
population, 20, 79–83, 104, 110, 126, 159
Port Hope, 117
Portugal, 42, 71, 79, 103, 225
Prague, 18
Princeton University, 17
Priory Hall, 95
privacy, 18, 42, 86, 182
private equity, 42
property management, 38, 92, 185, 222
Pruitt-Igoe Project, 121
public transport, 16, 31–2, 38, 165, 233
Purdue University, 111
Pyongyang, 34
Quebec (province), 58, 73, 165
Quito, 100
radon, 119, 143, 145, 232
real estate agencies, 48, 50, 172, 257
real estate agents, 33, 40–1, 47–55, 93, 105, 114, 137, 139, 142–3, 189, 191, 206–7, 211, 217, 258

real estate investment trusts (REITs), 42
real estate listings, 259
RealtyTrac, 35
Reason Foundation, 122
recreational property, 26–7, 30–1, 34, 79, 200, 236
Redfin, 94
Redmond, 82
religion, 80, 201
Remodeling, 157
renovations, 23, 73, 89, 92, 146, 149, 155–9, 192, 218, 238
rentals, 27–9, 33, 36, 38, 41, 84, 97, 105, 159, 168, 172, 175–6, 201, 216, 219–23, 225, 234–6
repairs, 23, 29, 35, 50, 52, 63, 86, 95, 97–8, 113, 125, 129, 138, 140, 143, 147–9, 156, 163, 166, 212, 218, 224, 238
Reporters Without Borders, 20, 91
research and statistics, 259
resident's cards, 189
resilience, 21
restaurants, 17, 27, 175, 233
retirement, 21, 30–1, 39, 79, 237
Rio de Janeiro, 20, 37
Romania, 81
Rome, 57, 87
Ronan Point, 95
roofs, 63, 89, 113, 145, 148, 159, 163, 166, 184, 224
Rotterdam, 98
Royal Canadian Mounted Police, 97
Royal Institute of British Architects, 165
Russia, 15, 54, 80–1, 112, 116
Sabana REIT, 43
sailing, 25, 164
Saint Kitts and Nevis, 42
sale and purchase (S&P) agreement, 33, 40, 49, 75, 114, 135–6, 138–9, 175, 193, 204, 208, 220, 226, 238
San Bruno, 110
San Francisco, 17, 28, 32, 34, 103, 122, 125
San Sebastián, 17
São Paulo, 17, 24, 37
Sarnia, 88
SARS (severe acute respiratory syndrome), 90
Saudi Arabia, 58, 90
Schimmack, Ulrich, 24

Scotland, 19, 25, 32, 57, 141
Seattle, 18,
section 106 agreements, 121
Senegal, 112
Senkaku Islands, 130
Seoul, 18, 39
separatist movements, 119–20
septic tanks, 143, 146, 174, 184
Serbia, 81
Setad, 102
sewers, 110, 146, 214–5, 235
Seychelles, 15, 112
"shadow inventory," 35
Shanghai, 16, 23, 95, 122, 125, 172, 220–1
shares, 27, 41–2
Sharia (Muslim law), 42, 58, 203
Shenzhen, 104, 127, 165
shopping, 22, 38, 125, 165, 170, 172, 233
sick building syndrome, 120–1, 232
Silver Bay Realty Trust, 36
Singapore: agents, 47–8; attractions and reasons to buy, 16, 20, 34–5, 38, 41–2; financing, 192, 206; insurance, 214; laws, 61; new homes, 172, 182, 185; property rights, 69; risk factors, 103, 112, 118–9, 122; tax, 221
skiing, 25, 79, 221
Skype, 40, 156
skyscrapers, 101
smartphones, 181
Snowden, Edward, 90, 182
social housing, 121–2, 170, 236
software, 182, 262
Sohag, 72
soil pollution, 122–3, 138, 232
solar power, 177, 180, 224
solicitors, 58–9, 61
Somalia, 80
South Africa, 15, 54, 103, 108, 112–3
South Korea, 15, 32, 38, 83, 116, 198, 225
Spain: attractions and reasons to buy, 17, 21, 28, 36, 42; demographics, 79; financing, 198, 202–3; negotiating, 75; new homes, 164, 173, 179; pre-owned homes, 153, 159; risk factors, 103, 118, 120; tax, 221, 225
Sri Lanka, 18, 57, 99, 103, 112, 120, 182–5
St. Bart's, 15

Stanford University, 17, 55
Stocker, Paul, 174–6
Stockholm, 18, 21, 81
Stockton, 106–7
Stradbally, 157–9
Stratfor, 18
student housing, 17, 36–7, 231
subprime crisis, 23, 35, 200–1
subsidence, 103, 124–5, 214–5, 232
subways, 31, 39–40, 109–10
surface rights, 65–7
Surrey, 36
sustainability, 18, 21, 114, 118, 125–6, 181
Sweden, 16, 18–20, 48–9, 81, 199, 225
swimming pools, 32, 63, 152, 163, 171, 175, 231
Swiss Re, 91
Switzerland, 16, 18, 20, 118, 198–9, 225
Sydney, 16, 20, 22, 103
Syria, 20, 80
Tahiti, 15, 49
Taipei, 123
Taiwan, 43, 112, 127, 225
Taleb, Nassim Nicholas, 15
Tampa, 104
Tanzania, 18, 81, 112
Taoism, 76
Tarion Corporation, 166
tax: annual tax on enveloped dwellings, 225; appeals, 222; capital gains, 29, 57, 223, 225–6, 235; council, 173; credits, 219, 224–6; deductions, 222, 224; evasion, 225–6; exemptions, 222–224; exit, 224; imputed income, 221; income, 41, 221–3; luxury, 221; occupant, 219, 221; property, 32, 70, 83, 151, 195, 200, 206–7, 219–222, 224, 232; sales, 53, 195, 220; value-added, 53, 137, 159
Tehran, 100
telephones, 62, 159, 181, 184, 207, 224, 233
television, 28, 31, 175, 184, 233
tenancy agreements, 59
tenders, 139–40
Tennessee, 83
termites, 126, 143, 232
Texas, 107, 127, 148
Thailand, 21, 91, 112, 117, 173–6

The Hague, 98
Thompson, Jim and Sally, 157–9
Times Higher Education, 17
timeshares, 26, 264
title, 20, 33–4, 40, 59, 63, 66, 68–72, 89, 93, 97, 136, 138, 140, 143–4, 162, 164, 173–4, 194–5, 203, 218, 237–8
title companies, 33, 66, 70, 136, 143
Tokyo, 16–8, 20, 39–41, 100–1, 123, 125, 169
Tokyo Bay, 100
Tokyo Electric Power (TEPCO), 116
Toronto, 20–1, 117, 206
Torrens system, 66, 68–70
traffic, 110, 126–7
translation, 60–1, 155, 157, 264
Transparency International, 16
transportation, 25, 31, 99, 108, 165, 172, 222, 233
TransUnion, 206
trusts, 27, 33, 42, 57, 59, 92, 105, 114, 139
tsunamis, 99, 103, 184, 215, 233
tuberculosis, 108–9
Turkey, 91, 100, 215
Twitter, 91
typhoons, 103, 112, 127, 233
U.S. Geological Survey, 100
U.S. Green Building Council, 181
Uber, 31
UBM's Future Cities, 18
Uganda, 18, 81, 112
Ukraine, 81
United Arab Emirates, 61, 118
United Kingdom: agents, 54; attractions and reasons to buy, 19–20, 36; demographics, 81; financing, 192, 202; new homes, 172, 182; pre-owned homes, 140–2; property rights, 64, 66, 68, 72; risk factors, 88, 104, 121; tax, 223, 225
United Nations, 18, 21, 80, 113
United States: agents, 47–9, 51, 54–5; attractions and reasons to buy, 19, 22–3, 28, 32, 34–5, 37–9; demographics, 79, 81–3; financing, 191–2, 194, 198, 200–1, 203, 206–7; insurance, 213, 215, 217; laws, 57–8; negotiating, 77; new homes, 163, 165–6, 182; pre-owned homes, 136, 142–4, 156–7; property rights, 63, 66, 68, 72; risk factors, 85–6, 89–90, 93–4, 96, 98, 101–2, 104, 106, 108–112, 116, 118–9, 121–2, 124, 128; tax, 223, 225
United States Northern Command, 108
universal design, 31, 237, 264
University of Colorado Boulder, 100
University of California, Berkeley, 17
University of California, Los Angeles, 17
University of Cambridge, 17
University of Oxford, 15, 17
University of Utah, 82
Urea formaldehyde foam insulation (UFFI), 128, 232
Uruguay, 21, 105
Uzbekistan, 71, 127
vacation clubs, 27
"vampire REOs," 35
Vancouver, 20–22, 88, 95, 145, 149
Venezuela, 193
Venice, 125
vernacular design, 156
Victoria (Australia), 102
video, 40, 149, 155, 167, 170, 172, 179, 181
Vienna, 18, 20, 121
Vietnam, 18, 25, 118
visas, 31–2, 42–3, 118, 189, 237
volatile organic compounds (VOCs), 120–1
Wales, 25, 69
Walk Score, 22
walkability, 22–3
Wall Street Journal, 16, 116
walls, 97, 113, 146, 148, 153, 170
warranties, 157, 163, 165–6, 216–7, 237
Washington, D.C., 21, 62, 110
water, 67–8, 83, 95–6, 101, 103–4, 106, 110, 118–9, 121, 123–6, 128–9, 143, 145, 148, 164, 166, 175, 177, 180, 184, 215, 233
water pollution, 116, 128
waterfront rights, 67–8
weather, 27, 91, 127–8, 155, 233, 265
Western Cape, 113
Wharton School, 23
Whistler, 221
WiFi, 18, 175
wills, 31, 59, 235, 239
Winchester, 36

windows, 97–8, 113, 145, 148, 163–4, 181
wiring, 96–8, 157, 166; aluminum, 85–6, 231; knob-and-tube, 111, 231
Wisconsin, 55
World Bank, 103–4
World Economic Forum, 20
World Health Organization (WHO), 85, 127
World's 50 Best Restaurants, 17
Wright, Frank Lloyd, 23
Wurster, Bernardi & Emmons, 32
WWII, 116, 129
Wyoming, 127
xenophobia, 107, 129–30
Yale University, 17
Yangon, 34, 80
Yemen, 127–8
YouTube, 91
Zambia, 81
Zimbabwe, 101
"zombie foreclosures," 35
zoning, 65, 75, 117, 130, 137, 177, 232
Zurich, 16, 21

ABOUT THE AUTHOR

Christopher Dillon is an entrepreneur and writer whose work has been recognized with several International Galaxy Awards.

In 2002, he bought and renovated a floor in an office building in Hong Kong's Central business district. He subsequently purchased and refurbished a luxury apartment on the west side of Hong Kong Island, transformed a derelict steam laundry into a multimedia studio and bought residential property in Japan. Christopher has served on the management committee of a 210-unit apartment complex in Hong Kong since 2012.

That experience inspired a trio of books: *Landed Hong Kong* (2008), *Landed Japan* (2010) and *Landed China* (2013). For more information, please see www.landedbook.com.

A native of Canada, Christopher lived in Tokyo from 1989 to 1992. He lives in Hong Kong.